THE
TOTALLY
USELESS

History

of the World

THE TOTALLY USELESS

HISTORY

of the World

IAN CROFTON

Quercus

First published in Great Britain in 2007 by

Quercus
21 Bloomsbury Square
London
WC1A 2NS

A CIP catalogue record for this book is available from the British Library

ISBN-10: 1 84724 403 3
ISBN-13: 978 1 84724 403 1

Printed and bound in China

10 9 8 7 6 5 4 3 2 1

Contents

The Emperor Caligula's floating palace on Lake Nemi, near Rome.

The Ancient World

Galactic Tyrant Peoples Earth 🙠 Tortoise Slays Playwright 🙠 The Case of the Missing Penises 🙠 Philosopher Urinates on Diners 🙠 The Rotting Emperor and the Putrid Fish 🙠 Seneca and the Armpit Plucker 🙠 Legalization of Flatulence 🙠 Sow's Womb and Mackerel Guts 🙠 Incest and Matricide 🙠 A Tax on Public Lavatories 🙠 On the Iniquities of Soap 🙠 Self-castration 🙠 Drowned in Rose Petals 🙠 Two Breasts on a Platter 🙠 A Fatal Evacuation of the Bowels 🙠 Thirty-Six Years on Top of a Pillar 🙠

75 million years ago

—

Galactic Tyrant Peoples Earth 🙾 According to the doctrines
of Scientology, the galactic tyrant Xenu kidnapped hundreds of billions of
individuals from other parts of the galaxy and sent them to planet Earth to be
exterminated. They arrived by craft that looked like Douglas DC-8s, but
which were in fact powered by rockets. The exiles were then exposed to
thermonuclear explosions, prior to being brainwashed by a 36-day-long 3-D
movie into believing that they were at the same time Jesus, God and the Devil.
The victims subsequently parasitized human bodies, and can apparently only
be removed by advanced Scientological techniques.

4004 BC

—

The Day of Creation 🙾 The date of Creation, according to James
Ussher, Protestant Archbishop of Armagh, in his 1650 work, *Annales veteris
testamenti, a prima mundi origine deducti* ('Annals of the Old Testament, deduced
from the first origins of the world'). More precisely, Ussher calculated – on the
basis of his interpretation of Biblical texts – that the Earth had been brought
into being on the evening preceding 23 October 4004 BC. It turns out that the
Earth is nearly a million times older than Ussher suggested.

616 BC

—

Burial Alive 🙾 Tarquinius Priscus became king of Rome. It was
Tarquinius who instituted the traditional punishment for any Vestal Virgin
who lost her virginity. The unfortunate woman was walled up alive in an
underground chamber called the Campus Scleratus, and was sometimes
supplied with food and water to prolong her slow death. Until the abolition
of the Vestal Virgins in AD 391, some 22 Vestal Virgins appear to have
suffered either immuration or burial alive.

532 BC

Leader Goes to War in Middle East Having Deliberately Misinterpreted the Intelligence 🍃 King Croesus of Lydia asked the Delphic Oracle if the signs were propitious for an attack on the Persian Empire. The Pythoness – the priestess of the Oracle – pronounced that 'If Croesus crosses the River Halys, a great empire shall be destroyed.' Insensitive to any ambiguity in this prophecy, Croesus attacked – and his army was utterly annihilated. The Oracle's pronouncement on this occasion was a model of clarity, compared to the usual wild ramblings that came from the Pythoness – whose trances may have been caused by natural emanations of methane, ethanol and carbon dioxide in her cave.

525 BC

On the Relative Puniness of Persian vs. Egyptian Skulls 🍃 At the decisive Battle of Pelusium, near Port Said, the Persians under Cambyses II defeated the Egyptians, and went on to conquer the country. In the 5th century, the Greek historian Herodotus visited the site and found the remains of the fallen still scattered across the battlefield. In the interests of impartial investigation, he noted that if you threw a pebble at a Persian skull it would make a hole in it, while even if you struck an Egyptian skull with a rock, 'you will scarcely break it in'. He ascribed the difference to the Egyptian practice of shaving the head from infancy, while the Persians covered theirs with folds of cloth.

———

Army Disappears in Desert 🍃 After his conquest of Egypt, Cambyses sent an army to the Siwa Oasis in Egypt's Western Desert, perhaps to persuade the Oracle of Amun to recognize his rule. But the 50,000 men never reached their destination, being overwhelmed, according to Herodotus, by a sandstorm. Exactly 2525 years later, geologists from Helwan University, prospecting for petroleum, found themselves among sand dunes littered with fragments of textiles and weapons, and the bleached bones of men who may once have belonged to the Lost Army of Cambyses.

circa 456 BC

Tortoise Slays Playwright ✦ The Greek dramatist Aeschylus died when an eagle dropped a tortoise on his bald head.

circa 434 BC

Sun Larger than the Peloponnese, Argues Greek Philosopher ✦ The Greek philosopher Anaxagoras was exiled from Athens for denying the divine nature of heavenly bodies. He asserted that the Sun was a great disc of blazing metal larger than the Peloponnese, and that the planets were lumps of rock torn from the Earth and set on fire by the rapidity of their rotation.

circa 430 BC

Volcanic Suicides ✦ The Greek philosopher Empedocles died by throwing himself into the active crater of Mount Etna. His intention had been that people should believe – in the absence of his body – that he had ascended to heaven as a god. His ruse was foiled when the volcano spewed forth one of his bronze sandals. The fate of Empedocles may have inspired the American tourist who, in 1859 – having received unhappy news from home – threw himself into a lava flow on the flank of Vesuvius, and was instantly incinerated.

415 BC

The Case of the Missing Penises ✦ (May) The Greek general Alcibiades was accused of knocking the phalli off all the hermai in Athens, a scandalously sacrilegious act. Hermai were pillars set up outside houses adorned with male genitals and topped with a head of the god Hermes (supposedly the inventor of masturbation). Alicibiades, who set off on an expedition against Syracuse shortly afterwards, was sentenced to death in his absence.

390 BC

Geese Save Rome 🐾 The sacred geese on the Capitoline Hill in Rome saved the city by making such a noise as the besieging Gauls attempted a covert night attack that the guards were roused and repelled the invaders.

circa 350 BC

Philosopher Urinates on Diners 🐾 The Greek philosopher Diogenes, disdaining the social niceties, lived like a dog – naked, scratching and defecating in the street – so earning the nickname 'the Dog' (Greek *kuon* – thus his followers became known as the Cynics, from the Greek *Kunikos*). The citizens of Athens indulged Diogenes' foibles, even throwing bones to him at a banquet. He showed his gratitude by urinating on their legs.

346 BC

If . . . 🐾 Having conquered much of the rest of Greece, Philip II of Macedon sent a message to the Spartans: 'You are advised to submit without further delay, for if I bring my army into your land, I will destroy your farms, slay your people, and raze your city.' They sent a one-word reply: 'If.' Their boldness paid off: Philip left them alone.

334 BC

Outwitting Alexander 🐾 Alexander the Great crossed the Dardanelles to begin his conquest of the Persian Empire. He was accompanied by one of his favourites, the rhetorician Anaximenes. Anxious to save his native city of Lampascus from destruction, Anaximenes asked for an audience with Alexander. Anticipating his request, Alexander swore an oath that he would deny Anaximenes' request. The cunning Anaximenes then spoke: 'My lord,' he said, 'I have only come to beg you to destroy Lampascus.' Alexander had no other choice but to honour his oath and spare the city.

331 BC

Guided by Crows 🦅 According to the contemporary historian Callisthenes of Olynthus, Alexander's army was guided through a desert by a flock of crows. The birds would fly ahead as the men followed them, or wait for them if they tarried. Even at night the crows called out to show the way.

274 BC

King Killed by Roof Tile 🦅 King Pyrrhus of Epirus was killed during the Siege of Argos when a poor old woman taking refuge on a roof threw down a tile onto his head. She was displeased at the way the king was setting upon her son, a man, according to Plutarch, 'of mean condition'. The tile hit Pyrrhus's helmet, which would have saved him had not the tile then ricocheted onto his neck, fatally fracturing his spinal column.

213 BC

Archimedes' Death Ray 🦅 During the Roman siege of Syracuse, Archimedes is said to have used arrays of polished shields to focus the Sun's rays onto the Roman ships, so setting them alight.

210 BC

The Rotting Emperor and the Putrid Fish 🦅 The first Chinese emperor, Shi Huangdi, died while searching for the Islands of the Immortals off the east coast of China. His chief minister, Li Si, was worried that if the imperial death became common knowledge there would very likely be a popular rebellion, so brutal and oppressive had been the emperor's rule. So during the two-month journey back to the capital, Li Si visited the emperor's carriage daily, giving the impression that he was discussing the affairs of the realm. And he disguised the smell of the emperor's bodily decay by positioning wagons full of fish before and after the emperor's carriage.

184 BC

Snake Bombs &While leading the Bithynians in a sea battle against the Pergamenes, the exiled Hannibal ordered his men to throw clay pots filled with snakes into the enemy galleys. The enemy, thus thrown into confusion, were readily defeated.

80 BC

The First Computer? & A cargo ship sank off the tiny Greek island of Antikythera, taking to the bottom the so-called Antikythera mechanism, recovered by sponge divers in 1904. The device, a complex assemblage of cogs, wheels and dials, is thought by some to be the first analogue computer, and was probably used to map the motions of the sun, moon and planets.

71 BC

Romans Crucify 6000 Slaves & After the defeat of Spartacus's slave revolt, the Appian Way was lined from Capua to Rome (a distance of more than 100 miles) with the crucified bodies of some 6000 captured rebels. Their decaying corpses were left in place for many years.

41 BC

The Most Expensive Banquet in History? ❧ When Mark Antony first met Cleopatra, at Tarsus in modern-day Turkey, their political discussions were lubricated with feast after feast. Indeed Cleopatra wagered Mark Antony that she would lay on the most expensive banquet in history. The next evening, as the banquet neared its end, Mark Antony observed that, though impressive, the meal had been no more lavish than the previous ones. At this Cleopatra took off one of her pearl earrings, extracted a huge pearl, ground it up and dissolved it in wine vinegar, then drank it down. The bet was won.

2 BC

Roman Family Values ❧ Julia, the daughter of the Emperor Augustus and wife of his heir Tiberius, shocked Rome and her father by her adulteries and participation in late-night drinking parties in the Forum. She was even said to have put her favours up for sale, and when asked how all her children resembled her husband, explained that she 'only took on new passengers when the boat was already full'. Augustus, who (despite his own infidelities) was determined to uphold family values, exiled his daughter to the tiny volcanic island of Pandataria (modern Ventotene), and forbade her wine and the company of men. Any visitors had to be approved by the emperor, who required details of their stature, complexion and any marks or scars on their body. Julia was allowed to return after five years, but when Tiberius became emperor he confined her to a single room, and may have had her starved to death.

AD 26

A Love of Animals ❧ The Emperor Tiberius retreated to Capri, never again to return to Rome. On the island he abandoned himself to vice, indulging, it is said, not only his taste for children, but also goats, donkeys and camels.

AD 31

Brutal Logic ❧ (18 October) The prefect of the Praetorian Guard, Lucius Aelius Sejanus – who had created a reign of terror in Rome and seduced Livilla, Tiberius's daughter-in-law – was executed for plotting against the emperor. First he was strangled, and then his body was thrown to the mob, who tore it to pieces. Sejanus's three children were likewise put to death, the young girl first being debauched by the public executioner, it being contrary to Roman law to kill a virgin.

AD 37

An Incestuous Emperor ❧ Caligula became Roman emperor, despite the prediction of an astrologer that he had no more chance of donning the purple than of riding a horse across the Gulf of Baiae. To show his contempt for this prophecy, Caligula had a pontoon bridge comprising scores of ships built across the Gulf, and proceeded to ride across wearing the breastplate of Alexander the Great.

Caligula turned out to be a mad and depraved despot, who slept with his sisters (and anyone else – of either sex – who caught his fancy), made it an offence for anyone to look at him (he was sensitive about his thinning pate and copious body hair), devised new methods of torture (such as covering the victim with honey, and letting loose a swarm of wasps), and (according to one story) appointed his favourite horse, Incitatus, to the consulship. Another story has it that when his sister Drusilla became pregnant by him, he was so impatient to see his child that he had it ripped from Drusilla's womb. Whether or not this story is true, Drusilla certainly died, whereupon Caligula declared her to be a goddess.

In AD 41 (24 January) Caligula was fatally stabbed in the genitals by two of his guards, whom he had humiliated. They went on to kill his wife, and smashed his baby daughter's head against a wall.

The Emperor Caligula fed his favourite horse, Incitatus, at his table from golden dishes. It was said that he also appointed Incitatus to the consulship, which had been the most senior position in the ancient Republic.

circa AD 40

—

Seneca and the Armpit Plucker &• The Roman playwright Lucius
Annaeus Seneca, a noted stoic, found himself bereft of his philosophy when

faced with the noises from the bath house next door to his lodgings. One might think of Roman baths as places of ease and quiet content, but in a letter Seneca tells a different story. 'Conjure up in your imagination,' he told Lucilius, his correspondent, 'all the sounds that make one hate one's ears.' Among these he numbered the grunts of the weightlifters, the slaps of the masseurs, the shouts of the ball-players and the cries of various vendors. Shrillest of all were the shrieks of that most specialized of craftsmen, the armpit plucker, who never desisted from his caterwauling except, according to Seneca, 'when he's doing his job and making someone else shriek for him'.

circa AD 43
—

Legalization of Flatulence ❧ The Emperor Claudius, worried that holding in flatulence might be injurious to health, passed a law permitting the unleashing of intestinal gases at banquets.

circa AD 50
—

Sow's Womb and Mackerel Guts ❧ By the 1st century AD, only one in ten people in Rome had access to a hearth where they could cook – so the purveyors of takeaway food did a roaring trade. For the wealthy who dined at home, popular items included roast dormouse, kale cooked in saltpetre, and sow's womb (served with or without udders). Spattered over everything was a ubiquitous fish sauce called garum, made from slow-cooked mackerel guts (production of the pungent, salty sauce within the city was prohibited on account of the stench). A dish for special occasions was the *porcus troianus* ('Trojan pig'), a whole roasted pig stuffed with fruit and sausages. Brought to the table standing on its legs, its belly was then cut open, letting spill the sausages as if they were the animal's entrails. By this time the earlier fashion of allowing one's fish to expire at table (preferably in a sauce) had gone out of favour.

The Body in the Bog ❧ In 1984 the well-preserved body of a man was found in a peat bog at Lindow Moss in Cheshire. At first it was thought he might have been the victim of a recent murder, but carbon dating placed his death at some time between 2 BC and AD 119. The man, thought to have been an ancient British nobleman from the care with which his hair and nails were trimmed, had suffered three blows to the head, a cut throat and strangulation by means of a knotted cord. He may have been the victim of a ritual execution, or just possibly a human sacrifice.

AD 54

Viper Flesh and Opium ❧ Nero became Emperor of Rome, in the wake of an epidemic of conspiracies and murders among the ruling Julio-Claudian dynasty: his predecessor, Claudius, was almost certainly poisoned, possibly with Nero's connivance. Aware of the risks attaching to his master's new job, Nero's physician, Andromachus, developed a poison antidote involving 64 ingredients, chief among them viper flesh and opium. This substance, known as theriac, derived from a concoction attributed to one of the ancient kings of Pontus, who used his prisoners as guinea pigs. Theriac became a popular remedy for more or less any ailment (particularly after the proportion of opium was increased), and was still on sale in Italy towards the end of the 19th century.

AD 58

Flames From Below Ground ❧ Tacitus reported that near Cologne in Germany flames shot out from vents in the Earth. The local tribesmen put out the fires by swaddling them in old clothes.

AD 59

___

Incest and Matricide ❧ The Emperor Nero ordered the death of his mother, Agrippina, with whom, according to Suetonius, he was on unusually intimate terms:

> Whenever he rode in a litter with his mother, he had incestuous relations with her, which were betrayed by the stains on his clothing.

By AD 59 Agrippina had taken against Nero's new mistress, Poppaea, and the feeling was mutual. Suetonius (not the most reliable of sources) gives the following account:

> At last terrified by her violence and threats, he [Nero] determined to have her life, and after thrice attempting it by poison and finding that she had made herself immune by antidotes, he tampered with the ceiling of her bedroom, contriving a mechanical device for loosening its panels and dropping them upon her while she slept. When this leaked out through some of those connected with the plot, he devised a collapsible boat to destroy her by shipwreck or by the falling in of its cabin. Then he pretended a reconciliation and invited her in a most cordial letter to come to Baiae and celebrate the feast of Minerva with him. On her arrival, instructing his captains to wreck the galley in which she had come, by running into it as if by accident, he detained her at a banquet, and when she would return to Bauli, offered her his contrivance in place of the craft which had been damaged, escorting her to it in high spirits and even kissing her breasts as they parted. The rest of the night he passed sleepless in intense anxiety, awaiting the outcome of his design. On learning that everything had gone wrong and that she had escaped by swimming, driven to desperation he secretly had a dagger thrown down beside her freedman Lucius Agelmus, when he joyfully brought word that she was safe and sound, and then ordered that the freedman be seized and bound, on the charge of being hired to kill the emperor; that his mother be put to death, and the pretence made that she had escaped the consequences of her detected guilt by suicide.

Suetonius also tells us that Nero 'castrated the boy Sporus and actually tried to make a woman of him; and he married him with all the usual ceremonies, including a dowry and a bridal veil, took him to his home attended by a great throng, and treated him as his wife. And the witty jest that someone made is still current, that it would have been well for the world if Nero's father Domitius had had that kind of wife.'

AD 66

—

Suicide of an Epicure ❧ Death of the Roman writer Petronius Arbiter. He had been Nero's 'director of elegance', but latterly fell out of the emperor's favour. To forestall arrest and execution, he took his own life in an appropriately tasteful fashion, slitting his veins and then having them bound up again to ensure a slow and easeful death. As his life gradually drained away, he pecked at dainty dishes, listened to music, and chatted with friends on untroubling subjects. He finally lay down as if to sleep, and so met his end.

AD 69

—

Pheasant Brain and Flamingo Tongues ❧ (17 April) Vitellius, a noted glutton, became emperor of Rome. Once in power he would send the navy to distant parts to obtain his favourite dishes, such as the brains of pheasants, the livers of pike and the tongues of flamingos. Such were the gustatory excesses of his banquets that one of his regular dining companions, who missed several days of feasting due to illness, reportedly sighed, 'Thank heaven I was sick, otherwise I would be dead.' By the end of the year Vitellius had been overthrown and killed.

circa AD 70

—

A Tax on Public Lavatories ❧ The Roman Emperor Vespasian imposed a tax on public lavatories. His son Titus was horrified at such an undignified measure, but Vespasian would have none of it. Thrusting a handful of coins under his son's nose he declared '*Pecunia non olet*' ('money does not smell'). In honour of the emperor, the public urinals that once graced many a street corner in French towns and cites were known as *vespasiennes*. The *vespasiennes*, however, *did* smell – pungently so.

AD 77

On the Iniquities of Soap ❧ Publication of Pliny the Elder's *Historia Naturalis*, in which he disapprovingly noted the use of soap among the German and Gallic tribes – especially the men. The Romans considered the stuff only good for a hair pomade, preferring to cleanse their skin by rubbing it with olive oil, and then scraping off both oil and grime with a special metal implement.

130

Of Beards and Buggery ❧ The lover of the Emperor Hadrian, a Greek youth called Antinous, drowned in the Nile in mysterious circumstances. One theory regarding his death holds that, having reached adulthood, Antinous was no longer an acceptable companion to the emperor: being sexually mature, it was thought he would not accept the role of passive partner.

Hadrian himself demonstrated his manliness by sporting a beard, setting a new fashion: prior to his reign, the emperors were all clean shaven, but those who followed him over the next century and a half were all bearded.

165

A Flare for Publicity ❧ The Cynic philosopher Peregrinus Proteus burnt himself alive at the Olympic Games. His popularity having diminished, he had apparently decided to make a sensational exit.

192

Strangled by Narcissus ❧ The Emperor Commodus was strangled in his bath on the orders of his mistress by the wrestler Narcissus. Commodus had shocked Roman society by fighting as a gladiator in the arena – a job thought fit only for the lowest of the low. What is more, he had charged the city of Rome 1 million sesterces per appearance.

circa 210

——

Self-Castration 🍂 Taking note of the words of Matthew 19:12 ('there be eunuchs, which have made themselves eunuchs for the kingdom of heaven's sake'), Origen, one of the Fathers of the Church, castrated himself.

217

——

Assassinated While Urinating 🍂 (8 April) The Emperor Caracalla was assassinated while urinating at the side of a road in Mesopotamia on his way to make war against the Parthians.

218

——

Drowned in Rose Petals 🍂 Elagabalus became emperor of Rome, and outraged Roman society by instituting a new religion with himself as high priest. He further offended traditionalists when he married a Vestal Virgin (*see* 616 BC). According to the contemporary (and hostile) historian Dio Cassius, Elagabalus was wont to:

> frequent the most notorious brothels, driving out the prostitutes and taking that role himself. Finally, he turned over a room in the palace for his indecencies, and here he would stand nude at the door, as harlots do, and shake the curtain which hung from gold rings, while in a soft melting voice he solicited passers-by.

Dio Cassius also records that the emperor had intended to cut off his genitals, but settled for circumcision.

Even his ambitious grandmother began to worry about his eccentric behaviour, and on 11 March 222 arranged for him and his mother to be assassinated in the imperial privy. Among the stories told about Elagabalus after he was dead was that he disposed of the guests at one of his banquets by smothering them with tons of rose petals falling from above.

circa 250

——

Two Breasts on a Platter ❧ For following the Christian faith, and rejecting the advances of a Roman prefect, St Agatha of Sicily was placed by the authorities in a brothel run by a madam called Aphrodisia, but all attempts on her virtue proved unsuccessful. She was then tortured on the rack, suffered the lash and had her sides torn with hooks. Subsequently her breasts were cut off, although these were miraculously restored. She finally expired after being dragged naked over hot coals. In Christian iconography she is often depicted carrying her amputated breasts on a plate. Agatha is the patron saint of wet nurses, bell-founders (echoing the shape of her breasts) and those suffering from breast cancer.

260

——

Emperor Humiliated, Then Flayed ❧ Death of the Roman Emperor Valerian. He had been captured by the Persian king Shapur I, and forced to work as this potentate's mounting block. When Valerian, sickened by his humiliation, offered to raise a massive ransom, Shapur had molten gold poured down his throat. The king then had the ex-emperor flayed and his skin stuffed with straw. This effigy was subsequently put on display in a temple.

304

——

Dealing with Unwanted Suitors – Part I ❧ Traditional date of the martyrdom of St Lucy of Syracuse. Legend has it that Lucy was wooed by a young man who complained that her beautiful eyes haunted him night and day. In response she cut out the offending orbs and sent them to him, begging that he now leave her in peace to pursue her devotions.

This painting by Bernardino Luini (c.1480–1532)
shows St Agatha, martyred c.250, carrying her
amputated breasts on a plate.

316

Flesh Torn by Combs 🐚 St Blasius or Blaize was martyred, his flesh
being torn by iron combs – hence his subsequent position as patron saint
of woolcombers.

320

Forty Frozen for their Faith &❧ At Sebaste in Armenia (modern Sivas in eastern Turkey), 40 Roman soldiers of the Twelfth Legion, the *Fulminata* or Thunderers, met an icy fate for persisting with their Christian faith. On one of the bitterest nights of the year they were left standing naked in the middle of a frozen lake, and instructed they could cross over to the welcoming fires that they could see flickering on the shore if only they would renounce Christ. If they did so, warm baths and blankets awaited them. Only one man broke and ran for the shore, but a soldier who witnessed the courage of the remaining men was so impressed that he stripped off and took the place on the frozen waters abandoned by the apostate.

336

A Fatal Evacuation of the Bowels &❧ The theologian Arius, deemed a heretic by the Council of Nicaea, met a spectacular end in Constantinople, as described by the historian Socrates Scholasticus (*fl.*5th century):

> As he approached the place called Constantine's Forum, where the column of porphyry is erected, a terror arising from the remorse of conscience seized Arius, and with the terror a violent relaxation of the bowels: he therefore enquired whether there was a convenient place near, and being directed to the back of Constantine's Forum, he hastened thither. Soon after a faintness came over him, and together with the evacuations his bowels protruded, followed by a copious haemorrhage, and the descent of the smaller intestines: moreover portions of his spleen and liver were brought off in the effusion of blood, so that he almost immediately died.

circa 400

Dealing with Unwanted Suitors – Part II ✺ The *Suda*, a 10th-century Byzantine encyclopedia, records the following story of how Hypatia – the Alexandrian neo-Platonic philosopher and mathematician – cured a lovesick admirer by showing him her sanitary towels:

> She was so very beautiful and attractive that one of those who attended her lectures fell in love with her. He was not able to contain his desire, but he informed her of his condition. Ignorant reports say that Hypatia relieved him of his disease by music; but truth proclaims that music failed to have any effect. She brought some of her female rags and threw them before him, showing him the signs of her unclean origin, and said, 'You love this, O youth, and there is nothing beautiful about it.' His soul was turned away by shame and surprise at the unpleasant sight, and he was brought to his right mind.

In March 415 there were anti-pagan riots in Alexandria, possibly stirred up by Bishop Cyril. Hypatia was stripped by a Christian mob, and scraped to death with what sources variously describe as tiles, potsherds or oyster shells. They may have been inspired by the Emperor Constantius, who had decreed that witches should have their flesh torn off their bones with iron hooks. Subsequently Hypatia became a heroine to Enlightenment figures such as Voltaire and Edward Gibbon.

401

Black Sea Freezes Over ✺ It became so cold that it was reported the Black Sea had frozen over.

405

Father of the Irish ✺ Death of Niall of the Nine Hostages, High King of Ireland. DNA research published in 2006 suggested that Niall was the ancestor of some 3 million men now alive, including 1 in 12 of the present male population of Ireland.

451

Death by Nosebleed &

At the Battle of Chalons, Attila the Hun prepared to meet his death, as here recounted by Sir Edward Creasy (*The Fifteen Decisive Battles of the World*, 1851):

> Expecting an assault on the morrow, Attila stationed his best archers in front of the cars and wagons, which were drawn up as a fortification along his lines, and made every preparation for a desperate resistance. But the 'Scourge of God' resolved that no man should boast of the honour of having either captured or slain him, and he caused to be raised in the centre of his encampment a huge pyramid of the wooden saddles of his cavalry. Round it he heaped the spoils and the wealth that he had won; on it he stationed his wives who had accompanied him in the campaign; and on the summit Attila placed himself, ready to perish in the flames, and balk the victorious foe of their choicest booty, should they succeed in storming his defences.

In fact Attila survived the battle and lived for another two years, until, in 453, he died of a nose bleed on his wedding night, after a heroic drinking bout. His followers, loathe to display such unmanly manifestations of grief as tears and lamentations, cut off their hair and slashed their bodies with knives, so that 'the greatest of warriors should be mourned with the blood of men'.

459

Thirty-Six Years on Top of a Pillar &

(2 September) Death of St Simeon Stylites, who had lived on top of a narrow pillar in the Syrian desert for 36 years. He found it was the only way to avoid the hordes of pilgrims who came to admire his asceticism.

The Emperor Kublai Khan in his hunting lodge, carried on the backs of four elephants (see 1292).

The Middle Ages

Torn Apart by Wild Horses 🐾 Debauched on the Altar 🐾 The Cadaver Synod 🐾 The Cucumber King 🐾 Pope Turns Palace into Whorehouse 🐾 Future King Defecates at own Baptism 🐾 Pontiff Makes Pact with Prince of Darkness 🐾 Eilmer the Flying Monk 🐾 Basil the Bulgar Slayer 🐾 Hakim the Mad 🐾 Rudolf the Sluggard 🐾 Comet Kills Cats 🐾 The Foreskin of Jesus 🐾 The Castration of Prince Arthur 🐾 Mass Flagellation 🐾 The Naked Brethren 🐾 A Hot Spit through the Secret Place Posterial 🐾 Bubonic Bombs 🐾 Crowning a Corpse as Queen 🐾

582

Blood Bath – Part I 🐦 It was said that it rained blood over Paris. In all likelihood the raindrops carried red dust from the Sahara – a common enough phenomenon in northwest Europe.

circa 585

Blood Bath – Part II 🐦 Near Vannes in France, a pond full of fish was reported to have turned into blood, which for days provided sustenance for flocks of birds and stray dogs.

589

Competition Among Miracle Workers 🐦 Death of St David. Among his miracles was that by which he cured St Kyned, a cripple, of his deformity, making him strong and straight. St Kyned, apparently something of a joker, demonstrated the power of his own prayers by miraculously restoring his various handicaps.

circa 600

Observing the Sabbath – Part I 🐦 The old chronicles known as the *Welsh Triads* alleged that one Gwrgi, a rogue Welshman at the court of Aethelfryth, King of Bernicia, became so fond of eating human flesh that he would have a male and female Welsh captive slaughtered for his table every day – and two of each on Saturdays, so as not to break the Sabbath.

613

Torn Apart by Wild Horses 🐦 Queen Brunhilda of Austrasia, hated for her cruelty and avarice, was eventually overthrown, at the age of 70.

Queen Brunhilda of Austrasia about to be torn apart (or possibly dragged to death) by wild horses.

The *Liber Historiae Francorum* details her fate: 'King Clotaire ordered that she be lifted on to a camel and led through the entire army. Then she was tied to the feet of wild horses and torn apart limb from limb. Finally she died. Her grave was the fire. Her bones were burnt.'

844

Pope Pig-Face 🐾 Sergius II was elected to the papacy. According to the 15th-century curator of the Vatican Library, Bartolomeo Platina, Sergius's original name meant 'Hog's-mouth'.

circa 850

The Origin of Coffee 🐾 An Arabian goatherd called Kaldi noticed that his flock became particularly perky when they fed on the berries of a certain bush. Thus was the property of the coffee bean first discovered – at least according to tradition.

855

Pope Joan ❧ According to legend, a woman called Joan became pope. The following account is found in the *Chronicon Pontificum et Imperatum* by the 13th-century Polish chronicler, Martin of Opava:

> John Anglicus, born at Mainz, was pope for two years, seven months and four days, and died in Rome, after which there was a vacancy in the papacy of one month. It is claimed that this John was a woman, who as a girl had been led to Athens dressed in the clothes of a man by a certain lover of hers. There she became proficient in a diversity of branches of knowledge, until she had no equal, and afterwards in Rome, she taught the liberal arts and had great masters among her students and audience. A high opinion of her life and learning arose in the city, and she was chosen for pope. While pope, however, she became pregnant by her companion. Through ignorance of the exact time when the birth was expected, she was delivered of a child while in procession from St Peter's to the Lateran, in a narrow lane between the Colisseum and St Clement's Church. After her death, it is said she was buried in that same place. The Lord Pope always turns aside from the street and it is believed by many that this is done because of abhorrence of the event. Nor is she placed on the list of the holy pontiffs, both because of her female sex and on account of the foulness of the matter.

870

A Spreadeagled King ❧ Edmund, martyr-king of East Anglia, was killed by the Vikings, possibly by the method known as the 'blood eagle' or 'spread eagle'. In this method of slow execution, the victim was held face down on the ground while his or her ribs were prised outward from the spine, until they stuck out either side of the body, like a pair of wings. The victim's still-breathing lungs were then pulled out, and salt rubbed into the wounds.

844

Debauched on the Altar ❧ During the siege of Salerno, the Saracens occupied the monastery church of St Benedict, where, according to Edward Gibbon, 'a mussulman chief spread his couch on the communion table, and on that altar sacrificed each night the virginity of a Christian nun. As he wrestled with a reluctant maid, a beam in the roof was accidentally or dexterously thrown down on his head; and the death of the lustful emir was imputed to the wrath of Christ, which was at length awakened to the defence of his faithful spouse.'

896

Gluttonous Moles in Ireland ❧ A shower of mole-like creatures fell on Ireland, and proceeded to devour everything in sight.

897

The Cadaver Synod ❧ The so-called Cadaver Synod took place in Rome in January 897, at a time of bitter political division in Italy. The previous pope, Formosus, who had been dead for nine months, was charged with breaking canon law by accepting the see of Rome (i.e. the papacy) while still bishop of another diocese, that of Porto. The current pope, Stephen VI, insisted that Formosus appear in person to answer charges, so the corpse of the dead pontiff was exhumed, dressed in papal vestments and propped up in a chair in court, a deacon answering the prosecution's charges on his behalf. Formosus was found guilty, his election declared invalid, his body stripped of the papal robes, and the fingers he used for blessing cut off. Ironically, Stephen himself had been bishop of another diocese, Anagni, when he became pope, but as it had been Formosus who had made the appointment, and all Formosus's acts as pope had been annulled, Stephen was let off the hook. Shortly afterwards, Stephen was deposed, imprisoned and strangled, and his successor, Theodore II, had Formosus' body buried and his pontificate reinstated.

921

The Uni-Corned Beast of the Steppes ❧ Ahamd ibn Fadlan set off as part of an embassy from the Caliph of Baghdad to the king of the Bulgars of the Volga region. He brought back reports he had heard of a mysterious creature on the steppes. It was, said the local people, larger than a bull, though smaller than a camel, and was possessed of a single pointed horn:

> Whenever it sees a rider, it approaches, and if the rider has a fast horse, the horse tries to escape by running fast, and if the beast overtakes them, it picks the rider out of the saddle with its horn, and tosses him in the air, and meets him with the point of the horn, and continues doing so until the rider dies. But it will not harm or hurt the horse in any way or manner.

Some have speculated that this unicorn-like creature might have been *Elasmotherium*, the giant rhinoceros that once lived in the region, but which almost certainly became extinct more than 100,000 years ago.

931

The Cucumber King ❧ Theinhko, king of Burma, was killed by an angry farmer after he had eaten his cucumbers without asking. The farmer then took over the throne as King Nyanng-u Sawrahan, known as 'the Cucumber King'.

circa 935

My Kingdom for a Lance ❧ Henry the Fowler, King of the Germans, exchanged a large swathe of his territory in what is now Switzerland for a holy relic, a lance said to have belonged to the Emperor Constantine. It may not have been such a bad bargain: his son carried it in 955 at Lechfeld, where the Germans scored a great victory over the pagan Magyars.

955

King Takes Nun as Mistress ❧ King Eadwig of England, then aged about 15, slipped away from his coronation feast to consort with a young noblewoman of easy virtue (and possibly also with her mother), only to be dragged back to the feast by an outraged St Dunstan, Abbot of Glastonbury. Eadwig was furious, and Dunstan was forced into exile. Dunstan had another run-in with the next king, Edgar, in 961, after the latter fathered a child by his mistress, a nun. Dunstan, by then Archbishop of Canterbury, refused to crown Edgar until 973 (at least that is one story as to why the king, who succeeded in 959, had to wait so long for his coronation).

964

Pope Turns Palace into Whorehouse ❧ (14 May) Death of Pope John XII. John, the son of Alberic II, ruler of Rome, had been elected pontiff in 955 on his father's orders. He was only 18 at the time, and was deposed less than a decade later. Among the charges levelled at him were that 'he had fornicated with the widow of Rainier, with Stephana his father's concubine, with the widow Anna, and with his own niece, and he made the sacred palace into a whorehouse'. Additionally, he had accepted payment for ordaining bishops (he made a 10-year-old boy Bishop of Todi), and 'toasted to the devil with wine'. It was said that Pope John was murdered by an irate husband whom he had cuckolded.

circa 968

Future King Defecates at Own Baptism ❧ In the Anglo-Saxon period, the holy water in baptismal fonts was not changed unless an infant defecated in it. Urination was, apparently, not a problem. According to one tradition, at his baptism *circa* 968, the future king of England, Ethelred the Unready, eased his infant bowels in the holy water. Dunstan, the Archbishop of Canterbury presiding over the ceremony, declared that this portent foretold the overthrow of the English monarchy. In 1013, Ethelred was forced off the throne by Sweyn Forkbeard, at the head of a Viking invasion.

circa 973

A Wolf Shortage in Wales ❧ King Edgar of England demanded a yearly tribute from the Welsh king Hywel of 300 wolves. Hywel kept up the payments for three years, after which he complained that he could find no more wolves.

999

Pontiff Makes Pact with Prince of Darkness ❧ Gerbert of Aurillac was elected pope as Silvester II. He had studied with Arab scholars in Spain, and had brought their knowledge of mathematics and astronomy to Christian Europe. It may have been Gerbert's familiarity with these arcane matters that led William of Malmesbury, writing in the 12th century, to conclude that Gerbert was a sorcerer who had made a pact with the Devil.

1010

Eilmer the Flying Monk ❧ Eilmer, a young monk at Malmesbury Abbey in Wiltshire, was inspired by the flight of jackdaws to make his own attempt to conquer the air. According to William of Malmesbury, writing in the following century, Eilmer constructed a pair of wings and launched himself from the top of the abbey tower. He apparently glided some 200 yards, but broke both legs on landing. The abbot disapproved of the young monk's levity, and forbade further attempts.

1014

Basil the Bulgar Slayer ❧ The Byzantine emperor, Basil II, ordered that 14,000 Bulgar prisoners captured in battle be blinded. He specified that one eye should be left per hundred men, so that the mutilated soldiers could be led home as a dire warning to their countrymen. Basil was for ever after known as 'Basil the Bulgar Slayer'.

1016

Death on the Privy ❧ (30 November) Death of Edmund Ironside, king of England. He most probably died of natural causes, but some sources say he was stabbed in the bowels while sitting on the privy by an assassin concealed therein, on the orders of Cnut, the Danish king who took over Edmund's kingdom.

1021

Hakim the Mad ❧ Death of Al-Hakim bi-Amr Allah, Caliph of Egypt, whose eccentric behaviour earned him the sobriquet Hakim the Mad. Hakim issued bans on the eating of grapes and water cress, and the playing of chess. Annoyed by the barking of dogs, he ordered that they all be killed, and also decreed that the people of Cairo work by night and sleep by day. If he caught a merchant cheating, he would have his slave Masoud sodomize him, while he himself himself stood on the man's head. The Caliph reserved a particular dislike for women, forbidding them to leave their homes, banning the making of women's shoes, and, on one occasion, having a group of noisy women boiled alive in a public bath. However, he had a great affection for his sister, Sitt al-Mulk, who became so alarmed at his incestuous intentions and his accusations of adultery on her part that she arranged for his disappearance. His blood-stained donkey was found near a well in the Muqattam Hills. The Druze sect claim that Hakim did not die, but was concealed by God, and that he will return as the Mahdi on Judgement Day.

1032

Rudolf the Sluggard ❧ (6 September) Death of the last king of Burgundy, Rudolf III, known as Rudolf the Sluggard because he failed to control his uppity nobles and could not stop the incursions of the Emperor Henry II into his territories.

1050

Ordeal by Fire ❧ Emma of Normandy, mother of Edward the Confessor, was accused of involvement in the murder of another son, Alfred (*see* 1053). Emma – who was also accused with carrying on with Alwyn, Bishop of Winchester – sought to prove her innocence by walking across nine red-hot ploughshares in front of the altar of Winchester Cathedral. This she did without apparent harm, thus establishing to everyone's satisfaction that she had had no share in these crimes.

1053

Choked on a Communion Wafer ❧ (Easter) Earl Godwine of Wessex swore a solemn oath that – contrary to popular opinion – he was not responsible for the murder of Alfred, brother of Edward the Confessor, who in 1036 had been blinded and then put to death by disembowelling. Taking a communion wafer to confirm his oath, Godwine choked to death.

1066

Speared in the Private Parts ❧ (25 September) At the Battle of Stamford Bridge, a single Norwegian held the bridge, holding back the English army, 'felling more than forty Englishmen with his trusty axe' – according to Henry of Huntingdon, the 12th-century chronicler. Henry continued: 'At length someone came up in a boat and through the openings of the bridge struck him in the private parts with a spear.' Victory for the English followed.

1066

Harold the Unrecognizable 🐾 (14 October) The body of King Harold was so horribly mutilated after his death at Hastings that only his mistress could identify him.

___

Riot in the Abbey 🐾 (25 December) During the coronation of William the Conqueror in Westminster Abbey, the congregation of Normans and Saxons shouted their approval in both French and English. The Norman soldiers outside thought an assassination attempt was being made inside the abbey, and set fire to the surrounding houses. Smoke filled the abbey and many of the congregation rushed outside, where rioting broke out. William was nevertheless successfully crowned.

1086

Comet Kills Cats 🐾 The chroniclers report that the passage of a comet proved fatal to all the cats of Westphalia.

1087

A Ruptured Conqueror 🐾 (9 September) William the Conqueror died, having ruptured his belly in a fall from his horse. As they attempted to bury him, the monks of Rouen found that William – who had become quite portly – was too large for the sarcophagus that had been prepared. As they tried to force the putrid carcase into its final resting place, it burst open, and even incense and perfumes failed to disperse the stench that filled the church.

circa 1110

The Foreskin of Jesus ❧ Among the gifts sent by the Byzantine emperor Alexius I Comnenus to Henry I of England was a scrap of what was said to be the prepuce of Christ.

1135

Philandering King 'Free from Carnal Desires' ❧ (1 December) Death of Henry I, apparently after eating a dish of lampreys that disagreed with him. Henry holds the record among English kings for having sired the most bastards: at least 20, by six different mistresses. The contemporary chronicler, William of Malmesbury, claimed that the king 'was wholly free from carnal desires', and that 'His intercourse with women was undertaken not for the satisfaction of his lusts, but from his desire for children.'

1157

Pitiful Fate of the Boy of Egremont ❧ William de Romilly, great-nephew of David I of Scotland and known as 'the Boy of Egremont', attempted to jump his horse across the Strid, a six-foot-wide chasm on the River Wharfe in Yorkshire. Like many others who have unsuccessfully attempted the jump, he was pulled by the raging waters down into deep underwater caverns, where he drowned.

1163

Lovers Reunited ❧ The *Chronicle of Tours* reported that when Heloise was laid to rest in the same grave as her lover, Peter Abelard, 21 years after his own demise, his corpse held out its hand to receive her.

1167

The Merman of Orford 🍂 Fishermen netted a merman off Orford, Suffolk, as described by the chronicler Ralph Coggeshall in 1207:

> Men fishing in the sea caught in their nets a wild man. He was naked and was like a man in all his members, covered with hair and with a long shaggy beard. He eagerly ate whatever was brought to him, but if it was raw he pressed it between his hands until all the juice was expelled. He would not talk, even when tortured and hung up by his feet. Brought into church, he showed no signs of reverence or belief. He sought his bed at sunset and always remained there until sunrise.
>
> He was allowed to go into the sea, strongly guarded with three lines of nets, but he dived under the nets and came up again and again. Eventually he came back of his own free will. But later on he escaped and was never seen again.

Coggeshall came to no definite conclusions as to the nature of the merman:

> As to whether this was a mortal man, or some fish pretending human shape, or was an evil spirit hiding in the body of a drowned man ... it is not possible to be precise; the more so because so many wonderful things of this kind are told by many to whom they have happened.

1189

Tarring and Feathering 🍂 As Richard I set off on the Third Crusade, he enacted a law by which any sailor caught thieving was to have his head shaved and then covered with molten pitch, and the feathers of a pillow shaken over it.

1191

Pontiff Kicks Off Emperor's Crown 🍂 (1 April) Pope Celestine III crowned Henry VI as emperor. To demonstrate his power over earthly

sovereigns, after he had placed the crown on the kneeling emperor, the pope then pushed it off with his toes.

1199
—

Saint Steals Relic ❧ St Hugh of Lincoln, visiting Fécamp Abbey in Normandy, carried off a piece of their best relic in his teeth. Theft of a relic was not then regarded as a crime, but rather as an expression by the dead saint of a desire for a change of scene.

—

French Bastards ❧ (12 December) Pope Innocent III put the kingdom of France under an interdict. In 1193 King Philip Augustus had married Ingeborg of Denmark, but found her repellent in the flesh, and applied to the pope for an annulment on the grounds of non-consummation. Ingeborg protested that the marriage *had* been consummated, and the pope refused to grant an annulment.

Ignoring this, in 1196 Philip Augustus married Agnes of Merania, and it was when he refused the pope's order to leave Agnes and return to Ingeborg that Celestine imposed the interdict. All the churches in France were shut up for nine months, and all children born in that period were deemed illegitimate, for so long as the king refused to sleep with his wife, 'it was not permitted to any of his subjects to sleep with theirs' (Isaac Disraeli, *Curiosities of Literature*, 1791–1823). The interdict continued until 7 September 1200.

1199
—

Fate of a Regicide ❧ (6 April) Death of Richard the Lionheart. He had been shot in the shoulder by an arrow while besieging Château Châlus, and the wound turned gangrenous, leading to septicaemia. As he lay dying, he asked to see Bertram de Gourdon, the man who had fired the fatal crossbow. 'What harm did I ever do thee,' asked the king, 'that thou should'st kill me?' Bertram replied: 'You killed with your own hand my father and two of my brothers, and you likewise designed to have killed me. You may take your revenge. I should cheerfully suffer all the torments that can be inflicted were I sure of having delivered the world of a tyrant who filled it with blood and carnage.' Richard was so impressed by the man's courage that he gave him his freedom and a hundred marks. But after Richard's death, his followers flayed Bertram alive.

1203

The Castration of Prince Arthur &❧ Presumed date of death of Arthur of Brittany, nephew of King John and his rival for the throne. It was widely thought that John was responsible for his murder. Arthur's jailer, Hubert de Burgh, later said that the youth, aged 15 or 16, was castrated by agents of the king and died of shock – but later withdrew this allegation.

1209

Old Testament God said to be Devil &❧ The Albigensian Crusade against the Cathars of southwest France began. The Church objected to most of the doctrines of the Cathars, who asserted that the God of the Old Testament was in fact the Devil. They also rejected all forms of killing, including war and capital punishment, and they avoided any food that might be regarded as resulting from sexual intercourse, such as meat, eggs and dairy products (fish were exempt).

The first major event of the Crusade was the capture on 22 July of the town of Béziers; Arnaud, the Cistercian abbot who commanded the Crusaders, was asked by his troops how they should tell Cathar from Catholic. 'Kill them all,' the abbot replied, 'God will recognize his own.' Arnaud reported to the Pope that some 20,000 persons had been put to the sword, 'regardless of rank, age or sex'.

1212

The Children's Crusade 🦜 According to later accounts, a boy in either France or Germany had a vision in which Jesus told him to lead the next crusade. Followed by some 20,000 children, he made his way to the Mediterranean, the waters of which he believed would part for him, allowing the crusaders to walk to Jerusalem. When this failed to happen, they boarded ships, but either died in shipwrecks or were sold into slavery.

Historians have now unravelled something of the truth behind the legend. The 'children' were actually dispossessed peasants, whom contemporaries patronizingly referred to as *pueri* (Latin, 'boys'), and there were two movements of such people, one originating in Germany and one in France. The first was led by a German shepherd called Nicholas, who led several thousand followers over the Alps into Italy, but when the waters failed to part, the group dispersed, and some may have ended up being sold as slaves in various Mediterranean ports. The second movement was led by a French shepherd boy called Stephen de Cloyes, who claimed to be in possession of a letter from Jesus to the king of France. Followed by 30,000 people, he travelled to Saint-Denis, but the king ordered them to disperse.

1226

Disregarding Doctor's Orders 🦜 As Louis VIII of France lay dying, his physicians sought to remedy his sickness by placing in his bed a beautiful young woman, who, when he awoke, offered the king her favours. But the king would have none of it. 'I prefer to die,' he said, 'rather than to save my life by a mortal sin.'

1227

The Extensive Progeny of Genghis Khan 🦜 (18 August) Death of Genghis Khan. His philosophy, as attributed to him, is summed up thus:

The greatest joy a man can have is victory: to conquer one's enemy's armies, to pursue them, to deprive them of their possessions, to reduce their families to tears, to ride on their horses, and to make love to their wives and daughters.

Research published in 2003 based on analysis of Y-chromosomes suggests that 8 per cent of men across a large area of Asia (about 0.5 per cent of the global male population) are descended from Genghis Khan.

1250

A Wild Man of the Woods In the *Konungs skuggsjá* ('king's mirror') written in Norway about this time there is a description of a strange sylvan creature:

> . . . a living creature was caught in the forest as to which no one could say definitely whether it was a man or some other animal; for no one could get a word from it or be sure that it understood human speech. It had the human shape, however, in every detail, both as to hands and face and feet; but the entire body was covered with hair as the beasts are, and down the back it had a long coarse mane like that of a horse, which fell to both sides and trailed along the ground when the creature stooped in walking.

1258

Rolled Up in a Carpet and Trampled to Death (10 February) Fall of Baghdad to a Mongol army under Hulagu, a grandson of Genghis Khan. Hundreds of thousands of citizens were slaughtered, and so many books were ransacked from the Grand Library and thrown into the Tigris that is was said a horse could walk across them. Arab historians recounted how the river 'ran black with scholars' ink and red with the blood of martyrs'. The Caliph himself was rolled up in a carpet and trampled to death by horses, in accordance with the Mongol belief that the Earth would be offended if tainted with royal blood. After the sack of Baghdad, such was the stench of decay coming from the city that the Mongols were obliged to move their camp upwind.

Flagellants atoning for their sins in Spain in the 16th century. The fashion
for mass flagellation first arose in 1259 in Italy.

1259

Mass Flagellation ❧ The first recorded outbreak of mass flagellation
occurred in Perugia, Italy, where processions of thousands of penitents
processed through the city thrashing themselves to the accompaniment of
hymns. Anybody who failed to join in was thought to be in league with the
Devil, and those more moderate priests who expressed reservations about
the goings-on were killed, together with many Jews. The Flagellant movement subsequently spread to other parts of Italy and elsewhere in Europe,
and was particularly strong at the time of the Black Death in the mid-14th
century.

1260

Observing the Sabbath – Part II ❧ According to the Tudor antiquary John Leland, a Jew in Tewkesbury refused to be rescued from the cesspool into which he had fallen because it was the Jewish Sabbath. The local baron, Richard de Clare, Earl of Gloucester, refused to countenance his rescue on the following day, that being the Christian Sabbath. Caught between these strictures, the unfortunate man died.

1264

Three Days on the Gallows ❧ (16 August) Henry III of England pardoned one Inetta de Balsham, who had been condemned to death for harbouring thieves. She had been hanged, but reportedly survived after three days swinging on the end of the rope.

1269

Dining with One's Husband's Heart ❧ On the death of John Baliol (father of the Scottish king), his widow Dervoguilla had his heart embalmed and placed in an ivory and silver casket, which she would place on the table while she ate her meals, calling it her 'sweet silent companion'. When she herself was buried in 1289, in New Abbey in Galloway, she had the casket placed over her own heart, and the site of her burial for ever after became known as Dolce Cor or Sweetheart Abbey.

1290

Medieval Manners ❧ Fra Bonvicino da Riva published a courtesy book in which he advised diners – who then customarily ate with their fingers from a shared bowl – not to poke their fingers in their ears while eating, let alone scratch 'at any foul part'. A century later another writer suggested that if 'you cannot help scratching, then courteously take a portion of your dress and scratch with that'.

1292

—

Tales of Kublai Khan ❧ Marco Polo returned from his 17-year stay in China, bringing back reports of the fabulous wealth of the emperor, Kublai Khan. The grounds of Kublai's palace at Khanbalig were dotted with man-made hills, covered in trees brought by elephant from all parts of the empire, and sprinkled with pieces of lapis lazuli. When out hawking, Kublai would travel in a hunting lodge carried on the backs of four elephants, while every three days his harem was replenished with a fresh batch of six carefully selected virgins.

1311

—

The Naked Brethren ❧ Pope Clement V condemned as heretical a sect known as the Brethren of the Free Spirit, which had spread across northern France and western Germany. The Brethren were pantheists who believed that 'all things are One, because whatever is, is God'. Thus sin could not exist, and everything was permitted. Some adherents were reported to celebrate mass while naked.

1313

—

Armour Barred from Parliament ❧ The *Statutum de Defensione portandi* was passed, banning members wearing armour from entering Parliament. The law is still in force.

1314

—

The Templar's Curse ❧ (18 March) Jacques de Molay, the last Grand Master of the Knights Templar, was slowly roasted to death over a hot, smokeless fire, on the orders of Philip IV of France, who had seized the considerable wealth of the order and tortured and put to death many of the knights, with the collusion of his puppet, Pope Clement V. Molay was said as he died to have challenged both king and pope to meet him before the judgement of God before the year was out. Both men indeed died in 1314, Clement on 20 April and Philip on 29 November, after a hunting accident.

1324

The Riches of Africa 🍂 Mansa Musa, the ruler of Mali, spent so much gold in Cairo on his way to Mecca that the currency was devalued as a result.

1327

A Hot Spit through the Secret Place Posterial 🍂 (20 or 21 January) Edward II of England was murdered in Berkeley Castle, while held prisoner by his estranged queen. It is said he was dispatched by a red-hot poker inserted into his anus ('with a hot spit put through the secret place posterial', according to the chronicler Ranulf Higden); but this may have been a fabrication.

1329

Following Another's Heart 🍂 (7 June) On his death Robert the Bruce, king of Scotland, asked his old friend and ally Sir James Douglas to take his heart on crusade to the Holy Land, in fulfilment of a vow that Bruce had been unable to keep in life. Douglas obliged, and on his way through Spain assisted the king of Castile in his fight against the Moors. Finding himself hopelessly surrounded in battle, Douglas flung the Bruce's heart in its casket into the fray and charged after, being rapidly overwhelmed. After the battle both the body of Douglas and the Bruce's heart were recovered, and returned to Scotland for burial.

1332

Autres Pays, Autres Moeurs ❧ (May) Ibn Battuta visited the court of the Khan of the Golden Horde near the Sea of Azov. The Arab traveller was shocked when the Khan invited his wives to sit down before he himself did. What was worse, the women wore no veils. That winter, Ibn Battuta had to don so many layers of clothes against the bitter cold of the steppes that he was unable to mount his horse unaided.

1336

A Curb on Banqueting ❧ The Sumptuary Act of Edward III forbade any person to eat more than two courses in one meal. The act made it clear that soup was to be considered as a full course, and not just a sauce. The following year Edward banned the wearing of fur by any man or woman, even the king.

1346

Bubonic Bombs ❧ The Tartars besieging Kaffa (modern Theodosia in the Crimea, then governed by the Genoese) catapulted the corpses of their own men who had died of plague into the city, in the hope that this would spread the disease to the defenders. It is thought that the Black Death may have spread to Europe via Genoese traders fleeing the city.

1349

Football Banned ❧ (12 June) Edward III, in a letter to the sheriffs of London, commanded that all able-bodied men practise archery in their spare time, and to this end banned 'the throwing of stones, wood, or iron, handball, football, bandyball, cambuck, or cockfighting, nor suchlike vain plays, which have no profit in them'.

circa 1350

The Costs of Keeping a Lion ❧ Accounts reveal that to keep a lion in the menagerie at the Tower of London cost sixpence a day, while to keep a prisoner in the Tower cost only a penny.

1351

Houses Made of Salt ❧ During his crossing of the Sahara en route to Mali, the Arab traveller Ibn Battuta arrived at the salt mine at Taghaza, where even the houses and mosque were built of salt.

1355

Crowning a Corpse as Queen ❧ (7 January) Inês de Castro, beloved and beautiful mistress of Dom Pedro, heir to the throne of Portugal, was assassinated by a group of royal councillors who had persuaded King Alfonso that his son and his mistress's family were plotting against him. After Alfonso's death Pedro became king, and subjected the assassins to horrific tortures, culminating in their hearts being torn from their bodies while they still lived. Pedro the Cruel – as he now became known – determined that Inês should take her rightful place as his queen. To this end he had her body exhumed, dressed in royal robes, and taken on a ceremonial, candlelit procession to the place of coronation, where it was anointed and crowned. The king ordered that his subjects all swear allegiance to their new queen, and one by one the nobles came forward, knelt, and kissed the cold and withered hand of the long-dead beauty.

1357

Abstention from Food and Drink Gains Pardon ❧ (25 April) Cecilia de Rygeway survived 40 days in Nottingham jail – where she was being held for the murder of her husband – without apparently taking any food or drink. So impressed was King Edward III that he gave her a pardon.

1360

Dead in the Saddle &- (14 April) *Stow's Chronicle* recorded that on this day 'King Edward [III] with his host lay before the city of Paris; which day was full dark of mist and hail, and so bitter cold, that many men died on their horsebacks with the cold; wherefore unto this day it hath been called the Black Monday.'

1363

Nightcaps Banned &- The Statute of Diet and Apparel forbade anyone with an annual income less than £20 from wearing a silk nightcap.

1376

The Pied Piper's Revenge &- (22 July) According to Verstegen, the Anglo-Dutch antiquary of the early 17th century, this was the day when the Pied Piper took his revenge on the ungrateful townspeople of Hamelin by leading 'a number of boys' of the town through a hole in the side of a hill, which then closed up. The Brothers Grimm put the disaster a century earlier, dating it to 26 June 1284. The legend may recall an outbreak of St Vitus dance, a disease (also known as chorea) characterized by jerky movements, or it may have been inspired by a landslide, or even the Children's Crusade (*see* 1212).

1379

Excess Baggage &- According to J.A. Farrer, in *Military Manners and Customs* (1885), 'When a fleet of English ships, under Sir John Arundel, on its way to Brittany, was overtaken by a storm, and the jettisoning of other things failed to relieve the vessels, sixty women, many of whom had been forced to embark, were thrown into the sea.'

circa 1380

A Confucian in a Coffin &● The first Ming emperor, Hongwu, issued an edict that none of his advisors was to criticize him, on pain of being beaten to death with a length of bamboo. There is a tale that one Confucian scholar was so determined to point out Hongwu's errors of policy that he brought a coffin with him to court, addressed the emperor in a forthright fashion, then climbed into the coffin, expecting to suffer instant execution. However, the emperor was sufficiently impressed with the man's courage to spare his life.

1381

The Order of Fools &● (12 November) Adolphus, Count of Cleves, founded the Order of Fools. Rather than being bent on mirth and misrule, members of the Order involved themselves in charitable work – although they did wear a badge with a picture of a jester.

1384

On the Immensity of Cairo &● An Italian traveller reported from Egypt that there were more people living in a single street in Cairo than in the whole of Florence.

1385

Naughty Nuns &● The nuns of St Helen Bishopgate in the City of London were reprimanded for kissing members of the public and wearing over-ostentatious veils; at the same time the prioress was ticked off for keeping too many lapdogs. This rebuke seems to have had little effect, for, in

1439, the nuns were told to desist from 'dancing and revelling', except at Christmas, and then only among themselves.

1386

Murderous Swine ❧ A sow in Normandy was executed for the murder of an infant. For its execution, it was dressed up in human clothes.

1388

Dead Man Wins Fight ❧ (15 August) At the Battle of Otterburn, the Scots, led by James, Earl of Douglas, defeated the English under Harry Hotspur. Douglas was mortally wounded, and commanded his men to conceal his body in a stand of bracken. It was to this stand of bracken that Hotspur formally conceded the battle. Hence the lines in the famous ballad about the battle:

> But I hae dream'd a dreary dream
> Beyond the Isle of Skye;
> I saw a dead man win a fight,
> And I think that man was I.

1392

A King Made of Glass ❧ (July) Charles VI of France suffered his first bout of madness while marching with his army. Believing he was about to be betrayed to his enemies, he set about him with his sword, killing at least one knight before his chamberlain and some soldiers could wrestle him to the ground. In later episodes Charles suffered the delusion that he was made of glass, and was likely to shatter into a thousand pieces.

1393

The Ball of the Burning Ones ✿ (28 January) For the *Bal des Sauvages* ('ball of the savages'), a masquerade at the Queen Mother's residence in Paris, Charles VI and five of his courtiers dressed themselves as wild men of the woods – a not inappropriate disguise, as during his intermittent fits of insanity the king refused to bathe and was known to howl like a wolf. On this occasion king and courtiers were chained together as if captive, and were thus unable to help themselves when a stray spark from a torch held by the king's brother, the Duc d'Orléans, ignited the hairy costume of one of the number. The king was saved when the Duchesse de Berry smothered the flames with her cloak, but several of the other men died. The masquerade was ever after known as the *Bal des Ardents* ('ball of the burning ones').

1413

Exit the King ✿ (20 March) Death of Henry IV of England. It having been prophesied that he would die in Jerusalem, the king had been planning to go on crusade to the Holy Land. Suddenly taken ill, he was moved to the Jerusalem Chamber in the Abbot's house at Westminster Abbey. When he recovered consciousness he asked where he was, and was told 'Jerusalem'. He knew then that he was going to die.

1415

Les Rosbifs on the Run ✿ (25 October) At the Battle of Agincourt many of the English archers – who paid such a key role in devastating the flower of French chivalry – were suffering from dysentery. Unable to leave their posts to relieve themselves, they fought naked from the waist down, and allowed nature to take its course.

1424

The General's Drumskin 🐌 (11 October) As he lay dying, the Czech Hussite general, Jan Zizka, ordered that his skin be turned into a war drum, so that he could still lead his men after death. The drum continued to be beaten at times of national emergency, such as the outbreak of the Thirty Years' War in 1618.

1428

A Remedy for the Servant Shortage 🐌 The Irish Parliament passed a law declaring that any servant attempting to leave Ireland was to be arrested. The law was only removed from the Irish statute book in 2006.

1437

The Mallard Song 🐌 A *schliwoppinge* (i.e. whopping great) mallard supposedly flew out of a 'sink or sewer' while the foundations of All Souls College, Oxford, were being dug. The event is marked every hundred years by a parade of the fellows led by a 'Lord Mallard' carried on a chair, while all sing the 'Mallard Song':

> Griffin, bustard, turkey, capon,
> Let other hungry mortals gape on;
> And on the bones their stomach fall hard,
> But let All Souls men have their MALLARD.
>
> *Oh! by the blood of King Edward,*
> *Oh! by the blood of King Edward,*
> *It was a wopping, wopping MALLARD.*

Death Down a Drain 🐌 (21 February) James I, king of Scotland, attempted to escape from his assassins by crawling down the outlet of the privy in his room. Unfortunately, the drain exit had been blocked off to prevent tennis balls rolling into it, and James was stabbed to death while attempting to negotiate an exit. In his ballad 'The King's Tragedy' (1881), Dante Gabriel Rossetti coyly refers to the privy as a 'vault' or 'crypt'.

1440

On the Corrupting Influence of the Court ❧ Henry VI founded Eton College, but forbade the boys to attend the royal court at nearby Windsor Castle lest they be corrupted.

The Original Bluebeard ❧ (21 October) Gilles de Retz, a French nobleman, confessed in court to the rape, torture, mutilation and murder of a large number of young boys, and some young girls. Estimates of the numbers of his victims range from 60 to 200. De Retz, the model for the stage villain Bluebeard, was executed five days later.

1445

Henry the Unsexed ❧ (23 April) Henry VI of England married Margaret of Anjou. It seems that his confessor advised Henry, for the sake of his soul, to abstain from sexual intercourse with his beautiful wife whenever possible. It was not until eight years after their marriage that Margaret bore their first child.

1451

Leeches Summoned to Court ❧ Representatives of the leeches resident in the vicinity of Lausanne on Lake Geneva were summoned to appear before a judge, who ordered them to leave the district within three days. Having ignored this injunction, the leeches were subjected to an exorcism, and this apparently did the trick.

1457

Golf Banned 🦊 A statute of the Scottish Parliament banned football and golf; this ban contained the first reference to the word 'golf'.

circa 1460

On the Irresistibility of Human Flesh 🦊 A family in Angus were arrested and burnt for cannibalism, with only the youngest daughter, about a year old, being spared. She was taken to Dundee where she was fostered until she grew to womanhood, when she was condemned and burnt for the same crime as the rest of her family. The historian Lindsay of Pitscottie reported that on the scaffold she told the crowd that 'If ye had experience of eating men and women's flesh, ye would think it so delicious, that ye would never forbear it again.'

1461

Royal Whimsy 🦊 (22 July) Louis XI succeeded to the throne of France. On one occasion, seeing a poor priest sleeping in the porch of a church, he raised him to a more elevated ecclesiastical position, solely to fulfil the proverb 'To lucky men good fortune will come even when they sleep.'

1462

Vlad the Impaler 🦊 Vlad III, Prince of Wallachia, had some 20,000 Turkish prisoners impaled on stakes to deter an Ottoman invasion of his realm, earning him the nickname 'Vlad the Impaler', and immortal fame as the original 'Dracula' (originally *Draculea*, meaning 'son of Dracul' – the byname of his father, and meaning 'the Dragon'). The episode in 1462 was just one in a lifetime of impaling, and Vlad typically liked to entertain his guests to a banquet while watching his victims slowly slide down their spikes (he made

Vlad the Impaler admires his handiwork while enjoying a light lunch.

sure that the points were not too sharp, so death should not come too quickly). Among the most prominent of Vlad's victims were the German merchants who had become powerful in his realm, and the accounts of his atrocities largely derive from contemporary German pamphlets – so the extent and method of Vlad's impaling activities may well be exaggerated.

1467

Wine Freezes in Flemish Winter It was such a severe winter in Flanders that wine had to be hacked up with an axe before it could be distributed to the troops stationed there.

circa 1470

A Porcine Organ The Abbot of Baigne invented a novel kind of musical instrument to amuse Louis XI of France. He assembled a number of pigs of different ages, placed them in a pavilion, and devised a kind of organ in which, when a particular key on a keyboard was pressed, a small spike would prod a particular pig, which would utter a cry of a particular pitch, depending on its size and age. According to one account, the abbot 'made 'em cry in such time and consort as highly delighted the king and all his company'. (For a cat piano, *see* 1650.)

1471

A Law for Thomas Cusake The Irish Parliament passed a law forbidding corn to be taken out of the country. In the same year it passed another law allowing a certain Thomas Cusake, bound for London to study law, to take with him corn for his subsistence.

1473

The Milk of Human Hatred ❧ Attacking the neighbouring Aztec city of Tlatelolco, the army of Axayactl of Tenochtitlán was surprised to be met by an army of naked women, who sought to distract their enemies by spraying them with milk from their breasts. However, this ruse did not save Tlatelolco, which was sacked, and many of its people rounded up and sacrificed.

1474

Henry the Impotent ❧ (11 December) Death of King Henry IV of Castile, called Henry the Impotent because, after a promising start, his reign degenerated into chaos.

The Cock that Laid an Egg ❧ At Basle, a cock was brought to trial for the crime of having laid an egg. Such an egg, argued the prosecution, was of inestimable value to sorcerers, and thus the cock must have made a compact with the Devil. The defence argued that there was no record of the Devil ever entering into a contract with a mere brute, and that the laying of the egg was an involuntary act, and quite without malicious intent. This argument was to no avail, and the court judged that the cock was a sorcerer or demon in disguise, and condemned both it and the egg to be burnt at the stake.

1477

Abandoned to the Wolves ❧ (5 January) Charles the Bold, Duke of Burgundy, was killed a the Battle of Nancy and his body abandoned to the wolves. His naked and mutilated corpse was found a few days later. It had been so badly gnawed by the wild beasts that only his physician was able to identify it, by certain old scars.

circa 1480

Ode to the Pubic Hair &. The Welsh poet Gwerful Mechain wrote her 'Ode to the Pubic Hair' ('*Cywydd y Cedor*'), in which she upbraids male poets for celebrating so many parts of a woman's body, but not the vagina. 'Let songs about the quim circulate,' she adjures her readers. As to the pubic hair: 'Lovely bush, God save it'.

1494

Cuba Not an Island &. (June) Christopher Columbus obliged his men to swear that Cuba was not an island, but the mainland of the American continent. He threatened anyone who recanted with having his tongue cut out.

1497

The Bonfire of the Vanities &. In Florence, Sandro Botticelli personally committed several of his paintings to the flames of the great bonfire lit in the Piazza della Signoria by the supporters of the austere Dominican monk Girolamo Savonarola, who had taken power in the city following the overthrow of the Medici. Savonarola's followers went from house to house adjuring the wealthy citizens to give up anything vain or immoral, from mirrors and make-up to pagan books and impious pictures. All were thrown on the bonfire. The flirtation of the Florentines with Puritanism did not last long, however, and in May the citizens revolted. Shortly afterwards Savonarola was excommunicated by the pope, and arrested as a heretic. On 23 May 1498 he and two close associates were hung naked in chains from a giant cross erected in the Piazza della Signori, and under them the executioner set light to another enormous bonfire.

—

Rubbing Urine into the Gums ❧ (25 December) Vasco da Gama sailed past an unknown land on the east coast of southern Africa, to which he gave the name Natal – Portuguese for 'Christmas'. So far from home, his crew were beginning to suffer from scurvy, for which they embarked on the then-standard treatment: trimming dead matter from their swollen gums with a knife, and rubbing the wound with urine.

1499
—

An Aged Widow ❧ Death of Agnes Skuner, who, according to the inscription on her grave in Camberwell Church, had reached the age of 119 – and outlived her husband Richard by 92 years.

Stories of cannibalism in the New World provided a justification for Europeans to claim both moral superiority and the lands of the native inhabitants.

The 16th Century

circa 1500

The Two Skulls of John the Baptist There is a possibly apocryphal tale of a traveller in France who, visiting a monastery, was shown the foundation's prize relic, the skull of John the Baptist. Raising an eyebrow, the visitor observed that he had been shown the skull of the saint only just recently at another monastery. 'Ah,' he was told, 'they have the skull of the saint when he was little more than a youth, whereas ours was his skull when he was an older and a wiser man.'

1505

Christian Charity The new Portuguese viceroy, Francisco d'Almeida, sailed for India via the east coast of Africa. His men mutilated every Arab they found, cutting off the right hands of the men and the ears and noses of the women. Arriving in Goa, they proceeded to slaughter all 8000 Muslims in the city.

Belief in Witch-Flight Held to be Heretical Publication of Samuel de Cassini's *Questione de le strie*, in which, *contra* the witch-hunting hysteria then sweeping Europe, he argued that those who held that witches flew at night were themselves guilty of heresy.

1506

Joanna the Mad (September) After the death of her husband, Philip the Handsome, Queen Juana of Castile insisted that his coffin accompany her wherever she went, even placing it on her bed as she slept. She had been passionately jealous of Philip while he lived, and was even more so after his death, insisting that no other woman should be allowed anywhere near the corpse. From time to time she would open the coffin, sometimes covering Philip's decomposing feet with kisses. She became increasingly *distraite*, and was eventually confined, her father, then her son, acting as regent. Joanna the Mad, as she is known to history, lived on until 1555.

1507

The Flying Abbot ❧ The alchemist John Damian, Abbot of Tongland Abbey, attempted to fly off the walls of Stirling Castle, themselves perched on top of considerable cliffs. The pioneer aviator met a predictable fate.

1509

Mammoth Mistaken for Man ❧ The remains of Chevalier Rincon were discovered at Rouen. It was said that his skull could hold a bushel (36 litres) of wheat, and that his shin bone was 1.2 m (4ft) in length. Many other such remains of 'giant men' were reported across Europe in the early modern period, and it was left to the great naturalist Baron Cuvier (1769–1832) to explain that such skeletons belonged to large extinct animals such as mammoths and mastodons.

1511

Demands Joyous ❧ Publication of *Demands Joyous* (i.e. 'merry questions'), a book of riddles by compiled by Wynkyn de Worde, which contained such side-splitters as: 'Q. How may a man discern a cow in a flock of sheep? A. By his eyesight.' Perhaps more to modern tastes is the following: 'Q. What beast is it that hath her tail between her eyes? A. It is a cat when she licketh her arse.'

1516

Over-Armed ❧ The Turks armed one of their galleys with an artillery piece so massive that when it went into action against the Portuguese, the recoil of the gun caused the vessel to capsize.

1517

Sumptuary Laws *re* Feasting

An English law set out the number of courses different ranks were permitted to eat during one meal. Thus cardinals were allowed nine, dukes and bishops seven, and so on, while those without a title but with an annual income of between £40 and £100 could ask for no more than three.

Luther Inspired on Privy

(31 October) Luther nailed his *Ninety-Five Theses* to the door of the Castle Church in Wittenberg. He said he had come to the conclusion that salvation is granted because of faith, not deeds, while '*in cloaca*' – in other words, while sitting on the lavatory. He was a lifelong sufferer from constipation and piles.

Butcher Blamed for Bad Bacon

A butcher who had been caught selling diseased and stinking bacon was paraded through the City of London with two sides of bacon tied to his person, two fletches of bacon borne before him, and a sign on his head proclaiming his crime, while pans were bashed to draw attention to his iniquities.

1520

Emperor Hog

The feckless Chinese emperor Zhu Houzhao, who took the name Zhengde, prohibited the raising of hogs, as the Chinese name for them was too similar to his family name of Zhu.

Land of the Big Feet

On his voyage of circumnavigation, Magellan named the southern part of South America *Patagonia*, after a Portuguese slang word meaning 'big foot'. The area, according to his chronicler, a Venetian

In the 16th century travellers brought back tales of all sorts of strange creatures from the New World. This headless couple are from Sir Walter Raleigh's account of Guyana, published in Nuremberg in 1599.

called Antonio Pigafetta, was inhabited by a people so tall that the Europeans only came up to their waists. They captured one of these giants to take back to Spain, but he died of scurvy while crossing the Pacific. His was only one of many deaths on the voyage. Pigafetta noted that when the bodies were thrown overboard, 'the Christians sank to the bottom with their face turned upward, while the Indians always sank with their face turned downward'.

1525

A Headless Warrior &♠ (24 February) At the Battle of Pavia, the Master of the King's Horseguards, Saint-Sevrin, had the top of his head cut off, but so firmly was he fixed in his saddle, that his corpse continued to ride about the battlefield, to the terror of his Spanish enemies.

1527

A Law Against Scotsmen 🦋 (31 August) The weavers of Newcastle were forbidden to take on any Scotsman as an apprentice.

1528

German Venezuela 🦋 The only German colony in the Americas was established when two banking families acquired the right to settle Venezuela from Charles V, Holy Roman Emperor and king of Spain. The Spanish resumed control in 1556.

1531

Appointment of the Governor of All Idiots 🦋 (January) Henry VIII appointed Sir William Paulet to the posts of 'Surveyor of the King's Widows, and Governor of All Idiots and Naturals in the King's Hands'.

Sea Monster 'Like Bishop' 🦋 It was reported that a sea creature 'taken in Polonia' bore a curious resemblance to a bishop.

1533

A Further Example of Christian Charity 🦋 (26 July) Faced with the prospect of being burned to death by the Spanish, Atahuallpa, the last emperor of the Incas, converted to Christianity. He was thus spared the flames, and was publicly garrotted instead.

1534

A Fashion for Mortality *&* After the death of her husband, Diane de Poitiers returned to court to became the mistress of the French Dauphin (the future Henri II). Because she was a widow decked in widow's weeds, all sorts of memento mori became the fashion at court, for example rings in the form of skeletons wrapped themselves round fingers, and time-pieces fashioned in the shape of skulls.

———

The Restoration of Men's Privy Parts *&* Around this time Bishop John 'Bilious' Bale, a reforming cleric, preached against the cult of St Walstan, whose well at Bawburgh near Norwich was a place of pilgrimage for farmers and agricultural labourers who sought a blessing on themselves and on their animals, particularly as regards fertility. Bale damned St Walstan as a disguised version of the Roman god Priapus (he of the impressively erect penis), and claimed that both men and beasts 'which had lost their Prevy Parts', if they visited the shrine, 'had newe Members restored to them, by this Walstane'. Rather than ridding East Anglia of this superstition, however, Bale's preaching had the opposite effect, as hordes flocked to the miraculous well.

1535

———

Pickling One's Father's Head in Spices *&* (August) A month after the execution of her father, Sir Thomas More, Margaret Roper passed in a boat under London Bridge, where his head was stuck on a pole. According to the 17th-century biographer and gossip John Aubrey, she cried, 'That head has lain many a time in my lap, would to God it would fall into my lap as I pass under!' Her prayer, according to Aubrey, was answered – although it is likely that she had in fact bribed the bridge-keeper to throw it down to her, rather than into the river, as was the usual custom. By whatever means she obtained it, she was brought before the council and briefly imprisoned for having her father's head in her possession, and during her trial she asserted that her father's head 'should not be food for fishes'. When she died in 1544, her father's head – which she had pickled in spices – was placed in her coffin.

1536

A Law Against Welshmen and Buggery 🙠 Henry VIII signed into law an all-purpose statute with the title:

> An Act for the Continue of the Statutes for Beggars and Vagabonds; and against Conveyance of Horses and Mares out of this Realm; against Welshmen making Affrays in the Counties of Hereford, Gloucester and Salop; and against the vice of Buggery.

End of the Kingdom of a Thousand Years 🙠 (22 January) Execution of John of Leiden, an illegitimate tailor's apprentice who in the city of Münster had set up his Kingdom of a Thousand Years, an Anabapist theocracy with himself as king. He had taken 16 wives, one of whom he publicly beheaded for showing him insufficient respect; he and his other wives then danced round the corpse. After fiercely resisting the efforts of the Church and the Emperor to crush his radical experiment, he was eventually captured by the Bishop of Münster. With spiked collars fastened round their necks, John and two of his associates had their flesh torn for an hour by red-hot pincers, before being finally dispatched with a dagger through the heart. Their mouldering cadavers were suspended in cages for some 50 years, and the cages can still be seen hanging from the tower of St Lambert's Church in Münster.

The Witch with Three Breasts 🙠 (19 May) Henry VIII's second wife, Anne Boleyn, was beheaded, having been accused of adultery, incest and witchcraft. In support of this last charge, it is said that she not only had

11 fingers but also three breasts – although the third 'nipple', supposedly used for suckling the Devil, was actually a mole on her neck.

———

Holy Duck's Blood 🐾 (Christmas Eve) Hailes Abbey in Gloucestershire was dissolved when the abbot and monks surrendered to Henry VIII's commissioners. The commissioners had declared that the abbey's famous relic, a phial of the Holy Blood – a great draw for pilgrims – in fact contained the blood of a duck, regularly refreshed.

1539

———

Having One's Cake ... 🐾 (7 December) Martin Luther and seven other doctors of divinity wrote a reply to Philip, Landgrave of Hesse, who had asked whether it would be possible to maintain two wives. He had tired of his original wife, Catherine of Saxony, but he wished to maintain her in public as his official consort; however, he now wished to have his relationship with his mistress, Marguerite de Staal, regularized by the Church. The good doctors concluded as follows:

> If your highness is thoroughly determined to marry a second wife, we are of opinion that it ought to be done secretly ... There is no opposition or real scandal to be dreaded here, for it is no unusual thing for princes to maintain mistresses ... and even though the people in general were scandalized, the most enlightened of the community would doubt the truth of the story, whilst prudent persons would always prefer this moderate course of procedure to adultery and other brutal actions.

Philip duly proceeded with the second marriage on 4 March 1540, the contract including the following:

> His Highness declares his intention of marrying Marguerite de Staal, notwithstanding that the princess, his consort, is still alive; and in order to prevent this proceeding being imputed to inconstancy or whim, to avoid scandal, and preserve the honour of the said Marguerite and the reputation of her family, he here swears before God, and on his soul and conscience, that

he neither takes her to wife through levity or caprice, nor from any contempt of law or superiors, but because he is compelled to this step by certain necessities so important and inevitable of health and conscience, that it is impossible for him to preserve his existence and live according to the law of God, unless he espouse a second wife in addition to the consort whom he already possesses.

1540

A Messy Business – Part I ✤ (28 July) Thomas Cromwell, formerly Henry VIII's chief minister, was beheaded. His vindictive master ordered that the execution be carried out by an inexperienced youth, who only succeeded on the third attempt. Cromwell's head was then boiled and displayed on London Bridge.

1541

On the Iniquity of Shove-Groat ✤ The game of shove-groat was declared illegal in England.

A Messy Business – Part II ✤ (27 May) The 67-year-old Margaret Pole, Countess of Salisbury, was led unwillingly to her execution at the Tower of London. As she struggled, the first blow of the axe hit her shoulder rather than her neck. She then leapt up from the block pursued by the headsman, who struck her 11 more blows before she fell down dead.

1542

Spaniard Assaulted by Amazons ✤ On his epic voyage down the Amazon, Francisco de Orellana was attacked by a tribe of tall, white women, 'with their privy parts covered' but otherwise unclothed. It was in honour of these warriors that Orellana gave the Amazon its name.

1546

The Sleeping Pot-Maker 🐾 (27 April) William Foxley, pot-maker for the Royal Mint in the Tower of London, fell asleep, and went on sleeping for a fortnight. According to the antiquarian John Stow (d.1605), Foxley 'could not be wakened with pinching, cramping, or otherwise burning whatsoever'. He seems to have been unharmed by the experience, living on for another 40 years.

1547

Stars Visible at Noon 🐾 (23 April) In England and other parts of northwest Europe 'the Sun appeared for three days as if it were suffused with blood while at the same time many stars were visible at noon'. The cause of this effect is unknown, although the astronomer Johannes Kepler believed it was caused by the 'diffusion of cometary matter'.

1549

A Charming Anagram 🐾 Birth of Marie Touchet, who became mistress of Charles IX in her late teens. Henry of Navarre (the future Henry IV of France) anagrammatized her name to '*Je charme tout*' ('I charm all'), with i becoming j.

1550

Keeper of the Papal Monkey 🐾 (7 February) When Julius III was elected pope, he made one of his servants a cardinal, as a reward for looking after his pet monkey.

1553

Secreted with the Excreted 🕭 The Catholic Mary Tudor became queen of England, forcing Protestants into a variety of subterfuges to conceal their faith. For example, the great-grandfather of Benjamin Franklin concealed the family's English bible by fastening it to the inside lid of a 'close-stool' (i.e. the wooden stool used to house a covered chamber pot). Franklin tells us how 'One of the children was stationed at the door to give notice if he saw an officer of the Spiritual Court make his appearance; in that case the lid was restored to its place, with the Bible concealed under it as before.'

1555

Dead Men 'Like Statues' 🕭 Two English ships, the *Bona Esperanza* and the *Bona Confidentia*, were found adrift in the Barents Sea, far to the north of the Arctic Circle, their crews of 70 men all dead. Under the command of Sir Hugh Willoughby, they had been searching for the Northeast Passage when they became trapped in the ice in the winter of 1553–4. The Venetian ambassador reported how the sailors who boarded the ships 'found some of [the dead mariners] seated in the act of writing, pen in hand, and the papers before them, others at table, platter in hand and spoon in mouth; others opening a locker, and others in various postures, like statues, as if they had been adjusted and placed in those attitudes'. It is likely that these men died of carbon monoxide poisoning from burning coal in a poorly ventilated space.

Ivan the Worst 🕭 Ivan IV, known as 'the Terrible', ordered the building of St Basil's Cathedral in Moscow. When it was completed he ordered the architects to be blinded, so that they would never design a more beautiful building. Ivan's reign was replete with such atrocities. One of his many supposed enemies, Prince Boris Telupa, was, according to a chronicler,

> drawn upon a sharp-made stake, which entered the lower part of his body and came out of his neck, upon which he languished in horrible pain for fifteen

hours, and spoke to his mother, brought to behold that woeful sight. And she was given to one hundred gunners, who defiled her to death, and the emperor's hungry hounds devoured her flesh and bones.

On another occasion Ivan – suspecting that the citizens of Novgorod were about to hand over their city to the Poles – had the Archbishop of Novgorod sewn up in the skin of a bear, and then set a pack of hounds upon him, and ordered that some 50,000 of the Archbishop's fellow citizens be drowned in the River Volkhov. In 1581 Ivan killed his own son in a rage – although in this instance he did show some remorse.

1560

The Lusty Ladies of Leith ❧ During the English siege of Leith, some soldiers from the French garrison disguised themselves as women and slipped out of a side gate. An English scout was so entranced by the prospect of female company that he left his post to join them. The assignation did not go quite as well as the Englishman had anticipated, for as soon as he was in their midst the demoiselles chopped off his head, took it back into the town and stuck it on top of a church spire, in full view of the besiegers.

1562

Embalmed Body Stands Trial ❧ (28 October) Death of George Gordon, the rebel Earl of Huntly, known as the Cock o' the North. It had been prophesied prior to the Battle of Corrichie fought that day that he would lie that night in the Tolbooth in Aberdeen without a mark on him. Huntly took this as a good sign, but just after the battle he suffered a fatal attack of apoplexy, and his body was duly laid out in the Tolbooth. Subsequently his embalmed body was obliged to stand trial for treason.

Some of the office-bearers in Hell at work in their various departments. Among the more senior of the devils, according to Johann Weyer's *Pseudomonarchia Daemonum*, published in 1563, are Moloch, Prince of the Country of Tears, and Pluto, Prince of Fire and Superintendent of Punishments.

1563
—

The Constitution of Hell 🐝 Publication of Johann Weyer's

Pseudomonarchia Daemonum, in which the author laid out the constitutional arrangements pertaining in Hell. According to Weyer (or Wier or Wierus) and other demonologists of the period, the Emperor of the Demons is Beelzebub, founder of the Order of the Fly. Beelzebub has apparently deposed Satan, who now heads the opposition. Among the great princes of Hell are: Eurynome, Prince of Death; Moloch, Prince of the Country of Tears, and member of the Imperial Council of State; Pluto, Prince of Fire and Superintendent of Punishments; Leonard, Grand Master of the Sabbaths and Inspector-General of Magic and Sorcery; and Prosperine, Archduchess of Hades and Sovereign Princess of the Evil Spirits. Weyer also names and outlines the responsibilities of the ministers of state, and lists the officers of the Household of the Princes, and Hell's ambassadors to France, England, Turkey, Russia, Spain, Italy and Switzerland. In all, the personnel of Hell (not counting its residential clients) are organized into 6666 legions, each comprising 6666 demons – giving a total of 44,435,556.

1568
—

Habsburg Inbreeding – Part I 🐝 (8 July) Death of Don Carlos,

heir to the Spanish throne, who had been imprisoned for his intrigues with the Dutch rebels. Don Carlos had long suffered from mental instability, probably due to excessive inbreeding among the Habsburg dynasty: he had only four great-grandparents (most people have eight), and two of his great-grandmothers were sisters; and he had only six great-great-grandparents (where most people have 16). Stories that his father, Philip II, had him killed – perhaps through jealousy, because Don Carlos had been betrothed to Philip's third wife, Elizabeth of Valois, before her father took her from him – are without foundation.

1569

The First National Lottery ❧ (11 January) The draw was made in first state lottery held in England. The profits were intended for the repair of the country's harbours and other public works. State lotteries continued in Britain until 1826. The publisher Robert Chambers, writing in the 1860s, commented, 'It seems strange that so glaringly immoral a project should have been kept up with such sanction so long.'

1574

Smoking Good for Your Health ❧ The distinguished Spanish physician Nicolas Monardes published a work (translated into English in 1596 as *Joyfull Newes out of the New-found Worlde*) in which he hailed the medical properties of tobacco, ensuring that the plant became a household remedy in western Europe for more than two centuries. Monardes' views were reinforced by Johann Neander in 1626, in his *Tabacologia*.

1577

The Massacre Cave ❧ When a gang of Macleods came to the Macdonald island of Eigg intent on rape and pillage, the Macdonalds caught several of their number and deprived them of their testicles. Outraged, the Macleods returned in force, trapped some two hundred Macdonalds who had taken refuge in a cave, and suffocated them by lighting a fire at the entrance. When Sir Walter Scott paid a visit to the island in 1814, he found that the 'Massacre Cave' contained 'numerous specimens of mortality'.

1580

Death by Tennis Ball

Death by Tennis Ball ❧ Publication of Montaigne's *Essays*. In Essay xvii, 'That to Study Philosophy is to Learn to Die', he describes how his brother was killed by a tennis ball:

> A brother of mine, Captain St Martin, a young man, three-and-twenty years old, who had already given sufficient testimony of his valour, playing a match at tennis, received a blow of a ball a little above his right ear, which, as it gave no manner or sign of wound or contusion, he took no notice of it, nor so much as sat down to repose himself, but, nevertheless, died within five or six hours after, of an apoplexy occasioned by that blow.

1582

Angel Suggests Free Love

Angel Suggests Free Love ❧ Dr John Dee, the mathematician, astrologer and hermetic philosopher, began to employ a man called Edward Kelley as an intermediary through whom he could contact the angels. In this way the angels dictated several books to Dee, for the service of humanity. The two men subsequently toured Central Europe, but Dee broke off their association in 1587 shortly after the Angel Uriel told Kelley that the two men should share their wives.

1584

Witches Mad not Bad

Witches Mad not Bad ❧ In *The Discovery of Witchcraft*, Reginald Scot argued that those accused of witchcraft were in fact suffering from mental illness. He held that the belief in witchcraft was 'contrary to reason, scripture and nature', and that his greatest adversaries were 'young ignorance and old custom'. In 1603 King James I and VI – a firm believer in the existence of witches – ordered that all copies of Scot's book were to be burnt.

1585

Scolding Becomes a Crime 🦅 Scolding was criminalized in England, and remained illegal until 1967, along with such offences as barratry (the vexatious incitement of quarrels or lawsuits), eavesdropping, challenging someone to a fight, and being a 'common night walker'.

The First Fagin 🦅 A gentleman called Wotton who had fallen on hard times opened an academy for pickpockets at an ale house near Billingsgate, London. Part of the training involved being able to empty a practice purse without sounding any of the little hawk's bells hanging on it.

Pope Fools Cardinals 🦅 Sixtus V, the son of an impoverished pig-dealer, was elected pope. Prior to his election he had given an impression of sickliness and imbecility, so many voted for him who hoped they could control him, and in the expectation that another election would soon be necessary. However, on donning the triple crown Sixtus cast away his walking stick, fixed his features in a stern glare and declared himself to be seven years younger than he had previously let on. He went on to conduct his pontificate with a rod of iron.

1586

Pressed to Death 🦅 (25 March) Margaret Clitherow of York was martyred for her Catholic faith. Hearing of her sentence to die by the *peine forte et dure*, she reportedly said, 'God be thanked, I am not worthy of so good a death as this.' She was then placed on the ground with her arms stretched out on either side, her hands tied to two posts. A sharp stone was placed under her back and a door across her torso, upon which more and more weights were added until the life was squeezed from her body. Her right hand is kept in St Mary's Convent, York. She was canonized in 1970.

1587

Curious Occurrences Attending the Beheading of Mary Queen of Scots ❧ (8 February) After the execution of Mary Queen of Scots, a contemporary account reported that 'Her lips stirred up and down a quarter of an hour after her head was cut off.' At the same time, Mary's little dog was found nestling under her skirts, and, having been pulled out, insisted on lying between her mistress's shoulders and her severed head.

1589

It is Hell that Created Me ❧ (1 August) Henry III of France was fatally stabbed by a fanatical Dominican friar, Frère Jacques Clement, a name that was promptly anagrammatized to '*C'est l'enfer qui m'a crée*' ('It is Hell that created me').

1590

Armies in the Air ❧ (13 March) On the eve of the Battle of Ivry, during the French Wars of Religion, an eyewitness called Davila left an account of a strange aerial phenomenon: 'The thunder and lightning, sometimes mingled with horrid darkness, added to their terrors; and such a flood of rain poured suddenly down, that the whole army was alarmed. A prodigious apparition, which appeared in the sky as soon as it had ceased to rain, increased the general dismay; for during the noise of the thunder, at which the boldest among them trembled, two great armies were distinctly seen in the air, that, after continuing some time engaged in fight, disappeared, covered with a thick cloud; so that the event of the battle was not seen.'

Crime Passionelle ❧ (16 October) The Italian composer and nobleman Carlo Gesualdo, Prince of Venosa and Count of Conza, murdered his wife, Maria d'Ava, the daughter of the Marquis of Pescara, and her lover, the Duke of Andria. Having long suspected their liaison, Gesualdo had pretended to go away on a hunting trip, but suddenly returned to his palace in Naples to find the two in bed together. He viciously stabbed them to death, Maria being struck 'in the parts it is best for a woman to keep modest', and then dumped the bodies in the centre of Naples. Gesualdo's noble birth kept him safe from prosecution.

1591

The Great Tun of Heidelberg ❧ Completion of the Great Tun of Heidelberg, a vast barrel measuring 5.5 m (18 ft) in diameter, and capable of holding 128 hogsheads (29,866 litres or 6750 gallons) of Rhenish wine.

The Popularity of Bear-Baiting ❧ The Lord Mayor of London issued an edict in which he complained, vis à vis the city's theatres, 'that in divers places, the players do use to recite their plays to the great hurt and destruction of the game of bear-baiting, and such-like pastimes, which are maintained for her majesty's pleasure'. In 1575 the Earl of Leicester, Queen Elizabeth's favourite, had entertained her on her visit to Kenilworth Castle by a display in which 13 bears were tied to stakes in the inner courtyard, and set upon by mastiffs.

1592

Wolves Roam Streets of Vienna ❧ Such was the severity of the winter that starving wolves were seen within the walls of Vienna.

The Devil's Drink ❧ Pope Clement VII, resisting those who would have him condemn coffee as the 'bitter invention of Satan' owing to its Arab/Muslim origins, supposedly declared, 'This Devil's drink is so good, we should cheat the Devil by baptizing it.'

1596

The First Flush ❧ Sir John Harington published his satire, *The Metamorphosis of Ajax*, which contains the first design for a flushing toilet. Ajax is a pun on *jakes*, 16th-century slang for a lavatory. Harington had already installed a flushing toilet for his godmother, Queen Elizabeth, in her palace at Richmond, Surrey, but publication of his Rabelaisian satire led to royal disapproval and exile.

1597

Mystery of Barnacle Geese Solved ❧ As no one had ever seen the nest or young of the barnacle geese that visited Europe every winter, it had for centuries been believed that the birds emerged from tiny shells growing on trees. The birds were thus regarded as fish, and it was therefore permissible to eat them on Roman Catholic fast days. The mystery was cleared up in the summer of 1597, however, when the nests of barnacle geese were found on the coast of Novaya Zemlya in the Arctic Ocean by sailors from William Barents's expedition.

1598

Royal Disdain ❧ (13 September) Philip III succeeded to the throne of Spain. He was intent on humbling his nobles, so would demand that they only address him while on their knees. He in turn spoke to them without

Werewolves as depicted by the 17th-century French painter Charles Le Brun.

completing words or sentences, upbraiding them should they misconstrue his meaning.

———

The Werewolves of Europe 🐾 The Gandillon family of the Jura Mountains were convicted of lycanthropy and burnt, their confessions having been extracted by torture. Only five years later a court in Bordeaux found that Jean Grenier's belief that he was a werewolf was a delusion. In the period 1520–1630 some 30,000 trials of supposed werewolves were held in Europe.

1599

A Nine Days' Wonder ✌ The comic actor Will Kemp danced a morris dance all the way from London to Norwich. He called it his Nine Days' Wonder – although the nine days of his dance were in fact spread out over a number of weeks.

Even in this age of Scientific Revolution, it was still believed that dragons haunted the Alps. This illustration is from Athanasius Kircher's *Mondus Subterraneus* (1678).

The 17th Century

On the Therapeutic Uses of Human Fat 🙰
Lion Lies Down with Lamb 🙰 Dead Man
Contradicts Executioner 🙰 The Grave Fart 🙰
Bathing in the Blood of Virgins 🙰 The Best
Bargain in History? 🙰 The Adventures of
Lord Minimus 🙰 Tradescant's Cabinet of
Curiosities 🙰 Centenarian Does Penance for
Fornication 🙰 Censors Crop Ears and Slit
Nostrils 🙰 The Pig-Faced Woman 🙰 Ibrahim
the Mad Drowns his Harem 🙰 A Cat Piano 🙰
Tracing One's Ancestry Back to Adam 🙰
Carrying Out One's Marital Obligations with a
Physician in Attendance 🙰 An Act Against
False Teeth and Bolstered Hips 🙰 On the
Merry Effects of *Bhang* 🙰

1600
—

Moll Cut-Purse and Morocco the Horse 🐎 The performing
horse Morocco was ridden by his master, a Scotsman called Banks, over the
roof of St Paul's in London. A servant wishing his master to see this
spectacle found him inside the cathedral and bid him come out to see for
himself. Gruffly his master replied, 'Away you fool, what need I go so far to
see a horse on the top, when I can see so many asses at the bottom?'

Morocco made another famous ride a year or two later, from Charing
Cross to Shoreditch, with the celebrated Moll Cut-Purse (née Mary Frith) in
the saddle. Moll was dressed in men's attire, for which she was condemned by
an ecclesiastical court to do penance at the door of St Paul's Cathedral. But
Moll – said to be the first woman in England to smoke tobacco – had
acquired a taste for cross-dressing, a taste she was to indulge for the rest
of her life.

1601
—

On the Therapeutic Uses of Human Fat 🐎 Beginning of the
three-year siege of Ostend, one of the bloodiest episodes in the Eighty Years'
War. During the siege Dutch physicians would slip out of the city at night to
strip the fat from the Spanish dead, and apply the fat to the wounds of their
own men, in the belief that it was an effective salve. Between them, two surgeons, Moerbeke and Courtmans, amputated more than 1700 arms and legs
during the siege. In the final phases, as the Spanish closed in, the Dutch, short
of earth, used dead bodies to shore up the ramparts.

1603
—

Robert Cary's Remarkable Ride 🐎 (March) Robert Cary rode
from London to Edinburgh, a distance of 400 miles, in a mere three days, to
take the news of Queen Elizabeth's death to her successor, King James VI
of Scotland.

1605

Lion Lies Down with Lamb (3 June) James I (as James VI was now known) and his family visited the Tower of London to see the lions there fight with dogs and bears. As a kind of curtain-raiser, some pieces of mutton and a live cock were thrown into the pit to gain the lions' attention. After they had consumed these, a live lamb was lowered down on a rope. A contemporary describes what happened next:

> Being come to the ground, the lamb lay upon his knees, and both the lions stood in their former places, and only beheld the lamb. Presently the lamb rose up and went unto the lions, who very gently looked upon and smelled on him, without any hurt. Then the lamb was very softly drawn up again, in as good plight as he was let down.

1606

Fool Fails to End Plague Bernard Bluet d'Arbères, former fool to the Duke of Mantua, starved himself to death in the mistaken belief that this would relieve the plague then raging in Paris.

Dead Man Contradicts Executioner (30 January) Execution of Sir Everard Digby, one of the conspirators in the Gunpowder Plot, by hanging, drawing and quartering. In his *Brief Lives*, John Aubrey, the 17th-century biographer and gossip, recounts that when the executioner, as was the custom, plucked out Digby's heart and held it aloft with the words 'Here is the heart of a traitor', Digby himself replied, 'Thou liest!'

The Martyrdom of Little John (2 March) Death of the Catholic martyr Nicholas Owen – known as 'Little John' because of his diminutive stature. He had been arrested for constructing 'priest holes' in various houses, and interrogated while hanging by his arms with weights attached to his feet.

He already suffered from a hernia, and inevitably his intestines burst through the rupture. The authorities let it be known that he had committed suicide by stabbing himself.

1607
—

The Grave Fart ⬥ Sir Henry Ludlow, MP for Wiltshire, said 'no' to a message brought from the House of Lords by the Serjeant by loudly breaking wind. The episode is referred to by Ben Jonson in his 'Epithalamion for Mr Jerome Watson':

> And sure, it was the Intent
> Of the grave Fart, late let in Parliament,
> Had it been seconded, and not in Fume
> Vanished away . . .

1608
—

An Arctic Mermaid ⬥ While attempting to find the Northeast Passage, two of Henry Hudson's crewmen spotted a mermaid: 'from the navel upward her back and breasts were like a woman's . . . Her skin very white; and long hair hanging down behind, of colour black: in her going down they saw her tail, which was like the tail of porpoise, and speckled like a mackerel.'

1613
—

On the Prevalence of Sorcery in the Basque Country ⬥ Pierre de Lancre, who had been sent by Henry IV of France to the Pays de Labourd in the Basque country to inquire into the extent of witchcraft in the region, reported that, out of a population of 30,000, virtually every family and virtually every priest was involved in sorcery.

1614

Bathing in the Blood of Virgins ❧ Death of the Hungarian noblewoman, Countess Elizabeth Báthory, while imprisoned in solitary confinement. She had been accused of the torture and murder of numerous young women, but the truth of this allegation has been swamped in legend, and it is possible that she was the innocent victim of a political frame-up. It is known, however, that she treated her own servants harshly, meting out brutal punishments if they infringed a rule. Among the numerous embellishments to her legend is that she bathed in the blood of virgins to attain eternal youth. The countess has been the inspiration for many later vampire tales.

1616

Compass Needle Points Southwest ❧ William Baffin, at the north end of the bay named after him in the Arctic, was astonished to find his compass needle pointing to the southwest, 'a thing almost incredible and matchless in the world beside'. At that period, no one realized that the magnetic pole is some distance from the geographic pole.

1619

Caught Copulating Under a Hedge ❧ William and Margaret Cripple of Somerset appeared at the local archdeacon's court, having been discovered copulating under a hedge.

Evidence of Witchcraft ❧ (11 March) Margaret and Philippa Flower, the so-called Witches of Belvoir, were hanged for practising their craft against the Earl of Rutland and his family. Their mother, Joan, had also been accused of witchcraft, and sought to clear herself by asking that she be given bread, stating that if she was guilty she would surely choke.

Unfortunately, the test went against her: having taken a mouthful of bread, she choked and died.

1620

A Prolific Breeder ❧ (10 May) Death of Mrs Honeywood, of Charing in Kent, at the age of 92. She had had 16 children, 114 grandchildren, 228 great-grandchildren, and 9 great-great-grandchildren. Lady Temple of Stow, who died in 1656, was said to have lived to see over 700 of her descendants.

1621

Londoner on Day Trip to Continent ❧ (17 July) Bernard Calvert left London at 3 o'clock in the morning, rode to Dover, took ship to Calais and back and returned by horse to London, where he arrived at 8 o'clock in the evening, having ridden 142 miles and sailed another 44.

Lugless Willie Lithgow ❧ The Scottish traveller William Lithgow, who is thought to have walked some 36,000 miles in the course of his career, was detained in Spain as a spy, and had his ears cut off by the Inquisition. That, at least, was his version of how he became known as 'Lugless [earless] Willie'. However, it is possible he suffered this mutilation at the hands of the family of a young woman he had debauched.

1622

Sultan's Stones Smashed ❧ (20 May) Sultan Osman II was killed in a palace coup. According to the Ottoman traveller and writer Evliya Çelebi (1611–82), Osman was put to death by the Grand Vizier Davut Pasha by having his testicles crushed, 'a mode of execution reserved by custom to the Ottoman sultans'.

1623

Ears of Bankrupts Nailed to Pillory 🙋 A law was passed by which all bankrupts had an ear nailed to the pillory for two hours, before it was cut off.

Spurned Suitor Calls for War 🙋 The future Charles I travelled incognito to Madrid to ask for the hand of the Spanish Infanta. Frustrated that he could not meet her alone, he leapt over her garden wall, much to her horror. Charles only retreated when the old marquis who guarded the infanta begged him on his knees to desist, as if the prince as much as addressed a word to his charge, the old man would lose his head. Following his final rejection, Charles left Madrid on 30 August, and on his return to England called for war with Spain.

1626

A Set-back in the Onward March of Frozen Food 🙋 (9 April) Death of the philosopher, statesman and essayist Francis Bacon, as a result of having contracted a chill while carrying out a scientific experiment involving stuffing a dead chicken with snow to see whether it would retard putrefaction.

The Best Bargain in History? 🙋 (24 May) Peter Minuit, the director-general of New Netherland, made a land deal with the local inhabitants. For trade goods worth 60 guilders (in today's values about $500–$700), the Dutch acquired an island called Manna-hata, later known as Manhattan. Jonas Michaelius, a Dutch minister, was not impressed with the inhabitants: 'I find them entirely savage and wild, strangers to all decency, yea, uncivil and stupid as garden stakes, proficient in all wickedness and ungodliness...'

King Charles I with his smallest courtier, Sir Jeffrey Hudson,
also known as Lord Minimus.

The Piece of Cod Which Passeth All Understanding ❧
(23 June) A codfish was cut open at the market in Cambridge and found to contain a book wrapped up in sailcloth. When unwrapped from its slimy covering, the volume turned out to be a theological work by John Frith, who was burnt at the stake in 1533 for his adherence to the reformed religion. An eyewitness of sorts, a Mr Mead, wrote to Sir M. Stuteville as follows:

> I saw all with mine own eyes, the fish, the maw, the piece of sail-cloth, the book, and observed all I have written; only I saw not the opening of the fish, which not many did, being upon the fish-woman's stall in the market, who first cut off his head, to which the maw hanging, and seeming much stuffed with somewhat, it was searched, and all found as aforesaid. He that had had his nose as near as I yester morning, would have been persuaded there was no imposture here without witness. The fish came from Lynn.

The Adventures of Lord Minimus ❧ At a banquet for Charles I
and Queen Henrietta Maria, the Duke of Buckingham served up Jeffrey Hudson, an 18-inch dwarf, in a pie, from which he burst dressed in a suit of armour. Hudson – aged only seven – was presented as a gift to Henrietta Maria, becoming known as 'Lord Minimus' or 'The Queen's Dwarf', and was painted with her by Van Dyck (the painting shows that, unusually for a dwarf, he had the proportions of a full-size adult). Hudson eventually tired of his mascot role, and in 1644, while exiled with the queen in France, challenged her master of horse, William Crofts, to a duel, after the latter had made some disparaging remark about his size. They fought with pistols on horseback, and Hudson shot Crofts dead. He was expelled from the court, and shortly afterwards was captured by Barbary pirates, spending 25 years as a slave in North Africa, until ransomed. Returning to England, he lived out the rest of his days in poverty. He died around 1682.

1627

—

A Divine Right of Kings 🙞 Charles I issued a proclamation that every household was to hand over its accumulated urine once every day in summer and once every two days in winter to an official collector so that the fluid wastes could be turned into saltpetre, an essential ingredient of gunpowder. The Crown also claimed as its property all soils impregnated with animal wastes, and gave permission to its agents – the so-called Saltpetre Men – to dig up the floors of dovecots, stables, slaughterhouses, etc., without the leave of the owners.

1630

—

The Glutton of Kent 🙞 Jeremy Taylor, a Thames waterman known as 'the Water Poet', gave the following account of Nicholas Wood, a glutton of Kent:

> Once ... he ate as much as would have served and sufficed thirty men, so that his belly was like to turn bankrupt and break, but that the serving-man turned him to the fire, and anointed his paunch with grease and butter, to make it stretch and hold; and afterwards, being laid in bed, he slept eight hours.

—

Textomania 🙞 At Oxford a comedy by Barton Holyday was presented before James I. Called *Textomania, or, The Marriage of the Arts*, it was an exercise in pedantry and dry-as-dust wit, featuring characters with names such as Physica, Historia, Ethicus, Geographus, Arithmetica, and so, laboriously, on. As an example of the writing the following may stand (Poeta is describing his new amour, Astronomia):

> Her *brow* is like a brave *heroic* line
> That does a sacred majestie inshrine;
> Her *nose*, *Phaleuciake*-like, in comely sort,

Ends in a *Trochie*, or a long and short.
Her *mouth* is like a pretty *Dimeter*;
Her *eie-brows* like a little-longer *Trimeter*.
Her *chinne* is an *adonicke*, and her *tongue*
Is an *Hypermeter*, somewhat too long . . .

The king apparently found the play itself more than 'somewhat too long', and tried to leave after the second act, but 'was prevailed to sit it out, in mere charity to the Oxford scholars'.

1631

Death of a Debauchee 🙰 (14 May) Mervyn Castleford, 2nd Baron Audley, was executed, having been found guilty of 'abetting a rape upon his countess, committing sodomy with his servants and commanding and countenancing the debauching of his daughter'.

White Slavers in County Cork 🙰 Barbary pirates carried off to slavery some 200 inhabitants of the fishing village of Baltimore, County Cork. Most of their captives were English, as the corsairs were reportedly too terrified of the Irish women to attempt their abduction. The event is preserved in the name of a local pub, The Algiers Inn.

Bottom in the Stocks 🙰 (27 September) A performance of *A Midsummer Night's Dream* was given privately at the Bishop of Lincoln's house in London. The play having been performed on a Sunday, the Puritans were outraged when they heard about it, and secured the conviction of the actor (a Mr Wilson) who had played Bottom. Wilson was duly sentenced to 12 hours in the stocks wearing his ass's head, with a pile of hay before him, and a placard bearing the following lines:

> Good people, I have played the beast,
> And brought ill things to pass;

I was a man, but thus have made,
Myself a silly ass.

1632

Famous Last Words ❦ (6 November) Death of Gustavus Adolphus, king of Sweden, at the Battle of Lützen. The king had refused to put on his cuirass, declaring 'The Lord God is my armour', and had then been killed leading a cavalry charge. However, the reason for his refusal to wear a metal cuirass may have been more to do with the old musketball that had been lodged in his neck for some years, which made wearing rigid armour extremely uncomfortable; instead, he favoured a more flexible but less resilient protective coat made of leather.

1634

Tradescant's Cabinet of Curiosities ❦ The gardener and botanist John Tradescant opened his Musaeum Tradescantium in a building called The Ark, in Lambeth, London. It was the prototype of the cabinets of curiosities that became so popular through the 17th and 18th centuries, and included in its collection such items as 'the hand of a mermaid' and 'a goose which has grown in Scotland on a tree'.

1635

Centenarian Does Penance for Fornication ❦ (15 November) Thomas Parr, the son of an agricultural labourer, was interred in Westminster Abbey. What earned Parr such an exalted place of burial was the fact that he was said to have been born in 1483, and had thus reputedly reached the age of 152 years old. He had waited until he was 80 before marrying, and at the age of 105 had been made to do penance at the church door for fornication with Catherine Milton, later his second wife. In the year of his death 'Old Parr' had been brought to London from his home in Aldebury,

Shropshire, by the Earl of Arundel, and was there presented to the king. It seems the excitement was too much for him, and within a few months he was dead.

1636

Bracken Fires Blamed for Rain 🔊 (1 August) The Earl of Pembroke and Montgomery wrote to the High Sheriff of Staffordshire asking him to ensure that the people desisted from burning 'fern' (bracken) while the king, Charles I, passed through the county, as there was a general belief that such fires caused rain, and it was wished 'that the country and himself may enjoy fair weather as long as he remains in those parts'.

1637

Censors Crop Ears and Slit Nostrils 🔊 A law was introduced forbidding the publication of any book without a licence from the ecclesiastical authorities. Anyone who infringed the law was likely to punished by being pilloried, branded, whipped, fined and having his or her ears cropped and nostrils slit.

1638

The Foundation of New Sweden 🔊 (29 March) A shipload of Swedish and Finnish settlers landed in the New World to found the colony of New Sweden. Centred on Fort Christina (on the site of the modern town of Wilmington, Delaware), Sweden's sole colony in North America was taken over by the Dutch in 1655.

1639

Mother Threatens to Shoot Son 🔊 During the First Bishop's War, the Duke of Hamilton commanded Charles I's forces in Scotland, and made

an unsuccessful attempt to land English troops behind the lines of the Covenanters. His mother, Lady Anne Cunningham, a staunch Covenanter, led her own troop of horses to Leith, and promised to shoot her son should the English troops land.

1640

—

On the Dangers of Alcohol and Tobacco 🍸 (9 February)
Death of the Ottoman sultan, Murad IV, from alcoholic cirrhosis of the liver. It was an ironic end for a ruler who had banned the use of both alcohol and tobacco, on pain of death, and who had been wont to roam the streets of Constantinople at night incognito, sword in hand, running through any person he found disobeying his ban. When he caught the royal gardener and his wife enjoying a smoke, he had their legs cut off, and let them bleed to death as they were pushed through the streets of the city on a wheelbarrow.

—

Monsieur or Mademoiselle? 🍸 (21 September) Anne of Austria,
queen consort of Louis XIII, gave birth to Philippe, duc d'Orléans, next in line to the throne after her first son, the future Louis XIV. Anxious that Philippe should not prove such a rebellious rival for power as Louis XIII's younger brother had turned out to be, Anne brought Philippe up as a girl, encouraging him to wear dresses and make-up, and steering him clear of the 'manly' pursuits of politics and soldiering. As an adult, Monsieur – as Philippe was known – showed a weakness for male favourites, and would continued to wear women's clothes in private. He also showed himself to be a capable military commander, in 1677 defeating William of Orange at Cassel. But Louis XIV was jealous of his brother's success, and ended his career with the army. Saint-Simon, the notorious gossip, recalled the older Monsieur as 'a little man propped up on heels like stilts, got up like a woman with rings, bracelets and jewels ... ribbons wherever he could put them, and exuding perfumes of all kinds'.

———

Bishop Falls from Grace ⁊ (5 December) John Atherton, Bishop of Waterford and Lismore in Ireland, was executed for committing an act of sodomy with his tithe collector, John Childe. The only witness was a disgruntled servant of Atherton's who had been discharged from his service. The servant later confessed to having perjured himself.

———

Like a Wheel Within a Wheel ⁊ During the Siege of Turin, the French held the citadel against Prince Thomas of Savoy, who held the city's outer walls; Thomas's Piedmontese were in turn surrounded by more French troops under Comte Henri Harcourt; and this French army was itself encircled by a Spanish army under the Marquis de Leganez. Prince Thomas surrendered to the French on 17 September, and the Spaniards were forced to withdraw.

1641

———

The Pig-Faced Woman ⁊ Publication in London of *A Certain Relation of the Hog-faced Gentlewoman*, which describes a Dutchwoman named Tanakin Skinker born at Wirkham, on the Rhine, in 1618. Miss Skinker had 'all the limbs and lineaments of her body well featured and proportioned, only her face, which is the ornament and beauty of all the rest, has the nose of a hog or swine, which is not only a stain and blemish, but a deformed ugliness, making all the rest loathsome, contemptible and odious to all that look upon her'. She was incapable of uttering any other noise than 'the hoggish Dutch ough, ough! or the French owee, owee!' The anonymous author wrote that £40,000 were on offer to any man who would marry her, and at the time of writing she was said to be somewhere in London, looking for a husband.

A similar rumour circulated in London in 1815, although this time the wealthy pig-faced woman in search of a mate hailed from Ireland, and ate from a silver trough. A more tangible pig-faced lady, by the name of Miss

In 1618 a wealthy Dutchwoman with the face of a pig was said to be seeking a husband in London. Despite the £40,000 dowry on offer, there were, apparently, no takers.

Stevens, was exhibited at the 1838 Hyde Park Fair. Miss Stevens proved, disappointingly, to be a bear with its face shaved to the skin.

1643
—

The Flooding of Hatfield Chase ❧ (February) The local inhabitants, angered that the new ditches and embankments constructed in Hatfield Chase by Flemish refugees had deprived them of their traditional livelihoods of wildfowling and fishing, pulled up the floodgates of Snow Sewer. This action, according to the contemporary account by the antiquary William Dugdale, 'by letting in the tides from the River Trent, soon drowned a great part of Hatfield Chase, divers persons standing there with muskets and saying they would stay till the whole level was drowned and the inhabitants were forced to swim away like ducks'.

1644

Rustic Oblivious to Conflict (2 July) Just before the Battle of Marston Moor, the decisive battle of the English Civil Wars, a Parliamentarian officer asked a labourer whether he supported the King or Parliament. 'Be them two fallen out, then?' the man replied.

1647

The Witch-Finder General Death of Matthew Hopkins, self-styled Witch-Finder General. Hopkins had travelled round eastern England, claiming to have a commission from Parliament and charging communities to find the witches hidden within them. One of his tests was to bind up the suspect and drop her into the village pond: if she sank, she was innocent; if she was guilty, she would float. The theory was that, as witches renounced their baptism, water would reject them. Hopkins also employed 'prickers', who would probe the suspect's skins with knives or needles for 'the Devil's mark', an area devoid of feeling and which would not bleed if pierced. Tradition has it that some villagers, having grown suspicious of Hopkins's claims, subjected him to his own water test. He failed, and was promptly hanged.

1648

Ibrahim the Mad Drowns his Harem (12 August) Ibrahim I, the recently deposed Ottoman sultan, was strangled with a bow string. Just before his overthrow Ibrahim – popularly known as Ibrahim the Mad – had had 278 members of his harem tied into weighted sacks and thrown into the Bosphorus; only one survived, her sack having been improperly tied. Ibrahim had been tipped off by his portly favourite, Sechir Para ('sugar cube'), that one of his concubines had been seduced by an outsider. Unable to find out the identity of the guilty party, Ibrahim had decided to proceed on the basis of collective guilt. (Ibrahim had a penchant for extremely large women: Sechir Para, a lady of Armenian origin, weighed in at 23½ stone (150 kg), and so impressed was the sultan that he appointed her to a provincial governorship.)

On the Dangers of Denying Haggai and Habakkuk ❧

(2 May) Parliament made it an offence to doubt that the last five books of the Old Testament – Habakkuk, Zephaniah, Haggai, Zecharia and Malachi – contained the word of God. The punishment was death.

A New Messiah ❧

Sabbatai Zevi, a Jew in Smyrna, declared himself to be the Messiah. He was expelled by the scandalized Jewish community of the city, a fate that befell him in a number of other cities around the eastern Mediterranean. Eventually settling in Cairo, he married a Polish-born Jewess who had been working as a prostitute in Livorno, and who had become convinced that she would become the bride of the expected Messiah. Many people across Europe and around the Mediterranean – both Jews and Christians – came to believe Sabbatai's claim that he was the one chosen to lead the Israelites back to the Promised Land in the prophesied year of 1666. At the beginning of that year Sabbatai travelled to Constantinople, the Ottoman capital, where he was promptly arrested and thrown into prison. He was released following his conversion to Islam, and became the doorkeeper to the sultan.

1649

King's Head Sewn Back On ❧

(30 January) Beheading of Charles I. It was a cold day, and Charles put on an extra shirt, so that the crowd should not think he trembled with fear. Contrary to the usual custom for those beheaded for treason, Cromwell gave permission for Charles's head to be

sewn back onto his body prior to burial. After the Restoration, Charles II showed less respect for Cromwell's corpse. He had it dug up from its grave in Westminster Abbey, and ordered the head to be cut off and stuck on a pole on top of Westminster Hall, where it remained for 20 years. The rest of Cromwell's remains were hanged from a gibbet at Tyburn.

Monarchs Guilty of Treason?

(17 March) Parliament made it illegal to claim to be king. If this act had received the royal assent, all monarchs since Charles II, including the present Queen, would have been guilty of high treason.

Reverend Gentleman Claims 'Concubines Without Number'

The Revd. Abiezer Coppe, an Oxford graduate and initially a Presbyterian and then an Anabaptist minister, began to preach in the pulpit while wearing no clothes. The following year he published *The Fiery Flying Roll*, in which he declared: 'I have concubines without number, which I cannot be without. I can, if it be my will, kiss and hug Ladies, and love my neighbour's wife as myself, without sin.' He was subsequently arrested, and, despite pleading insanity, imprisoned. He denied responsibility for fathering numerous children, avowing that he would 'turn them out of doors, and starve them to death'. He celebrated his release by publishing *Coppe's Return to the Ways of Righteousness*.

1650

Surviving the Gallows

Anne Green, a servant girl, was condemned in Oxford to hang for child murder. After she was cut down from the gallows, and just as the anatomists were about to begin the dissection of her corpse, she gave a sign of life. She later fully revived, was pardoned, and went on to marry and bear three children. Eight years later, in the same city, a Mrs Cope also survived her hanging, but this time the authorities insisted on mounting a second attempt the following day, which proved successful.

The cat piano described by Athanasius Kircher in 1650. Pressing a particular
key on the keyboard would drive a spike into a particular cat's tail,
prompting it to caterwaul. The device proved successful in relieving
an Italian prince of his melancholy.

A Cat Piano 🐾 Publication of *Musurgia Universalis* by the German Jesuit
scholar Athanasius Kircher, in which he describes an unusual musical
instrument:

> In order to raise the spirits of an Italian prince burdened by the cares of his
> position, a musician created for him a cat piano. The musician selected cats
> whose natural voices were at different pitches and arranged them in cages side
> by side, so that when a key on the piano was depressed, a mechanism drove a
> sharp spike into the appropriate cat's tail. The result was a melody of miaows
> . . . who could not help but laugh at such music? Thus was the prince raised
> from his melancholy.

(For a porcine organ, *see* 1470.)

The Devil's Bark 🐾 The bark of the cinchona tree – the origin of
quinine, and an effective means to control fevers – was introduced to England

in the 1650s. Because it had been brought from South America to Europe by Spanish missionaries, it was known as Jesuits' bark, and the ardently Protestant Oliver Cromwell refused to use it on the grounds of its Catholic associations, referring to it as 'the Devil's bark'. As a result, Cromwell suffered badly from the malaria he had contracted in his native fenlands of eastern England.

1651

The Giant of Brockford Bridge 🦶 While digging gravel in the road between Brockford Bridge and Ipswich, two men came across the body of a giant. According to a contemporary account, 'from top of his skull to the bottom of the bones of his feet was ten foot . . . the circumference of one of his thigh bones of the bigness of a middle-sized woman's waist . . . When the finding of this wonder of men was noised abroad, many of the people of the adjacent towns resorted to see it, and divers out of mere folly, I think, than discretion, broke the skeleton to gain part, or small pieces of bones, to brag they had part of him.' Thus we will never know whether this was a genuine giant, or, in fact, the bones of an ox or a woolly rhinoceros.

1652

The Cavalier Highwayman 🦶 Execution of Captain James Hind, the Cavalier highwayman. Hind had earned his reputation for gallantry when, on his first outing in his chosen profession, he had allowed his victims to keep £1 out of the £15 he had taken, to cover the expenses of their onward journey.

Tracing One's Ancestry Back to Adam 🦶 Publication by Sir Thomas Urquhart, the Scottish Cavalier and scholar, of *Pantochronoachanon; or, A Peculiar Promptuary of Time*, in which he traced his ancestry back through 153 generations, via Noah, to the lump of clay from which God formed

Adam. Some hold that Urquhart was only joking. It was said that when Sir Thomas was informed of the Restoration of Charles II in 1660 he laughed so much that he died.

1654

Repelled by Crabs ❧ The British attempt to capture Jamaica from Spain was thwarted when the invaders retreated in the belief that the loud rustling in the reeds along the shore was the sound of soldiers waiting to ambush them. It turned out the sound was made by large numbers of land crabs scuttling about.

1655

'Bad Wine is Sudden Death' ❧ Death at the age of 82 of Sir Theodore Mayerne, noted bon viveur, cookery writer (he created the City of London Pie, involving marrow bones and sparrows) and physician to four kings: Henry IV of France, and to James I, Charles I and the future Charles II of England. On his deathbed Mayerne attributed his demise to the bad wine he had drunk in an inn on the Strand: 'Good wine is slow poison,' he said. 'I have drunk it all my lifetime, and it has not killed me yet; but bad wine is sudden death.'

A Century of Inventions ❧ Publication of *A Century of Inventions*, by Edward, Marquis of Worcester. This collection of futuristic projects (none realized, or even designed in detail) included ideas for floating gardens, automatons, a watch that would never need winding, a cannon that could be fired six times in a minute, flying machines, a device for lighting fires and candles at predetermined times, a calculating machine, and a 100-foot-high ladder that could be carried in one's pocket.

During the Civil War the marquis had held Raglan Castle for Charles I, and when a troop of Parliamentarians approached he set in motion some hydraulic machines of his devising, and these made such a roaring noise the attackers were convinced that the defenders had let loose a pride of lions, and fled.

1656

Punishment for Blasphemy ❧ (October) The breakaway Quaker preacher, James Nayler, rode into Bristol in a re-enactment of Christ's entry into Jerusalem, while his followers sang 'Holy, holy, holy', and strewed his path with their garments. In December he was convicted of blasphemy, flogged, branded on his forehead with the letter B, imprisoned for two years of hard labour, and had his tongue pierced with a hot iron.

1657

Old Ironsides Plays the Fool ❧ (18 November) Mary Cromwell, daughter of the Lord Protector, married Lord Falconbridge. The father of the bride, despite his puritanical reputation, laid on lavish entertainment, and himself danced till five in the morning. The same month, Cromwell's other daughter, Frances, married Mr Rich, and Cromwell amused himself by seizing off the bridegroom's wig, pretending to hurl it into the fire while in fact concealing and then sitting upon it, all the while mourning its loss.

1659

Keeping the Congregation Awake ❧ Richard Dovey left a bequest to pay a poor man to keep dogs out of the church of Claverley in Shropshire, and to keep the congregation awake during Sunday sermons.

1661

Midwinter Spring ❧ (20 January) Samuel Pepys noted in his diary: 'It is strange what weather we have had all this winter; no cold at all; but the ways are dusty, and the flies fly up and down, and the rosebushes are full of leaves, such a time of the year as was never known in this world before here.'

———

The Queen is Not Yet Shaved 🐾 With the Restoration in England

women actors began for the first time to play female roles on the stage. One of the last male actors to take female parts was Edward Kynaston, who played the Queen in *The Maid's Tragedy* in 1661. One day King Charles arrived earlier than expected at the theatre, and became impatient that the play had not started. The manager, thinking honesty the best policy, was obliged to explain to his majesty that 'the Queen is not yet shaved'.

———

Carrying Out One's Marital Obligations with a Physician in Attendance 🐾 (20 June) Cosimo III Medici, Grand Duke of Tuscany,

married Marguérite Louise d'Orléans, cousin of Louis XIV. Cosimo was so concerned that sexual intercourse might be injurious to health that on the one night a week when he visited his wife's chamber he was accompanied by a physician. Despite this unromantic circumstance, Marguérite Louise did manage to bear Cosimo three children, although such was her loathing of her husband that during all three pregnancies she attempted to induce miscarriages.

Marguérite Louise eventually managed to escape back to France in 1674. After this, Cosimo's mother – who had shared her son's dislike of her daughter-in-law – increasingly influenced state policy, and was responsible for a number of edicts designed to enforce public morality. An example was the Ordinance on Low Windows:

> Since permitting young men to enter one's house to court the young girls, and allowing them to banter in the doorway or at the window, are enormous incentives to abduction, abortion and infanticide, it is hereby prohibited to allow young men inside, or to allow them to court, with or without permission, in the doorway or at the low windows.

A Battle of Precedence ❧ (30 September) For many years the ambassadors of France and Spain claimed precedence over each other at the courts of Europe. The matter came to a head in London on the day that the new ambassador from Sweden arrived. He was to travel in the king's carriage from Tower Wharf, and whoever followed immediately behind the king's carriage would have precedence. The carriages of the French and Spanish ambassadors arrived at the Wharf, both accompanied by scores of armed men. A running fight ensued through the streets of London, as one carriage tried to get in front of the other, much to the amusement of the populace. Swords were drawn and shots fired, and by the end of the day up to a dozen men lay dead. The Spanish coach ended up the winner. However, Louis XIV threatened Philip IV with war if he did not cede precedence, and Spain in the end conceded.

1662

The Penalties of Bestiality ❧ A man convicted of bestiality in New England was obliged to watch as the objects of his affections – a cow, two heifers, three sheep and two sows – were put to death in front of him, before he himself was executed.

1663

The Trial of the German Princess ❧ (4 June) A certain Mary Carleton, a woman of great wit and spirit, was brought to trial at the Old Bailey for bigamy. Born Mary Moders, the daughter of a Canterbury fiddler, she had passed herself off in London society as a German princess, Henrietta Maria de Wolway. Her landlady introduced her to her brother, John Carleton, an impecunious lawyer, who in turn passed himself off as an English nobleman, and in this guise wooed and won her. After a few weeks Carleton was alarmed at his wife's extravagant spending, and at the non-appearance of the riches he had expected to accompany the match.

Investigations were made, and reports soon came from Dover that Mrs Carleton already had two husbands in that town. However, Mrs Carleton persuaded the court that she was an entirely different person to the bigamist of Dover, and was acquitted. She subsequently appeared as herself on stage in a play based on her story, but did not manage to sustain this career, turned to various criminal scams, and was eventually hanged at Tyburn for the theft of a watch.

1664

A Human Mount ❧ A gentleman called Lionel Copley was charged with assault, having forced a saddle and bridle onto a man of lower social rank, and then ridden him round Sheffield.

1665

Madness in the Plague Year ❧ During the Great Plague of London, it was said that some citizens, once they were infected, became so distracted that they threw themselves out of windows, or shot themselves, or killed their own children.

1666

A Dishonourable Device ❧ George Villiers, Duke of Buckingham, avoided a duel with Lord Ossory (whose nation, Ireland, Buckingham had insulted in Parliament) by having his opponent locked up in the Tower of London.

1667

Marquis Threatens to Infect King with Pox ❧ Madame de Montespan became the mistress of Louis XIV. Her outraged husband, the Marquis de Montespan, a fiery and impoverished Gascon, let it be known that he intended to visit the most unsalubrious brothels, infect himself with the nastiest of poxes, and pass on his infections to his wife and thence to the king. To avert this unpleasant outcome, Montespan was arrested, and sent into exile.

1670

An Act Against False Teeth and Bolstered Hips &
The English Parliament passed an act with the following strictures:

> Be it resolved that all women, of whatever age, rank, profession, or degree; whether virgin maids or widows; that shall after the passing of this Act, impose upon and betray into matrimony any of His Majesty's male subjects, by scents, paints, cosmetics, washes, artificial teeth, false hair, Spanish wool, iron stays, hoops, high-heeled shoes, or bolstered hips, shall incur the penalty of the laws now in force against witchcraft, sorcery, and such like misdemeanours, and that the marriage, upon conviction, shall stand null and void.

1671

The Case of Colonel Blood & (15 March) Colonel Thomas Blood,
disguised as a cleric, was arrested while attempting to steal the crown jewels from the Tower of London. Charles II subsequently offered Blood a pardon and a position at court, leading to speculation that the theft was on the king's commission, in order to raise some badly needed cash.

Intention to Cut Noses a Hanging Offence & An act of
Parliament made it a capital offence to lie in wait with intent to mutilate a person's nose. The law followed an assault along these lines on Sir John Coventry. The act took an equally dim view if the intent was to cut out a tongue, put out an eye, cut off a lip or otherwise maim or disfigure a person. The law was repealed in 1828.

1672

A Remarkable Fire-Eater ❧ (8 October) John Evelyn recorded in his diary the extraordinary performance of a man called Richardson:

> He devoured brimstone on glowing coals before us, chewing and swallowing them; he melted a beer-glass and ate it quite up; then taking a live coal on his tongue he put on it a raw oyster; the coal was blown on with bellows till it flamed and sparkled in his mouth, and so remained until the oyster gaped and was quite boiled. Then he melted pitch and wax with sulphur, which he drank down as it flamed: I saw it flaming in his mouth a good while; he also took up a thick piece of iron, such as laundresses use to put in their smoothing-boxes, when it was fiery hot, held it between his teeth, then in his hand, and threw it about like a stone; but this I observed he cared not to hold very long. Then he stood on a small pot, and, bending his body, took a glowing iron with his mouth from between his feet, without touching the pot or ground with his hands, with divers other prodigious feats.

Richardson's career eventually came to an end when his servant disclosed the secrets of his trade.

1674

A Nauseous Puddle of Water ❧ The anonymous *Women's Petition Against Coffee* condemned the beverage 'as a little base, black, thick, nasty, bitter, stinking, nauseous puddle of water', for which people should not trifle away their time or their money.

1675

On the Merry Effects of *Bhang* ❧ Around this time the English explorer, Thomas Bowrey, wrote what is thought to be the first account of cannabis use by a Westerner. While trading along the coast of Bengal, he and some of his shipmates experimented with *bhang*, an infusion of cannabis seed and leaf. Most found it worked 'merrily' upon them, as they lay across carpets spread around the room, 'complimenting each other in high terms, each man fancying himself no less than an emperor'. However, some reacted differently: one man sat on the floor and 'wept bitterly all the afternoon', another became so terrified that he stuck his head in a 'great jar' for four hours or more, while a third became 'quarrelsome and fought with one of the wooden pillars of the porch until he had left himself little skin upon the knuckles of his fingers'.

Coffee and Scandal 🐚 The government issued a proclamation for the suppression of all coffee houses in England, on the grounds that they were hotbeds of political dissent, rumour-mongering and libels against the king's ministers. The coffee merchants raised a petition, and the government relented, on condition that the owners of the coffee houses 'should prevent all scandalous papers, books, and libels from being read in them; and hinder every person from declaring, uttering, or divulging all manner of false and scandalous reports against government, or the ministers thereof'. As this proved quite impossible to enforce, the government's proscription was deemed laughable, and generally ignored.

Cromwell the Turk 🐚 The City goldsmith Robert Viner, who had received a knighthood from Charles II in return for lending him money, decided in his gratitude to honour Charles with a statue, and, being more a businessman than a patron of the arts, went about acquiring it by the quickest and cheapest method possible. To this end he purchased an old marble statue of the Polish king John Sobieski, whose horse was trampling a Turk. Viner then employed a not-very-skilled sculptor to do his best to turn John into Charles and the Turk into Oliver Cromwell. The result was generally considered risible, especially as Cromwell still wore the Turk's turban.

1676

The Marchioness and the Poisoned Biscuits 🐚 (17 July)
Execution by beheading of the Marchioness of Brinvilliers, who, in collaboration with her lover and a servant, had poisoned her father and two brothers, in order to obtain a large inheritance. Prior to these crimes, the Marchioness had tried out her methods on the poor of Paris, to whom she gave poisoned biscuits.

1677

A Cure for the Wombling Trot 🐚 Publication of *The Woman's Prophecy, or the Rare and Wonderful Doctrines*, in which the popular quack, Mrs Mary Green, offered to cure such afflictions as 'glimmering of the gizzard, quavering of the kidneys and the wombling trot'.

1678

The Musical Coalman 🐚 Thomas Britton, a London charcoal seller (known as the Musical Small Coal Man) began a series of public concerts in the loft above his shop. He attracted personages as august as the Duchess of Queensbury, who had to climb up a ladder to listen to the music. The concerts would continue for 36 years, and latterly involve the composer Handel.

In 1714 Britton was introduced (unwittingly) to Mr Honeyman, a ventriloquist. When Mr Honeyman launched into his act, Britton was so taken aback that he died of shock on the spot.

1679

Poet Laureate Set Upon by Ne'er-Do-Wells 🐚 (17 December) The poet John Dryden was attacked in the streets of London, as recorded by a contemporary newspaper: 'Upon the 17th instant, in the

evening, Mr Dryden, the great poet, was set upon in Rose Street, in Covent-Garden, by three persons, who called him a rogue, and other bad names, knockt him down, and dangerously wounded him, but upon his crying out "Murther!" they made their escape. It is conceived that they had their pay beforehand, and designed not to rob him, but to execute on him some cruelty, if not popish vengeance.' Apparently the poet's offence had been to pen a satire against Lord Rochester.

1680

___

The 'Dog Shogun' 🐾 Tokugawa Tsunayoshi became shogun of Japan. Having been born in the Year of the Dog, the new shogun introduced laws outlawing any cruelty to dogs. Some of those who broke his laws were put to death.

1682

___

Musical Lothario Meets Untimely End 🐾 (25 February)
The Italian composer Alessandro Stradella, a notorious philanderer, was stabbed to death by an assassin presumed to have been hired by the nobleman with whose mistress he had eloped.

___

Peter the Anatomist 🐾 (7 May) Death of the sickly and childless Tsar
Fyodor III of Russia. He had been married for a year to his second wife Martha Apraksina, and on her death some years later, Fyodor's successor, Peter the Great, sought to satisfy his curiosity (and his ambitions as an anatomist) by personally dissecting her body to see whether she had died a virgin.

___

On Puritan Vices 🐾 The anonymous author of *A Letter from New England* denounced the people of Boston, Massachussetts, especially the Puritans, in round terms:

ON THE USELESSNESS OF AMERICA

Messalina was chaste in comparison of their lewd and repeated fornications and adulteries. For lying and cheating, they outvie Judas, and all the false merchants in hell; and the worst of drunkards may here find pot-companions enough, for all their pretences to sobriety. In a word, no sect of men upon the face of the earth are so unmannerly, in their outward disclaiming against vices in particular, and more punctual in the practice of all in general.

1683

—

On the Uselessness of America ❦ (5 August) After René La Salle had travelled from the Great Lakes to the mouth of the Mississippi and claimed the whole area for France, calling it Louisiana in honour of his king, an ungrateful Louis XIV wrote, 'I am convinced the discovery of Sieur de la Salle is very useless, and that such enterprises ought to be prevented in future.'

1685

—

A Cruel Judge ❦ At the infamous Bloody Assizes following the failure of Monmouth's Rebellion, the notorious Judge Jeffreys threw the pardon of one of the convicted traitors to his official jester, and told the man's friends that they could buy it from him if they pleased.

—

On Hawking and Spitting ❦ Publication of the anonymous *Rules of Civility*, which advises its readers, while at table, to 'forbear hawking and spitting as much as you can'. If it cannot be helped, then one should turn one's back and spit into one's handkerchief rather than on the floor.

1686

—

Royal Society Declines to Publish Newton ❦ (2 June) The council of the Royal Society, London, having a limited publication budget, declined to fund the printing of Newton's *Principia Mathematica*, in favour of Willoughby's *History of Fishes*.

1687

—

An Occupational Hazard 🙠 (8 January) The French composer Jean-Baptiste Lully wounded himself in the toe while beating time with a staff – as was then the practice – during a performance of a Te Deum. The wound became septic, but Lully refused to have it amputated, and on 22 March he died of blood poisoning.

1688

—

The Mermaids of Dee 🙠 The *Aberdeen Almanac* for the year advised its readers that if they were to go to the mouth of the River Dee on certain dates through the spring and summer, and into October, 'they will undoubtedly see a pretty company of MARMAIDS, creatures of admirable beauty, and likewise hear their charming sweet melodious voices'. These mermaids, it would appear, favoured songs of cither a pious or a patriotic bent.

1689

—

Proof of the Damnableness of Quakers 🙠 Cotton Mather, in his *Memorable Providences, relating to Witchcrafts and Possessions*, recounted the story of the Goodwin children, who, when under the influence of witchcraft, could not read the Bible – although they could manage Quaker tracts without difficulty.

circa 1690

—

A Changeling Child Who Cries like a Cat 🙠 An advertisement appeared in London for the exhibition of a 'Changeling Child':

> To be seen next door to the Black Raven, in West Smithfield, being a living skeleton, taken by a Venetian galley from a Turkish vessel in the Archipelago: This is a fairy child, suppos'd to be born of Hungarian parents, but chang'd

The belief that even the most respectable of ladies could be a witch was still widely prevalent at the end of the 17th century. Here the goat under the draperies gives the game away.

in the nursing, aged nine years and more, not exceeding a foot and a half high. The legs, thighs, and arms are so very small, that they scarce exceed the bigness of a man's thumb, and the face no bigger than the palm of one's hand; and seems so grave and solid, as if it were threescore years old. You may see the whole anatomy of its body by setting it against the sun. It never speaks. And when passion moves it, it cries like a cat. It has no teeth, but is the most voracious and hungry creature in the world, devouring more victuals than the stoutest man in England.

1692

On the Hollowness of the Earth &• Edmund Halley proposed in the *Philosophical Transactions of the Royal Society* that the Earth was hollow, containing a number of concentric spheres each with its own atmosphere and rate of rotation. He came up with the hypothesis to account for anomalies in compass readings.

The Most Drunken Synod &• Peter the Great established the Most Drunken Synod, a drinking club that parodied the rituals of the Russian Orthodox Church. In his diary, J.G. Korb, the Austrian Secretary of Legation in St Petersburg, explained the nature of the Synod:

> They were a sham patriarch and a complete set of clergy dedicated to Bacchus ... He that bore the assumed honours on the Patriarch was conspicuous in the vestments proper to a bishop ... Cupid and Venus were the insignia on his crosier, lest there should be any mistake about what flock he was pastor of. The remaining rout of Bacchanalians came after him, some carrying great bowls of wine, others mead, others again beer and brandy, that last joy of heated Bacchus.

Peter had an inordinate appetite for buffoonery, particularly if it involved some element of cruelty. Voltaire, in his *History of the Russian Empire under Peter the Great*, tells us how the Tsar conceived the idea of marrying Zotov, his 84-year-old jester – and the Patriarch of the Drunken Synod – to a widow of a similar age:

The guests were invited by four stammerers; some decrepit old men escorted the bride; while four of the fattest men in Russia served as runners. The band was on a cart drawn by bears goaded with steel points, which, by their roaring, provided a bass worthy of the tunes being played on the wagon. The bride and groom were blessed in the cathedral by a blind and deaf priest wearing spectacles. The procession, the wedding ceremony, the nuptial feast, the disrobing of the bridal couple, and the ritual of putting them to bed were all equally appropriate to the buffoonery of the entertainment.

Only Peter laughed at some of his japes. When his former wife, Eudoxia, supposedly confined to a nunnery, took a lover, a certain Stepan Glebov, Peter had the unfortunate man impaled. The episode is referred to in Dostoevsky's *The Idiot*: 'He was fifteen hours on the stake in the frost, in a fur coat, and died bearing no ill-will towards any man.' The fur coat was a touch added by Peter, to ensure that Glebov's sufferings were not prematurely ended by the extreme cold of the Russian winter.

1694

Punishment for Adultery ❧ The Swedish adventurer, Count Philip von Königsmark, disappeared. He had been the lover of Sophia Dorothea of Celle, the young wife of Georg Ludwig, Duke of Brunswick-Lüneburg – the future George I of Great Britain and Ireland. Inevitably it was believed that the Count had been killed on George's orders. George proceeded to divorce his wife, and then had her locked up in the castle of Ahlden for the remaining 32 years of her life, forbidding her to see any visitors, even her own children.

1695

A Stabbing on Stage ❧ At the age of 17 George Farquhar accidentally wounded a fellow actor on stage during a performance of Dryden's *The Indian Emperor*, having mistaken a real sword for a foil. After this shock he abandoned acting, and turned his hand to writing plays, with considerable success.

A Moveable Feast ❧ (30 December) Death of Sir Samuel Morland, a man of great ingenuity, credited with the invention of the speaking-trumpet, the fire-engine, an improved steam engine and the country's first drinking fountain (installed in Hammersmith in 1685). His most intriguing innovation was a carriage equipped with a kitchen, which, aided by clockwork machinery, could produce soup, broil steaks and roast joints as he travelled about.

1697

White Woman Scalps Indians ❧ Mrs Hannah Dustin, a settler in Haverhill, Massachusetts, together with her baby and a friend called Mary Neff were captured by Indians. They killed the baby, but enslaved the two women. One night some weeks later, while their captors slept, the two women got hold of the tomahawks of the Indian braves and proceeded to slaughter them. Mrs Dustin then took their scalps – ten in all – for which she received a reward of £50.

1699

Billiard Player Takes Over French Finances ❧ (5 September) Louis XIV made Michel Chamillart controller-general of finances, allegedly on the grounds that he was the only man who could beat him at billiards. Despite this qualification, Chamillart proved unable to recover France's finances from the terrible mess into which Louis had plunged them.

An early illustration of the aurora borealis, from Johann Scheuchzer's *Biblia Sacra* (1718).

The 18th Century

The Man Who Could Dislocate His Own Back 🐾 Brothel Madam Employs Chaplain 🐾 A Fellatrix Meets her Maker 🐾 Cat Urges Servant Girl to Destroy Herself 🐾 A Buccaneering Bishop 🐾 Female Pirates Narrowly Avoid Sapphic Encounter 🐾 The Pitiful Fate of the Infant Prodigy of Lübeck 🐾 The Dragons of the Alps 🐾 Young Lady Believes Herself Infested with Imps 🐾 The Woeful End of Mother Clap 🐾 The Rabbits of Godalming 🐾 A Treatise on Flogging 🐾 Perspiration from the Bowels of the Earth 🐾 Sow-Gelder Attempts to Spay Wife 🐾 Spontaneous Combustion of Humans 🐾 Loose, Idle, and Disorderly Persons 🐾

1700

The Man Who Could Dislocate His Own Back 🙋

Approximate date of the death of Joseph Clark, of London, 'a man whose suppleness of body rendered him the wonder of his time,' according to *Curiosities of Human Nature*, an 1849 work by 'the author of Peter Parley's Tales'. The author continues:

> Though he was well made, and rather gross than thin, he could easily exhibit every species of deformity. The powers of his face were even more extraordinary than the flexibility of his body. He would suddenly transform himself so completely as not to be recognized by his familiar acquaintances. He could dislocate almost any of the joints of his body, and he often amused himself by imposing upon people in this way.
>
> He once dislocated the vertebrae of his back and other parts of his body, in such a manner, that Molins, the famous surgeon, before whom he appeared as a patient, was shocked at the sight, and would not even attempt a cure. On one occasion, he ordered a coat of a tailor. When the latter measured him, he had an enormous hump on his left shoulder; when the coat came to be tried on, the hump was shifted to the right side! The tailor expressed great astonishment, begged a thousand pardons, and altered the coat as quickly as possible. When he tried it on, the deformity appeared in the middle of his back!

Brothel Madam Employs Chaplain 🙋

The most exclusive brothel of the period in London was run by a certain Mother Wisebourne, whose clients included at least two secretaries of state. So respectable was her establishment that a chaplain was maintained on the premises. Among those who worked for Mother Wisebourne was Sarah Pridden. That was the peak of her career; Sarah died in Newgate prison of brain fever in 1723, and her life became the inspiration of Hogarth's *Harlot's Progress* (1732).

Minister Slits Boys' Throats 🙋

The Revd Thomas Hunter, while out on a nature ramble near Edinburgh, cut the throats of the two boys to whom he was tutor. He was annoyed that they had discovered him the previous day *in flagrante delicto* with the servant girl, a circumstance they had communicated to their father. The reverend gentleman's revenge was judged unduly harsh, particularly as the boys' father – although dismissing the servant girl – decided to maintain Hunter in his post. Hunter was hanged.

———

City Mob Whips Women as if Horses &

(October) A mob assembled in the City of London, lined up on both sides of the road and whipped every woman who passed by. Should a woman be accompanied by her husband, he was forced to ride on her back, while the mob whipped his unfortunate mount.

———

Habsburg Inbreeding – Part II: Charles the Bewitched &

(1 November) Death of Charles II, the last Habsburg king of Spain. Contemporaries knew him as *El Hechizado* ('the bewitched'), and royal exorcists tried in vain to rid him of his disabilities: he was sickly, mentally retarded, and was barely able either to walk or speak. His speech was not helped by a lower jaw that massively outgrew the upper, and a tongue so large that he constantly dribbled. In 1697 the English ambassador recounted:

> He has a ravenous stomach, and swallows all he eats whole, for his nether jaw stands so much out, that his two rows of teeth cannot meet; to compensate which, he has a prodigious wide throat, so that a gizzard or liver of a hen passes down whole, and his weak stomach not being able to digest it, he voids in the same manner.

All this was as a result of excessive inbreeding among the Habsburgs – for example, his father's parents were also his mother's grandparents, and he himself was descended from Joanna the Mad (*see* 1506) by 14 different lines. Charles's inability to father an heir by either of his two wives led to the War of the Spanish Succession.

———

A Pious Eye 🐌 (December) It was reported in *The English Post* that the iris of one eye of a child living near Somerset House in the Strand, London, bore the message *Deus meus* (Latin, 'my God'). The other eye, if inspected by candlelight, carried various Greek and Hebrew characters, to which, however, no meaning could be ascribed.

1702

Governor Dons Female Attire 🐌 John Cornbury Hyde, Earl of Clarendon and governor of New York, opened the colonial assembly wearing a blue silk frock. He argued that as he was representing a woman, Queen Anne, he should dress in an appropriate fashion.

1703

———

The Great Storm 🐌 (27 November) The Great Storm hit England, causing much devastation and many deaths, among whom were the Bishop of Wells and his wife, who were killed in bed by a falling chimney. The biggest loss of life occurred in the Downs off the east coast, where a Royal Navy fleet recently returned from the Mediterranean was devastated, with the loss of 1200 men. Two hundred sailors were stranded on the Goodwin Sands, and their lives threatened as the tide rose. The mayor of Deal, learning of their peril, busied himself with trying to arrange a rescue. The local boatmen were too concerned with collecting valuable materials from the wrecks to help, while the custom house officers said it was not their job to send their boats out to save imperilled men. Infuriated, the mayor rounded up some sympathetic townsfolk and they took the customs boats by force, and rescued as many sailors as they could. The mayor then applied to the Royal Navy agent in Deal for help in looking after the rescued men, but he claimed his job was only to look after wounded sailors, not those who had been shipwrecked. The mayor had perforce to dig into his own pockets to clothe and feed the men, and bury the dead. Only after lengthy petitioning was he reimbursed by the government, and the wives and children of the dead awarded pensions.

———

Defoe in the Pillory ❧ (29–31 July) Daniel Defoe was held for three days in the pillory as punishment for writing his satirical *Shortest Way with Dissenters*. But such was his popularity that the crowd threw flowers at him, rather than rotten eggs and cabbage stumps.

———

The First Formosan ❧ A man arrived in London claiming to be the first Formosan to visit England. He had been converted to Christianity, he said, and his name was George Psalmanazar. He caused a sensation, eating spiced raw meat, and wearing a snake around his neck to keep him cool, as was the habit of his country. He explained his pale skin by recounting how those of high caste, such as himself, lived underground, shaded from the harsh sun. In 1704 he published *An Historical and Geographical Description of Formosa*, in which he described how Formosan men walked naked apart from a disc of gold or silver to cover their private parts. Polygamy was the norm, and husbands could eat their wives if they were unfaithful; however, if a husband took more wives than he could maintain, he would be beheaded. Anyone who struck the king or a governor was hung up by their feet and torn to pieces by four dogs attached to his body. The diet of the Formosans included the flesh of serpents, which they drain of venom 'after this manner: They take them when they are alive and beat them with Rods until they be very angry; and when they are in this furious passion, all the Venom that was in the Body ascends to the Head, which being then cut off, there remains no more Poison in the Body, which may therefore be safely eaten.' The Formosans also kept pet snakes, 'which they carry about their body', and had also domesticated rhinoceroses, which were 'very useful for the service of Man'. The hearts of some 18,000 boys were sacrificed to their god each year, and the priests ate their bodies. Psalmanazar described the Formosan language, and printed this version of the Lord's Prayer:

OUR Father who in Heaven art, Hallowed be
Amy Pornio dan chin Ornio vicy, Gnayjorhe
thy Name, Come thy Kingdom, Be done thy Will
sai Lory, Eyfodere sai Bagalin, jorhe sai domion
as in Heaven, also in Earth so, Our bread
apo chin Ornio, kay chin Badi eyen, Amy khatsada
daily give us today, and forgive us
nadakchion toye ant nadayi, kay Radonaye ant
our trespasses, as we forgive our trespassers,
amy Sochin, apo ant radonern amy Sochiakhin,
do lead us not into temptation, but deliver us from
bagne ant kau chin malaboski, ali abinaye ant tuen
Evil, for thine is the Kingdom, and Glory, and
Broskacy, kens sai vie Bagalin, kay Fary, kay
Omnipotence to all ages. Amen.
Barhaniaan chinania sendabey. Amien.

Eventually Psalmanazar was challenged by Edmund Halley and others, and admitted he was actually a Frenchman. He had derived the name Psalmanazar from Shalmaneser, the king of Assyria mentioned in 2 Kings; however, he never admitted his real name. Psalmanazar later learnt Hebrew, published an annotated edition of the Psalms, and became a friend of Samuel Johnson.

1706

—

Justice Delayed – Part I 🏴 In Virginia, a woman called Grace Sherwood was found guilty of using witchcraft to cause another woman to miscarry. The verdict was delivered after she had her thumbs tied to her toes and was plunged into a river; the fact that she floated demonstrated the truth of the allegations. Her punishment is unknown, but she escaped execution and lived to the age of 80. Three hundred years later, in 2006, the governor of Virginia, Timothy Kaine, quashed the conviction.

1709

Rescue of Stranded Mariner ❧ (2 February) HMS *Duke* picked up

a stranded mariner from a remote Pacific island. The man, who had survived alone for over four years, was dressed in goat skins, talked wildly and was so fit he could outrun the ship's bulldog. The island was Juan Fernández, 600 km (400 miles) off the coast of Chile, and the man's name was Alexander Selkirk – the inspiration for Daniel Defoe's *Robinson Crusoe*.

A Fellatrix Meets her Maker ❧ (9 October) Death of Barbara

Villiers, Duchess of Cleveland and one-time mistress of Charles II. She was said on one occasion to have bitten off the penis of a bishop while performing fellatio, but this may have been mere tittle-tattle broadcast by Lord Coleraine.

A Flying Ship ❧ (20–22 December) The London *Evening Post* carried a

report that a priest in Brazil had petitioned the king of Portugal to grant him a patent for his invention of a 'flying ship'. The newspaper printed a helpful illustration of this machine, which appears to be half boat and half bird – and wholly fantastical.

1710

Ducking and Diving ❧ Jenny Diver, the celebrated pickpocket, was

hanged at Tyburn. Among her stratagems was one involving a dress with false arms and hands, which she would don to attend church services. Here she would place herself between two wealthy old women, relieving them of their valuables while appearing to hold both hands demurely together in her lap. She achieved immortality as a character in John Gay's *Beggar's Opera*, and in Brecht's modernized version, *The Threepenny Opera*.

1711

Rippingdale vs Rembrandt ❧ In *The Examiner*, John Hunt opined that 'Rembrandt is not to be compared in the painting of character with our extraordinarily gifted artist Mr Rippingdale.'

1712

Cat Urges Servant Girl to Destroy Herself ❧ Jane Wenham, a resident of Walkerne in Hertfordshire, was condemned to death for witchcraft, having been accused by a servant girl called Ann Thorn of having turned into a cat. This cat then offered the girl a knife, and suggested she kill herself. During the trial, Miss Wenham's inability to recite the Lord's Prayer without stumbling was taken by the jury as proof of her guilt, despite the strong doubts expressed by the judge. It later transpired that Miss Thorn made up the whole thing while suffering from boyfriend trouble, and Jane Wenham was given a royal pardon. She was not, as is sometimes reported, the last woman to be condemned to death for witchcraft in England: on 28 July 1716 Mary Hickes and her daughter, aged nine, were also hanged for the crime in Huntingdon.

Duellists Kill Each Other ❧ (15 November) The Duke of Hamilton and Lord Mohun fought a duel in Kensington Gardens, both suffering fatal sword wounds. Such was the rancour between the principals (at heart political – Hamilton was a Jacobite and Mohun a Whig) that their seconds also drew swords – although with less fatal consequences.

1714

A Jolly Doctor ❧ Death of the physician John Radcliffe, a man so witty that people would feign illness in order to obtain his company.

—

Strumpet Dragged Across Bay ❦ (17 March) On the Isle of Man,
Katherine Kindred was found guilty of being 'a notorious strumpet', and was sentenced to be dragged behind a boat across the harbour at Peeltown.

—

The Personal Hygiene of King George ❦ (18 September)
George I arrived in London to take the throne of Great Britain. A great lover of horses, women and food, he brought with him 18 cooks – but only one washerwoman.

—

A Meeting of Mistresses ❦ (20 October) At George I's coronation,
Lady Dorchester, who had been a mistress of James II, noticed that also present in Westminster Abbey were the Duchess of Portsmouth, a mistress of Charles II, and Lady Orkney, William III's mistress. Lady Dorchester then turned to her companion, Lady Cowper, and remarked, 'Good God! Who would have thought we three whores would have met together here!'

1716
—

A Buccaneering Bishop ❦ Lancelot Blackburne was appointed
Bishop of Exeter. Earlier in his career he had been padre on board a pirate ship in the West Indies, administering to the spiritual needs of his shipmates while claiming his share of any plunder. Blackburne crowned his career as Archbishop of York, in which office he was celebrated more for his amatory exploits than his attention to his clerical duties. On his death the balladeers repined:

> All the buxom damsels in the North
> Who knew his parts lament his going forth.

1718

'There Were Giants in the Earth . . .' 🐑 A French academician called Henrion published a work in which he described how the average stature of the human race had undergone a steady decline since the Creation. Adam, he claimed, was 37.72 m (123 ft 9 in) tall, and Eve 36.2 m (118 ft 9 in). Noah, by contrast, only managed 8.2 m (27 ft), Abraham 6 m (20 ft) and Moses 4 m (13 ft). By the time of the late Roman Republic, men such as Julius Caesar grew to a mere 1.5 m (5 ft), and it was only the coming of Christ, according to Henrion, that prevented humanity from shrinking to microscopic proportions.

A Ban on Ovine Faeces in Coffee 🐑 The Irish Parliament passed the Coffee Adulteration Act, by which it was forbidden (among other things) to attempt to pass off sheep dung as coffee beans.

A *Coup de Foudre* 🐑 (31 July) At Stanton Harcourt in Oxfordshire, a pair of lovers engaged to be wed, John Hewit and Sarah Drew, were hit by lightning as they worked together in the fields. The poet Alexander Pope, who was staying nearby, wrote them an epitaph.

Blackbeard the Pirate 🐑 (22 November) Death of the pirate Edward Teach, better known as Blackbeard. He was killed in an engagement with the Royal Navy, having sustained 25 wounds. He had earlier shown his disdain for both Man and Devil by challenging his crew to experience a foretaste of Hell. This he created by taking some of his men down into the hold, shutting the hatches, and setting light to pots full of brimstone. Blackbeard, naturally, held out the longest, being, according to some, in his natural element. He had 14 wives (some of them shared among his crew), and in battle would enhance his demonic image by sticking lighted tapers in his hair and beard. After his death, his head was cut off and hung from the mast; legend said that his headless body, thrown into the sea, swam several times around the ship before sinking. Another legend recounts how his skull, repatriated to his native Bristol, was turned into a punch bowl.

1719

Hangman Hanged ☙ The London hangman, William Marvel, was himself hanged, having been found guilty of stealing ten silk handkerchiefs.

1720

Four Pints of Gin and an Early Grave ☙ (February) In Spitalfields, London, a sailor entered a pub completely sober, and within two hours, having downed four pints of gin, was dead.

Female Pirates Narrowly Avoid Sapphic Encounter ☙ Death in prison of Mary Read, of a fever. Mary Read was a noted pirate, who had disguised herself as a boy. On her ship, the *Revenge*, she conceived a passion for a fellow pirate, but when she confessed her desires, it transpired that the object of her attentions was also a woman, called Anne Bonny.

1721

Bite Not the Glove ☙ A young Scotsman died in a duel near Selkirk, in the Scottish Borders, having no notion as to why he had issued the challenge that led to his death. What had incensed him was the fact that his glove bore a rent in its fabric. Sir Walter Scott, in a note to *The Lay of the Last Minstrel*, explains the circumstance:

> To bite the thumb or the glove seems not to have been considered, upon the Border, as a gesture of contempt, though so used by Shakespeare [in *Romeo and Juliet*], but as a pledge of mortal revenge. It is yet remembered that a

young gentleman of Teviotdale, on the morning after a hard drinking bout, observed that he had bitten his glove. He instantly demanded of his companions with whom he had quarrelled? and learning that he had had words with one of the party, insisted on instant satisfaction, asserting that, though he remembered nothing of the dispute, yet he never would have bitten his glove without he had received some unpardonable insult. He fell in the duel . . .

—

The Pitiful Fate of the Infant Prodigy of Lübeck ❧

(6 February) Birth in Lübeck of Christian Heinecker. By the age of one year old he could recount the principal events in the Pentateuch; at two he was master of nearly all of Biblical history; at three he had mastered Latin and French, and could answer 'most questions' regarding universal history and geography; by the age of four he had studied religion and the history of the church, and could enter into rational debate upon these subjects. All this was too much for the infant frame, for on 27 June 1725, when less than four-and-a-half years old, he died.

1722

—

A Considerate Criminal ❧

The highwayman Benjamin Child was hanged. His was a generous soul: on one occasion he had used his illegal earnings to discharge all the debtors in Salisbury prison.

1723

—

The Dragons of the Alps ❧

Johann Scheuchzer, professor of natural philosophy at the University of Zurich, published his comprehensive study of the Swiss Alps, *Itinera per Helvetiae Alpinas Regionas*. In this he described how some chamois have a stone in their stomachs that renders them immune to the bullets of the hunter. He also listed the types of dragon that inhabit the upper slopes, including one with the head of a cat, the tongue of a snake, legs covered in scales and a forked tail covered with hair.

1724

Rumours of Death Much Exaggerated 🐌 (3 March)

The *Caledonian Mercury* carried the following paragraph: 'We hear that my Lord Arniston, one of the ordinary lords of session, is dead.' The following week the newspaper was obliged to print an apology: 'It was by mistake in our last that we stated Lord Arniston was dead, occasioned by the rendezvous of coaches hard by his lordship's lodging, that were to attend the funeral of a son of the Right Honourable the Earl of Galloway; wherefore his lordship's pardon and family is humbly craved.'

1725

Wild Boys 🐌 Peter the Wild Boy, a feral child, was found living in

woods near Hanover. He lived off plants, and could not be taught to speak. George I brought him to England, where he became the object of much curiosity. He lived until 1785, and is buried by St Mary's Church, Norchurch. Another feral child, Victor, known as the Wild Boy of Aveyron, was found living in woods near Toulouse in 1797. It was found that he could be taught to understand various words and phrases, although all he could say was *lait* ('milk') and *O Dieu* ('oh God'). Victor died in Paris in 1828.

1726

Young Lady Believes Herself Infested with Imps 🐌

A young lady in Canterbury became convinced she was bewitched, and fell into a fever of quite fantastical dread. She had one day sat on a public bench, and subsequently felt an itching and pricking all over her body. On being told that the bench had shortly before been occupied by an impoverished old woman noted for her deformities, she leapt to the conclusion that she was a victim of a witch's spell, and 'even fancied crooked nails and bits of iron were coming up her throat'. When her servants took her home and stripped her to establish the source of her distress, a swarm of lice were revealed. The servants had no doubt that they had migrated from the old woman's clothing, but the young lady was convinced they were imps under the Devil's command. Several local matrons then visited the old woman, and subjected her to an examination. They were in search of 'unnatural teats' where the Devil might suck; finding none, they concluded that the Devil had rendered them invisible. There is no record of any further harm coming to the old woman. How long the young lady remained a victim to her vaporous fantasy is unknown.

The Woeful End of Mother Clap &⬧ (July) 'Mother' Margaret Clap was convicted of running a homosexual brothel in Holborn. Her defence, that as she was a woman 'it cannot be thought that I would ever be concerned in such practices', cut no ice, and she was sentenced to a fine, a jail term and a spell standing in the pillory. Such was the vicious indignation of the mob, she did not survive this latter punishment.

Punishment for Exploring Windward Passage &⬧ (September) According to *The British Gazette*, a certain Thomas Doulton was pilloried at Charing Cross 'for endeavouring (according to the canting term) to discover the *Windward Passage* upon one Joseph Yates, a seafaring person'.

The Rabbits of Godalming &⬧ (19 November) Mist's W*eekly Journal* carried the following report:

> From Guildford comes a strange, but well attested piece of news. That a poor woman who lives at Godalming, near that town, was, about a month past, delivered by Mr John Howard, an eminent surgeon and man-midwife, of a creature resembling a rabbit; but whose heart and lungs grew without its belly. About fourteen days since she was delivered by the same person of a perfect rabbit; and, in a few days after, of four more; and on Friday, Saturday, and Sunday, the fourth, fifth and sixth instant, of one in each day; in all nine.

Hogarth's print, *The Wise Men of Godalming*, depicts Mrs Mary Toft, a poor
woman of Godalming, giving birth to a considerable number of rabbits
before several witnesses.

They died all in bringing into the world. The woman hath made oath, that two
months ago, being working in a field with other women, they put up a rabbit;
who running from them, they pursued it, but to no purpose: This created in
her such a longing to it, that she (being with child) was taken ill, and miscar-
ried; and, from that time, she hath not been able to avoid thinking of rabbits.

The report caused such a sensation that King George I ordered that the
woman, Mrs Mary Toft, to be attended by two distinguished surgeons from
the capital, both of whom witnessed her giving birth to several more rabbits
(all dead). They explained that impressions received by expectant mothers
could have an effect on the foetus: thus Mrs Toft's obsession with rabbits
during her pregnancy no doubt accounted for her furry progeny.

Mrs Toft was subsequently exposed as a fraud, arrested and made a full
confession, demonstrating how she smuggled the infant creatures into the
appropriate part of her anatomy by sleight of hand. For a while roast rabbit

and jugged hare disappeared from the tables of England, and those who traded in rabbits threatened to sue the woman they believed to be responsible for their misfortune. The authorities subsequently decided that there were no grounds for a prosecution. The affair inspired Hogarth's satirical print entitled *The Wise Men of Godalming*.

1727

A Year of Marvels &⋅ In an editorial, *The Craftsman* newspaper commented on a year of marvels, including 'the wild human youth brought forth by an old oak, in a desert, uninhabited forest abroad'. Also of note were 'black swans, white bears, six-legged cows, men with two heads, flying horses, speaking dogs and dancing elephants' – not to mention 'the prodigious three-legged eagle' captured in Kent, and 'the wonderful young man', who was delivered of a baby girl in Fetter Lane.

Inventor of Cat Flap Dies &⋅ (31 March) Death of Sir Isaac Newton, known for his invention of the cat flap.

The Amazons of Dahomey &⋅ King Agadja of Dahomey deployed an all-female regiment – the so-called Dahomey Amazons – in his conquest of the neighbouring kingdom of Savi. The regiment derived from the all-female bodyguard – the so-called 'elephant huntresses' – of Agadja's father, King Houegbadja (ruled 1645–85), and continued in existence through the 19th century, by which time they comprised around a third of the army of Dahomey, and were armed with knives and rifles. Some were volunteers, while others were women whose husbands had complained about them to the king, and who were forcibly conscripted as a result. All were expected to remain celibate. The last survivor of the all-female regiment died in 1979.

A Treatise on Flogging 🦞 The publisher Edmond Curll was arrested for publishing *Venus in the Cloister or The Nun in her Smock* by the Abbé du Prat and *A Treatise of the Use of Flogging in Venereal Affairs* by Johann Heinrich Meibom, professor of medicine at the University of Helmstedt. In his defence Curll claimed that the former was a true account of the goings on in French convents, and that the latter was a genuine work of medical science. The court was unimpressed, imposing a fine of £100 and a spell in the pillory.

1728

Gallows Humour 🦞 (28 February) Lord Islay, in his judicial capacity as an Extraordinary Lord of Session in Edinburgh, issued a death sentence thus:

> I, Archibald, Earl of Islay, do hereby prorogate and continue the life of John Ruddell, writer in Edinburgh, to the term of Whitsunday next, and no longer.

1729

Perspiration from the Bowels of the Earth 🦞 (20 May) A waterspout swept ashore at Bexhill-on-Sea, Sussex, and transformed itself into a tornado, cutting a swathe of destruction 19 km long by 350 m wide (12 miles by 380 yards) as it sped inland. Contemporaries blamed it on 'Flatus, or ... a kind of Perspiration from the Bowels of the Earth'.

1730

Sow-Gelder Attempts to Spay Wife 🦞 (22 August) The *London Journal* reported that a sow-gelder in Somerset had been brought to court for attempting to spay his wife. The assault followed a session in the local public house with other married men, all of whom complained of the fecundity of their spouses, and the concomitant expense thereof. The sow-gelder determined to see whether his professional skills might resolve the problem by assaying an experiment upon his wife, but, having forcibly bound and gagged her, and made an incision in her belly, 'found there was some difference between the situation of the parts in the rational and irrational animals', and was obliged to abandon the experiment. The case against him was dismissed when his wife refused to testify.

1731

An Irish Hoax ❧ A certain E. Conid carved his name and the date on the side of a horizontal stone at the Hill of Tara, traditionally held to be the seat of the high kings of Ireland. Later in the century the antiquary Charles Vallencey opined that the inscription read 'BELI DIVOSE', held to mean 'To Belus, God of Fire'. In addition to wishful thinking, Vallencey's error may be attributed to the fact that the inscriber had etched his name upside down, presumably while reclining on the stone.

———

Spontaneous Combustion of Humans ❧ Giuseppe Bianchini, a prebendary of Verona, published an account of the spontaneous combustion of the Countess Cornelia de Baudi Cesenate. Six years earlier in France the surgeon Le Cat reported on a case in which a man was convicted of his wife's murder, but appeal to a higher court resulted in his acquittal, on the grounds that the unfortunate woman had burst into flames without outside help. Charles Dickens cites these cases in his preface to *Bleak House*, defending his depiction of the spontaneous combustion of Mr Krook therein.

———

Swiftian Scatology ❧ In Jonathan Swift's poem 'Strephon and Chloe', the hero is shocked at the noises his young bride makes while urinating:

> *Strephon* who heard the fuming Rill
> As from a mossy Cliff distil,
> Cry'd out, ye Gods, what Sound is this?
> Can *Chloe*, heav'nly *Chloe* —?

To make matters worse, Chloe proceeds to break wind.

> The little *Cupids* hov'ring round,
> (As Pictures prove) with Garlands crown'd,
> Abasht at what they saw and heard,
> Flew off, nor evermore appear'd.

1733

Augustus the Energetic (1 February) Death of Augustus II of Poland, known as 'the Strong' because of his ability to break horseshoes with his bare hands, hold men in the air at arm's length, and other such feats of physical prowess. True to his byname Augustus sired what for a European monarch might well be a record number of bastards – estimates range between 365 and 382. It is said that, unable to keep track of his many and varied offspring, he inadvertently took one of his daughters as his mistress. Via the most notable of his illegitimate children, Maurice de Saxe, Marshal of France, Augustus was great-great-grandfather of the novelist George Sand, who, appropriately enough, took as her lover the Polish composer Frédéric Chopin.

1735

Credit Encouraged in Irish Public Houses The Irish Tippling Act prevented landlords from over-zealously seeking to recover money owed to them for ale.

The Irish Hellfire Club Foundation of the Irish Hellfire Club, on which the later English club of the same name was modelled. The members met in the Eagle Tavern in Dublin, and in a hunting lodge on Montpellier Hill to the south of the city. In these two locations all kinds of rakish, hellraising and diabolical goings-on were practised – heroic drinking bouts, black Sabbaths, the sacrifice of cats, and a goodly variety of

transgressive sexual practices. The lodge on Montpellier Hill was burnt down when the members deliberately set it alight to get some foretaste of the climate of Hell, or, according to another account, when one member became so annoyed with a footman that he poured brandy over the unfortunate fellow and set him alight.

1736

A Puzzle &. An anonymous wit published an engraving entitled 'The Puzzle', accompanied by the following challenge: 'This curious inscription is humbly dedicated to the penetrating geniuses of Oxford, Cambridge, Eton, and the learned Society of Antiquaries.' The illustration showed a group of learned men peering at a stone on which is carved:

BENE

A.T.H. TH. ISST

ONERE. POS. ET

H.CLAUD,COSTER.TRIP

E.SELLERO

F.IMP

IN.GT.ONAS.DO

TH. HI.

S.C.

ON. SOR

T.I.A.N.E

If one ignores the layout and the punctuation, this reads: 'Beneath this stone reposeth Claud Coster, tripe-seller of Impington, as doth his consort Jane.'

1737

Prince's Sedan Chair Used for Fornication &. (February) A riot broke out in Covent Garden after the coachman of the manager of the Theatre Royal attempted to requisition the sedan chair of the Prince of Wales in order to fulfil his amorous purposes with a local prostitute.

1738

A Predicted Demise 🍂 (10 September) Death of Dr Thomas Sheridan, friend of Jonathan Swift and grandfather of the playwright Richard Brinsley Sheridan. He had been dining at a friend's house when the conversation turned to matters meteorological. Sheridan opined the following: 'Let the wind blow east, west, north, or south, the immortal soul will take its flight to the destined point.' Having uttered this, he leant back in his chair and died.

1739

Ladies and Gentlemen Gain Separate Facilities 🍂 The first segregated toilets for men and women were made available, at a ball in Paris.

The War of Jenkins's Ear 🍂 The pro-war party in Parliament invited a certain Captain Jenkins to appear before MPs, together with his severed ear, which he kept pickled in a jar. The ear had been cut off by the Spanish eight years previously, and was adduced as evidence of the ill-will of Spain towards His Majesty's subjects. The pro-war party carried the day, and the subsequent hostilities were known as the War of Jenkins's Ear.

Stoned to Death in a Bullring 🍂 In Cuenca, Ecuador, Jean Senièrgues, the physician on a French scientific expedition to the Equator, upset the local populace by appearing at the bullring with another man's fiancée. The spectators proceeded to stone and hack Senièrgues to death, while his companions were obliged to run for their lives. Prior to this unfortunate turn of events, Senièrgues had administered the then current treatment for malaria to one of his colleagues: half a lemon stuffed with gunpowder and Guinea pepper, inserted into the anus and changed twice daily.

—

Scotia Nostra ❧ (September) At the end of the Russo-Turkish war the commissioners of both sides – Marshal James Keith (a Jacobite exile) for the Russians, and the Grand Vizier for the Turks – met to discuss peace terms, talking through interpreters. As the two were about to part, the Grand Vizier grasped Keith by the hand, and declared that he was 'unco' happy to meet a fellow countryman who had done so well for himself. 'Dinna be surprised,' the Grand Vizier explained, 'I'm o' the same country wi' yoursel'. I mind weel seein' you and your brother, when boys, passin' by to the school at Kirkcaldy. My father, sir, was bellman o' Kirkcaldy.'

1740
—

The Vagaries of Fortune ❧ A man called William Duell, hanged for the murder of Sarah Griffin, was about to be dissected by students at Surgeons Hall when he gave signs of life. Having fully revived, his sentence was commuted to transportation. A cow in France was less fortunate: having been brought to court on a charge of murder, it was convicted and executed – the last such animal trial on record.

—

A German Giant ❧ Death of the German giant, Maximilian Christopher Miller, who grew to 2.49 m (8 ft), and whose hand measured 30 cm (1 ft).

1741
—

The Popularity of *Pamela* ❧ So mesmerized were the people of Slough by the public readings given by the town blacksmith of Samuel Richardson's epistolary novel *Pamela* that they rung the church bells to celebrate the eventual marriage of the heroine with Mr B.

Pushing the Envelope ❧ The Earl of Rosse, one of the founders of the Irish Hell-Fire Club, received a letter from a neighbouring cleric upbraiding him for his many and varied sins. Unperturbed, Rosse, having noted that the letter was simply addressed to 'My Lord', forwarded it to the notably pious and virtuous Earl of Kildare.

Homo Vulpi Lupus Est ❧ The Russian expedition led by Vitus Bering, weakened by cold, hunger and scurvy, overwintered on Bering Island, a bleak spot in the Bering Sea off the east coast of Kamchatka. They dug trenches in which to shelter, but these proved no defence against the Arctic foxes that preyed upon the dead and dying alike. In revenge, the fitter men would torture any unfortunate fox they caught, blinding it, cutting off its tail, burning its paws and part-flaying it before letting it go as a warning to its fellows. Bering himself died on the island.

1743

A Putrified Overgrown Body ❧ Death of Dr George Cheyne, a pioneer of the modern diet industry. Cheyne had in his early years gorged himself on vast quantities of rich food and drink, so that he became, in his own words, 'a putrified overgrown Body from Luxury and perpetual Laziness'. He adopted a diet of fruit, vegetables and milk, and recommended this to all persons who were overweight. His only dietary lapse was dictated by his profession: in order to make a diagnosis he would draw some blood from his patient, dip in his finger, and taste it.

1744

Loose, Idle, and Disorderly Persons ❧ (January) Two men were condemned in London to a month's hard labour 'for singing of seditious ballads, and being dress'd in a ridiculous manner, with paper stars and garters, and horns tipp'd with gold in their hats, and for being loose, idle, and disorderly persons, not having any visible way of living'.

___

Son of Footman Marries Great-Granddaughter of King 🙿
Henry Fox eloped with Lady Caroline Lennox. Horace Walpole commented:

> The town has been in a great bustle about a private match ... His father was a footman, her great-grandfather, a king ... All the blood-royal have been up in arms.

Lady Caroline was the daughter of the 2nd Duke of Lennox, whose father, the 1st Duke, was an illegitimate son of Charles II. Henry Fox was the son of Sir Stephen Fox, a man of yeoman stock who had started his career in the household of the Earl of Northumberland. Henry Fox went on to make a fortune as Paymaster of the Forces during the Seven Years' War, and was ennobled as Baron Holland in 1763. His son was Charles James Fox, the leading Whig politician.

___

Desist from Gobbling, Advises Lamb of God 🙿 The Swedish
scientist, Emanuel Swedenborg, was dining at an inn in Bishopsgate, London, when he saw Jesus Christ in the corner of the room. The Lord limited his remarks to an injunction to eat more slowly. According to Caroline Fox, writing a century later, 'This was the beginning of all his visions and mysterious communications.' Swedenborg abandoned science, and proceeded to visit both Heaven and Hell, where he discoursed with angels, devils and other spirits.

1746
___

The Etiquette of the Scaffold 🙿 (18 August) As the two Jacobite
rebels, the Earl of Kilmarnock and Lord Balmerino, faced execution on Tower Hill for their part in the '45 Rising, the former volunteered to defy

precedence and allow Balmerino, a peer of inferior rank, to meet his fate first. However, the sheriffs objected to this disregard for the etiquette of the scaffold, and insisted that the senior peer take precedence on the block.

1747

On the Cooking of Eggs

Publication of *The Art of Cookery Made Plain and Easy* by Hannah Glasse, who derided the decadent French for using six pounds of butter to cook a dozen eggs, when anybody who understands cooking knows 'that half a pound is full enough'.

Man Pisses in Another's Hat

(15 May) A labourer, John Swan, brought a case before the magistrates in Wiltshire, complaining that a certain James Alexander had passed water in his hat. The case was settled when Alexander agreed to pay for a new item of headgear.

1748

Anglo-French Relations – Part I: Regarding the Vulgarity of Shakespeare

Voltaire, a French philosopher, offered his opinion of *Hamlet*:

> It is a vulgar and preposterous drama, which would not be tolerated by the vilest populace of France, or Italy ... One would imagine this piece to be the work of a drunken savage.

Anglo-French Relations – Part II: Regarding the Roast Beef of Old England

William Hogarth, the English artist, was arrested in France as he sketched the gate of Calais, and charged with being a spy. The governor of the town informed him that had not peace negotiations then been underway between their two countries, he 'should have been under the disagreeable necessity of hanging Mr Hogarth on the ramparts'. As it was, the painter was put under armed guard and placed on a ship back to England. Hogarth's revenge took the form of a painting of the Gate of Calais, titled *Oh, The Roast Beef of Old England*, in which a side of beef is carried into the port for the consumption of English tourists, while various feeble and emaciated Frenchmen look on. This work was exhibited in the Louvre in 2006.

The Roast Butter of Old England &⬦ Publication of *The Art of Cookery*, by 'A Lady'. The book includes a recipe on 'How to Roast a Pound of Butter'.

1749

Person Promises to Squeeze Himself into Quart Bottle &⬦ (16 January) Crowds flocked into the Haymarket Theatre, London, in response to an advertisement promising that a man would squeeze himself into a quart (1 litre) bottle, and, while there, 'sing several songs'. The bill continued: 'that if any spectator should come masked, he would, if requested, declare who they were; and that in a private room he would produce the representation of any person dead, with which the person requesting it should converse some minutes, as if alive.' Once the theatre was full, the audience began to stir with impatience, there being no sign of the performance beginning. At this point the manager appeared on stage to offer a refund, to which one wag shouted that he would pay double if were to see a man squeeze into a pint bottle. The audience then erupted in fury, and set about the destruction of the interior of the theatre, tearing out seats and fittings, and dragging them out into the street to be burnt – egged on, so it was said, by the Duke of Cumberland, the king's younger son.

The Ugliest Man in London &⬦ Death of John Heidegger, the Swiss opera impresario who claimed to be the ugliest man in London. Lord Chesterfield had bet him that he could find an uglier person, and duly produced a fearful old crone. Witnesses were about to acclaim her the marginal winner when Heidegger seized the old woman's bonnet and put it on his own head – and so clinched the prize.

___

Miss Chudleigh's Undress ❧ At the Venetian ambassador's ball at Somerset House, Elizabeth Chudleigh, the noted society beauty and maid of honour to the Princess of Wales, appeared in a startlingly revealing costume. 'Miss Chudleigh's undress was remarkable,' noted Mrs Elizabeth Montague. 'She was Iphigenia for the sacrifice, but so naked the high priest might easily inspect the entrails of the victim.'

1750

A Widow in Masquerade ❧ (2 June) A Royal Marine by the name of James Gray revealed that he was actually a widow called Hannah Snell. 'Had you known,' she teasingly told her shipmates, 'who you had between the sheets with you, you would have come to closer quarters.' Snell had just returned from active service in India, where she had been wounded several times in the legs and groin. The latter wound she would not let the surgeons touch, for fear of exposure; she dealt with it herself, plunging finger and thumb into the wound to extract the musket ball that had made it. On another occasion, she had been stripped to the waist and flogged for some misdemeanour, the boatswain remarking that her breasts 'were most like a woman's he ever saw'. Still no one guessed her true sex. On her discharge Snell was granted a pension by an admiring government, and opened a pub in Wapping called The Female Warrior (or, in some accounts, The Widow in Masquerade).

1751

The Last Fatal Witch-Dipping ❧ (April) The last fatal witch-dipping in England took place at Tring, Hertfordshire. Later trials by water are recorded, for example that of a suspected wizard in the River Debden at

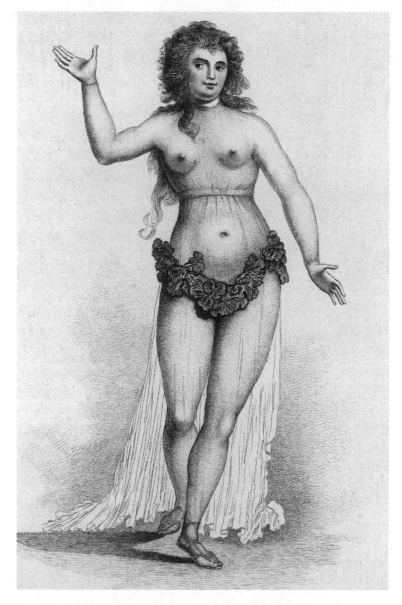

Elizabeth Chudleigh, maid of honour to the Princess of Wales and the future Countess of Bristol, appeared in this fetching costume at the Venetian ambassador's ball in 1749.

Farnham, Suffolk, in 1776. However, when, bound hand and foot, he sunk to the bottom, a 'humane spectator' intervened to save him, and the crowd, 'ashamed of themselves and angry at their own weakness and credulity', dispersed.

___

A Diet of Water ❧ (November) Christina Michelot, a young French girl, became ill with a fever, and survived on nothing but water for nearly four years, until July 1755 – as attested by a number of physicians.

1752

On the Benefits of Tar Water ❧ George Berkeley, Bishop of Cloyne and founder of the *esse est percipi* school of philosophy, published *Further Thoughts on Tar Water*, a substance he held to be a universal panacea if consumed in adequate quantities. A contemporary wag penned the following quatrain in homage to the great man:

> Who dare deride what pious Cloyne has done?
> The Church shall rise and vindicate her son;
> She tells us all her bishops shepherds are,
> And shepherds heal their rotten sheep with tar.

___

Eleven Days That Never Were ❧ (3–13 September) These days went missing as Britain and its colonies replaced the Julian calendar with that introduced by Pope Gregory XIII in the 16th century, with the aim of keeping more in phase with the solar year. Catholic Europe had adopted the Gregorian calendar, but Protestant Europe largely kept with the old system introduced by Julius Caesar, which began the year on 25 March, and which by the 18th century was 11 days behind the Gregorian calendar. Things had been getting so out of hand that when it was 1 January 1750 in London it was 12 January 1751 in Paris. Despite these anomalies, many in Britain agitated against the reform, with the slogan 'Give us back our eleven days!'

—

The Kraken Wakes ✒ In his *Natural History of Norway* (1752–3), Erik Pontoppidan, Bishop of Bergen, described the vast sea creature known as the Kraken, an animal 'the size of a floating island', capable of dragging the largest ships down to the depths. However, a greater danger to shipping was the whirlpool set in motion as the creature lowered itself beneath the surface. It is possible that the legend of the Kraken was inspired by underwater volcanic activity around Iceland, such as smoke and bubbles coming up from the depths, and even the creation of new islands by the extrusion of ash and lava.

1753
—

Bishop Engages in Serial Polygamy ✒ On the occasion of his fourth marriage, Dr John Thomas, Bishop of Lincoln, had his wedding ring inscribed with the motto:

> If I survive,
> I'll make it five.

1754
—

Berwick's Electors Shipped to Norway ✒ In his first attempt to enter Parliament, the radical politician, pamphleteer and libertine John Wilkes stood for the seat of Berwick-upon-Tweed. Entering into the spirit of 18th-century electioneering, Wilkes bribed the captain of a ship bringing electors from London to take them to Norway instead. Even this stratagem failed to win him the seat.

—

The Sultan Who Kept Clear of his Wives ✒ Osman III became sultan of the Ottoman Empire. Although he lived near the harem in his palace, he so disliked the company of women that he wore iron-soled shoes so that any member of the opposite sex would be alerted to his approach, and make herself scarce.

It was either this Sultan Osman, or an earlier one, who was so impressed by the skill with which a gardener planted a cabbage, that he made him viceroy of Cyprus.

1755

Shetland Covered in Black Dust (20 October) Vast quantities of sulphurous black dust fell on Shetland, blackening the face of anybody working out of doors. The previous day there had been a big volcanic eruption in Iceland, 1000 km (600 miles) away.

1756

Birth of Long-Lived Tortoise This was possibly the birth year of Adwaita ('the only one'), a giant Aldabra tortoise that became the pet of Clive of India. It was presented to Alipore Zoo in Calcutta in 1876, and died there in March 2006, at an estimated age of 250 years.

A Game of Chicken During the French and Indian Wars, the American officer Israel Putnam was challenged to a duel by a British officer. Putnam told his opponent that he was not much of a pistol man, but suggested that they each sit on a keg of gunpowder attached to a burning fuse. Honour obliged the Briton to agree, but as the fuses burned shorter and shorter he eventually leapt up and fled. Only later did Putnam reveal that the kegs were filled not with gunpowder but with onions.

King of Corsica Ends Up in Debtors' Prison (11 December) Death in London of King Theodore of Corsica. Theodore Neuhoff, a Westphalian soldier of fortune, had, in 1736, aided the Corsicans in their revolt against their Genoese masters, and had been invited by them to be their king. After a number of months on the throne, his popularity began to wane, and he decided it would be more expedient to rule his kingdom from overseas. King Theodore never managed to reclaim his realm, despite attempts in 1738 and 1742, and ended up in London, where before long he was imprisoned as a debtor. He eventually secured his release by making over the kingdom of Corsica to his creditors. He was buried in St Ann's, Westminster, and Horace Walpole wrote his epitaph, which ends:

> Theodore this moral learned ere dead:
> Fate poured its lessons on his living head,
> Bestowed a kingdom, and denied him bread.

Subsequently, 'King Theodore of Corsica' became a slang name for gin, along with such terms as 'Cuckold's Comfort' and 'Ladies' Delight'.

1757

Hideous End of a Regicide 🐚 (5 January) A fanatic, Robert-François Damiens, stabbed Louis XV, the French king, but without causing any significant harm. He became the last person in France to suffer the traditional punishment for regicides. He was taken to the Place de Grève in Paris, where he was tortured with red-hot pincers, then the hand that had held the knife was burnt, before molten wax, lead and boiling oil were poured into the wounds. He was then torn to pieces by four horses, one being harnessed to each limb. Finally his armless and legless body, in which the last breath of life was not yet extinguished, was burnt at the stake.

1759

A Proposal to Grow Vines in the Bogs of Ireland 🐚 Death of Richard Pockrich, the Irish inventor. Among his many unsuccessful schemes was one for the planting of Irish bogs with vines. He also proposed an act of Parliament whereby anybody reaching the age of 999 years should be considered legally dead, so that their heirs might inherit.

1760

The Last Aristocrat to be Hanged in England 🕮 (5 May)
Death of Earl Ferrers, the last aristocrat to be hanged in England. Ferrers had shot his steward when the latter had failed to comply with his lordship's wishes regarding the rents from the family estates, which were in the hands of trustees. Ferrers conducted his own defence before his peers in the House of Lords, unsuccessfully entering a plea of insanity. It was said he was hanged by a silken cord to mitigate the shame of his fate, and that his family had contrived a scaffold with a drop, so that he should not swing from a cart like a common criminal. The death was also quicker, Horace Walpole recalling, 'There was a contrivance for sinking the stage under him, which did not play well; and he suffered a little by the delay, but was dead in four minutes.'

Death on the Po 🕮 (25 October) George II died of a ruptured aortic
aneurysm while straining at stool. His aorta – the major artery from the heart – was said to have exploded with such a bang his valet thought he had broken wind. Two years previously, George had been gravely ill, and was thought likely to die, particularly as the oldest lion in the Tower of London had just expired: it had long been held that the fate of the lions in the Tower – who were named after kings – was tied up with that of the reigning monarch.

1761

Rancour Maintained Even in Death 🕮 (15 or 16 July) A French
officer called Fenestre had his head blown off at the Battle of Vellingshausen. Decades of enmity between him and a fellow officer (a man called d'Agay, with whom he had fought a number of duels) thus came to an end – but not before a shard of Fenestre's skull struck d'Agay in the eye, blinding him.

———

A Calamitous Coronation ❧ (25 September) The coronation of George III was not auspicious. The coronation chairs for the king and queen were missing, as was the sword of state, and a jewel fell out of the crown.

1762

———

The First Jigsaw Puzzle ❧ Lady Charlotte Finch became governess to George III's children after the birth of the Prince of Wales. She is credited with having made one of the first known jigsaw puzzles, in the form of chopped-up maps, which she used to teach the royal children geography.

———

A Tribute to Folly ❧ After his death, the Corporation of Bath voted to erect a statue of Beau Nash, who had been master of ceremonies at the spa since the turn of the century. The statue was placed in the Pump Room between the busts of Newton and Pope, Lord Chesterfield waspishly commenting:

> The statue placed these busts between
> Gives satire all its strength;
> Wisdom and Wit are little seen,
> But Folly at full length.

1763

———

Broiled Like a Chicken in a Mine Shaft ❧ (8 November) A young man came to an unpleasant end near Glasgow when, in the dark, he fell into a deep pit of water. As this pit was above a coal shaft that had been on fire for some years, the water was boiling 'like a cauldron'. He was not found until morning, when the flesh fell off his bones, like a broiled chicken.

1764

A Musical Prodigy ❧ Wolfgang Amadeus Mozart composed his first symphony, at the age of eight.

1765

Thirty Miles of Rope in Man o' War ❧ Completion of HMS *Victory*. In all, the ship used 30 miles (48 km) of rope.

An Absence of Enlightenment ❧ (1 July) The Chevalier de la Barre was beheaded then burnt at Abbeville, France, for blasphemy, having mutilated a statue of Christ on a bridge in the town. On the scaffold his only remark was: 'I did not believe they could have taken the life of a young man for so small a matter.'

1766

Fishing While Disguised as a Tree ❧ Death of Thomas Birch, keeper of books at the British Museum. Birch, a keen angler, was wont to go fishing disguised as a tree.

A Vigorous Old Scot ❧ (3 May) The *Edinburgh Courant* reported that the wife of Sir William Nicolson of Glenbervy, then aged 92, had just been delivered of a daughter.

1767

The Human Ox ❧ (1 October) The *Annual Register* reported:

We have the following extraordinary account from Wimbourne, in

Dorsetshire. A few days ago died here Roger Gill, shoemaker, and one of our singing-men, aged about sixty-seven, remarkable for chewing his meat or cud twice over, as an ox, sheep, or cow. He seldom made any breakfast in his latter days; he generally dined about twelve or one o'clock, ate pretty heartily and quickly, without much chewing or mastication. He never drank with his dinner, but afterwards about a pint of such malt liquor as he could get; but no sort of spirituous liquor in any shape, except a little punch, but never cared for that. He usually began his second chewing about a quarter or half an hour, sometimes later, after dinner; when every morsel came up successively, sweeter and sweeter to the taste. Some-times a morsel would prove offensive and crude, in which case he spat it out. The chewing continued usually about an hour or more, and some-times would leave him a little while, in which case he would be sick at stomach, troubled with the heartburn, and foul breath. Smoking tobacco would sometimes stop his chewing, but was never attended with any ill consequences. But on the 10th of June last, the faculty entirely left him, and the poor man remained in great tortures till the time of his death.

1769

An Academic Sinecure ❦ Bishop Richard Watson was elected professor of chemistry at Cambridge. It says something for the state of England's universities at the time that Watson should later confess: 'At the time this honour was conferred upon me, I knew nothing at all of chemistry, had never read a syllable on the subject, nor seen a single experiment in it.'

———

A Recipe for Albatross ❦ Joseph Banks, chief scientist on Captain Cook's first voyage, noted down his recipe for cooking albatross: 'The way of dressing them is thus: skin them overnight and soak their carcases in salt water till morn, then parboil them and throw away the water, then stew them well with very little water and when sufficiently tender serve them up with a savoury sauce.' Although he shot a number of albatrosses, Banks, unlike Coleridge's Ancient Mariner, suffered no ill fortune as a consequence: he

The outrageous dandies known as macaroni were one of the
wonders of London in the early 1770s.

returned from the voyage a celebrity, pursued a successful scientific career, and was for many years President of the Royal Society.

———

Gallantry No Guarantee Against the Gallows 🍃 (18 December) The *London Gazette* carried a story from the British attack on St Fernando de Omoo, on the Mosquito Coast of Central America. One of the attacking party, a sailor, had equipped himself with two cutlasses, one in each hand, and in the dark and confusion became separated from his fellows. An unarmed Spanish officer appeared, and, rather than cutting him down, the sailor, scorning to take an unfair advantage, presented the Spaniard with one of his cutlasses, so they should fight on an equal footing. So impressed was the Spaniard by this gallantry, that he promptly surrendered himself. The sailor was promoted to boatswain, but a few weeks later became intoxicated, struck a lieutenant, and was hanged for his pains.

1770

———

The Advent of the Macaroni 🍃 A new species of dandy arrived on the London scene – the macaroni (so-called because they met at the Macaroni Club, where the dish in question was always served). They wore tight-cut clothes and tiny cocked hats, carried staffs adorned with long tassels, and bore on the backs of their heads great knots of artificial hair. A contemporary versifier wrote:

> Each tries the other to outvie,
> With foretops mounting to the sky,
> And some you oft with tails may spy,
> As thick as any pony:
> Insipid gait, affected sneer,
> With side-curls high above the ear,
> That each may more the ass appear
> Or shew the macaroni.

Another contemporary writer opined of the species: 'His hat, like his understanding, is very little ... He has generally an abundant quantity of hair, and well he may, for his head produces nothing else ... '

———

The Devil's Trill 🪶 (26 February) Death of the Italian composer and violinist Giuseppe Tartini. He claimed that his most famous work, the violin sonata in G minor, better known as 'The Devil's Trill', was inspired by a dream in which the Devil played him a remarkable piece of breathtaking virtuosity. On awaking, Tartini wrote down what he could remember of the music, including the extraordinarily difficult double-stopped trills of the last movement, but claimed that what he could recall did not match the brilliance of the original. Some said that Tartini possessed a sixth finger on his left hand.

———

A Lack of Carnal Knowledge 🪶 (16 May) Marriage of the French Dauphin, the future Louis XVI, then aged 15, to Marie-Antoinette, who was a year younger. At the marriage feast, his father had to tell Louis to slow down his eating. 'Why?' his son responded. 'I always sleep better on a full stomach.' It seems that sleep is what the Dauphin did on his wedding night, and for many a night thereafter. The couple remained childless for seven years, neither apparently having any idea concerning the activities appropriate to the marital bed. It was not until Marie-Antoinette's brother, the Emperor Joseph II, visited Paris in April 1777 and quizzed the couple about the absence of an heir that it became clear what the problem was. Joseph presumably provided the necessary guidance, as the following year the queen announced that she was pregnant.

1771

Lightning Cures Deafness 🪶 (30 August) A man in Irvine, Ayrshire, was struck by lightning, and the deafness he had suffered from for 20 years was instantly cured.

The First Automobile Accident ❧ The first automobile accident occurred when a steam-powered tractor built by Nicholas-Joseph Cugnot for the French army crashed into a wall. Its top speed was around 4 kph (2.5 mph).

Princess Proves an Imposter ❧ High society in Virginia was thrilled to find in its midst Princess Susanna Carolina Matilda, sister of Queen Charlotte, with whom she had reportedly quarrelled. The grandees of Virginia were only too delighted to entertain the princess and to subsidize her needs, having been led to believe in her extensive powers of patronage. The princess was eventually apprehended at gunpoint at a soirée, it having been established that she was in fact Sarah Wilson, one-time servant of a lady-in-waiting to Queen Charlotte. Miss Wilson had been found guilty of stealing some of the queen's jewellery and one of her dresses, and had been transported as an indentured servant to Maryland, from where she had escaped to Virginia. Following her exposure, Miss Wilson was obliged to return to a life of servitude, but again escaped, and eventually married a British army officer.

1772

A Serial Polygamist ❧ There occurred in Bordeaux the death of a man who had been married 16 times. The same year, a woman aged 85 married her sixth husband at the church of St Clement Danes in London.

Heads Fall into Street ❧ The heads of two English Jacobites, Francis Townley and George Fletcher, which had been fixed on top of poles on Temple Bar, London, since their execution in 1746, fell down into the street.

———

An Ancient Transvestite ❧ (14 April) A very old person known as Elizabeth Russell was buried in Streatham. While preparing the corpse, it became clear that it was anatomically male, and it was assumed to belong to one or other of Elizabeth's brothers, William and John, who were baptized respectively in 1668 and 1672. 'Elizabeth' Russell had travelled widely with a band of gypsies, and was renowned as a healer, seamstress and astrologer. In his later years he was visited by Dr Johnson.

———

Well-Travelled Goat Laid to Rest ❧ (28 April) Almost certainly the first goat to have twice circumnavigated the globe died in Mile End, London. Her first voyage had been with Captain Wallis, and her second with Captain Cook. The Lords of the Admiralty subsequently made her a pensioner of Greenwich Hospital.

(For another notable naval goat, *see* 1812.)

1773

A Recipe for Cucumbers ❧ Dr Johnson offered his recipe for cucumbers: 'They should be well sliced, and dressed with pepper and vinegar, and then thrown out, as good for nothing.'

———

Shocking Spectacle in the South Seas ❧ (18 December) Ordinary Seaman Jem Burney, brother of the diarist and novelist Fanny Burney, recorded the sight that met him and his companions when he landed on Tahiti. He was investigating the fate of his shipmates from HMS *Adventure*, who had come ashore the previous day to take on provisions. He found 'such a shocking scene of carnage and barbarity as can never be mentioned or thought of but with horror; for the heads, hearts and lungs of several of our people were seen lying on the beach, and, at a little distance, the dogs gnawing their entrails'.

1774

The Last Appearance of the Wandering Jew? ❧ (22 April) A

man called Isaac Laquedem appeared in Brussels and claimed to be the Wandering Jew of Christian legend. The story tells how during Christ's journey to Calvary, he stopped for a rest, but a shoemaker pushed him in the back and shouted, 'Go quicker, Jesus, why do you loiter?' Christ turned to the man and calmly replied, 'I am going, and you will wait till I return.' The man was thus destined to wander the Earth until the Second Coming. Reports of the Wandering Jew crop up across Europe throughout the Middle Ages (the chronicler Matthew Paris describes his meeting at St Albans in 1228 with the Archbishop of Armenia, who claimed he had entertained the Wandering Jew at his table). The appearance in Brussels in 1774 seems to be the last on record.

The End of Day ❧ (22 June) A country millwright called John Day

perished in an ill-advised experiment in Plymouth Sound. Day had become convinced that he could survive under the surface of the sea in a watertight box, and, with the aid of a colleague, a gambling man called Blake, took bets that he could stay for 12 hours at a depth of 30 m (100 ft), and then return to the surface. With the aid of Plymouth shipwrights, Day eventually completed his box, the base of which was screwed to an old boat. The plan was that after 12 hours, Day would loosen the screws from inside the box, which would then rise up safely to the surface. On the day in question, Day entered his box, which was equipped with a bed, some biscuits and water, a watch and . . . a taper. The boat was sunk, and, naturally, as the taper and Day himself consumed all the oxygen within the sealed box, the unfortunate millwright, having asphyxiated himself, was never seen again.

Copycat Killings ❧ Publication of Goethe's novel, *The Sorrows of Young*

Werther, a tale of sensitive artist who kills himself over a girl. It was an immense success, and throughout Europe young men adopted Werther's style of dress, as described in the book. The novel also inspired a fashion for suicide: it was said that some 2000 young men were moved by the book to take their own lives.

___

The Calumnies of Colonel Luttrell &. In the Middlesex by-election, John Wilkes, the well-known radical and rake, defeated Colonel James Luttrell, a man of equally lax morals. On one occasion Luttrell turned up at a fancy-dress ball given by a Mrs Cornely costumed as a corpse, and bearing a label describing how he had died from the pox he'd contracted from the same Mrs Cornely. On another occasion he turned down a challenge issued by his father, Lord Irnham, on the grounds that his father was not a gentleman.

1776

___

The Part Played by Cheese in the Founding of the United States &. The Americans chose as their national motto 'E pluribus unum' (Latin, 'out of many, one'). The phrase came from a poem attributed to Virgil, and referred to a recipe involving cheese, garlic and herbs.

1777

___

Mozartian Scatology &. Wolfgang Amadeus Mozart wrote to Maria Anna Thekla Mozart thus:

> Mamma said to me: 'I bet that you have let one off.' 'I don't think so, Mamma,' I replied. 'Well, I am certain that you have,' she insisted. Well, I thought, 'Let's see,' and put my fingers to my arse and then to my nose and – *Ecce, provatum est*! Mamma was right after all.

Meanwhile, in England, William Crotch, at the age of two years and three weeks, played 'God Save the King' on his father's handmade organ.

—

A Swinging Vicar ❧ (27 June) The Revd Dr William Dodd, a fashionable preacher of extravagant habits, was hanged at Tyburn for forging a bond to the value of £4200 in the name of his former pupil, Lord Chesterfield. Many among the middle classes were shocked that a respectable clergyman should meet such a fate. Among Dr Dodd's supporters was Samuel Johnson, who campaigned fruitlessly on his behalf, and wrote his address from the gallows.

—

Woman Marries Three Other Women ❧ (5 July) A woman called Ann Morrow was sentenced in London to the pillory and six months imprisonment for dressing as a man, marrying three different women, and defrauding them of their money and their clothes. It was only this same year that an act had been passed forbidding any woman from 'disguising herself in men's clothing and courting other women'. The unfortunate Ann Morrow was blinded by the fierce pelting directed at her in the pillory.

—

Pirates Show Their Respect for Scholarship ❧ (12 December) Death of the Swiss scholar and scientist, Albrecht von Haller. Such was his great reputation during his lifetime that a case of books addressed to him, seized by pirates from a ship, was forwarded by them to the great professor as soon as they made port.

—

The Hazards of Fashion ❧ The mode for extravagant female headdresses in England reached its apogee, with ladies manipulating their hair into constructions in excess of a foot and a half tall, and sometimes up to a yard wide. These headdresses might include 'wool, hair, powder, lawn, muslin, net, lace, gauze, ribbon, flowers, feathers, and wire'. Such constructions could be a hazard: that worn by Lady Laycock brushed too close to a candle and caught fire, with unfortunate results, as recorded by *The New Bath Guide*:

Yet Miss at the Rooms
Must beware of her plumes,
For if Vulcan her feather embraces,
Like poor Lady Laycock,
She'd burn like a haycock,
And roast all the Loves and the Graces.

Many years later, in 1835, Frances, the 85-year-old Marchioness of Salisbury, died in a fire at her home in Hatfield. The fire had started when the vast and elaborate hairstyle she had maintained since her youth accidentally ignited when it came into contact with a chandelier.

1778

A Remarkable Prediction ❧ The 15-year-old Joséphine Rose Tascher de la Pagerie, the daughter of a plantation owner on Martinique, had her fortune told by an old mulatto woman, who made the following predictions:

> You will marry a fair man. Your star promises you two alliances. Your first husband will be born in Martinique, but will pass his life in Europe, with girded sword. An unhappy lawsuit will separate you. He will perish in a tragic manner. Your second husband will be a dark man, of European origin and small fortune; but he will fill the world with his glory and fame. You will then become an eminent lady, more than a queen. Then, after having astonished the world, you will die unhappy.

In 1779 Joséphine's family arranged for her to marry Alexandre, Vicomte de Beauharnais, a native of Martinique, and the couple settled in Paris. It was not a happy union. The jealous Beauharnais issued a lawsuit against his wife on the basis of her conduct prior to their marriage, and the two lived apart for three years. In 1794, during the Terror, Beauharnais was charged with having defended Metz inadequately the previous year, and guillotined. In 1796 his widow married a dark Corsican of humble origins called Napoléon Bonaparte, and in 1804 Joséphine became his empress. But in 1810 Napoléon, impatient for an heir, had the marriage annulled, and the following year married Marie Louise of Austria. Joséphine died in 1814.

1779

Mud Baths and Celestial Beds
Dr James Graham opened his Temple of Health in the Adelphi, London. Here he advertised the benefits of bathing in mud by publicly immersing himself in the substance, accompanied by a young lady purporting to be Vestina, Goddess of Health, but in fact Amy Lyon, the daughter of a blacksmith and later more familiar as Emma Hamilton, mistress of Lord Nelson. Dr Graham subsequently moved his operation to Pall Mall, where the Temple of Health also became a Temple of Hymen. Here Graham offered to cure the impotent and infertile by means of various electrical and magnetic devices, most notably his 'grand celestial state bed'. This induced 'a superior ecstasy never before experienced: the barren must certainly become fruitful when agitated in the delights of love'. Sadly, business could not keep up with Graham's lavish expenditure, and the 'last of the unblushing quack-doctors' died in poverty in Glasgow in 1794.

Attempt to Beat Out One's Own Brains
(7 April) Miss Reay, mistress to the Earl of Sandwich, was shot dead outside the Theatre Royal, Covent Garden. Her assassin, a lovestruck officer called Hackman, then turned the pistol upon himself, but failed to inflict a mortal wound. The frenzied young man then beat himself about the head with the pistol butt, but without fatal effect. It was left to the gallows at Tyburn to finish the job, less than a fortnight later.

The Melancholy Fate of Sodomites and Suicides
(July) Two men were found guilty at Bury St Edmunds of 'sodomitical practices'. A contemporary newspaper describes their fate:

> On Wednesday William Snell and John Carter stood on the pillory at Bury previous to which Snell took several doses of arsenic which he said he had

kept for several years, it had no effect on him till he was being carried back to the gaol when it began to operate and he expired about 7 in the evening. The coroner's verdict was self murder in consequence of which he was to be buried in the King's highway and a stake driven through his body. Snell was severely pelted by the populace but Carter came through unhurt nothing being thrown at him the fury of the people having subsided.

Suicide was deemed to be a breach of the laws of both God and Man, and no suicide could be buried in hallowed ground. Instead, the corpse was usually buried at a crossroads, it being thought that that this would enable the Devil to escape more readily. A stake through the heart, meanwhile, was proof against the soul of the suicide from haunting the living.

1780

Riding Backwards through the Himalaya ❧ George Bogle, Britain's first emissary to Tibet, drowned while taking his morning bath. On his travels through the Himalaya he had learnt that the best way to counter altitude sickness was 'to chew garlic and face backwards on one's mount', this being the best way to avoid the 'poisonous mountain vapours'.

The Origin of Quiz ❧ Around this date, Mr Daly, manager of a Dublin theatre, proposed a wager by which he would introduce a new word into the language and have everybody using it within 24 hours. Accordingly, he and his associates scrawled the word 'QUIZ' on walls all over the city, and in no time at all the citizens of Dublin were asking what these letters meant. The wager was won. Sadly, some of our duller lexicographers doubt the veracity of this tale.

1781

A Planet Called George ❧ (13 March) The astronomer William Herschel, a recipient of the patronage of King George III, discovered the planet Uranus. He suggested that the new celestial body be named *Georgium Sidus* ('the Georgian Star'), but in the end the tradition of naming planets after classical gods and goddesses was maintained.

—

Mass Murder on the *Zong* 🐚 (29 November) On the orders of Captain Luke Collingwood, the crew of the slaveship *Zong* threw 183 sick African slaves into the sea, en route from Africa to Jamaica. His reason was that his insurance did not cover the loss of slaves from disease, but it did cover the loss of slaves by drowning. The relevant clause read:

> The insurer takes upon him the risk of the loss, capture, and death of slaves, or any other unavoidable accident to them: but natural death is always understood to be excepted: by natural death is meant, not only when it happens by disease or sickness, but also when the captive destroys himself through despair, which often happens: but when slaves are killed, or thrown into the sea in order to quell an insurrection on their part, then the insurers must answer.

The insurance claim was rejected by the British courts, but no one was ever prosecuted. However, the case did give a major impetus to the anti-slavery movement.

1782

—

Girl Hanged for Consorting with Gypsies 🐚 In England, a 14-year-old girl was hanged for being found in the company of gypsies.

—

A Gentle Soul 🐚 (March) The young Maximilien Robespierre, later known as the instigator of the Terror in which thousands lost their heads, was appointed as a judge in Arras. He resigned shortly afterwards, explaining that he could not bring himself to pronounce the death penalty.

The Last Alchemist ❧ (6 May) James Price, a member of the Royal Society, began a series of experiments in which he claimed to have transmuted mercury into silver and gold. The experiments, which continued until 25 May, were conducted in the presence of a number of distinguished persons, including fellow chemists, lawyers, and peers of the realm. Price presented some of the resulting gold to King George III, and the University of Oxford awarded him a degree of M.D. However, the Royal Society was more sceptical, and invited Price to repeat his experiments in their presence. Price prevaricated, on the grounds that the work was 'difficult, tedious and injurious to health', and that, in addition, the value of the resulting gold was much less than the cost of producing it. The Society persisted, and at last Price invited three members to his laboratory in Guildford. On their arrival on 3 August 1783, Price promptly took a draft of laurel water, then one of the most effective poisons known to man, thus swiftly bringing his life to its end.

1783

Umbrellas on Mont Blanc ❧ After three guides failed to reach the summit of the as-yet unclimbed Mont Blanc, one of them concluded that the only equipment required was an umbrella and a bottle of smelling salts.

The Montyon Prize for Virtue ❧ Baron de Montyon established a prize for examples of great virtue among the labouring classes, to be awarded by the Académie Française. Typical winners of the prize were servants who recognized the 'higher birth and superiority of natural condition' of their masters or mistresses, and thus continued to serve and support them after the latter had declined into abject poverty. The 1823 winner, a poor old man, had for 11 years given up his only bed to a distressed gentlewoman of his acquaintance who had become ill and impoverished. Despite her constant ill-temper and peevishness, he had spent his slender income on dainties for her to eat, while he himself survived on the discarded scraps of others.

———

An *Annus Horribilis* ❧ Gilbert White, the English naturalist, recorded that 'the summer of the year 1783 was an amazing and portentous one, and full of horrible phenomena'. Beginning in February, a 'dry fog', which some said had an unpleasant smell, and others said was luminous by night, spread from Sicily up through Italy and across Europe. It was also recorded in the Americas and parts of Asia. The fog was accompanied by frequent thunderstorms and a number of natural disasters: Calabria was devastated by an earthquake that killed 30,000; in Iceland, vast lava flows caused the deaths of 9500 people, a fifth of the population, from asphyxiation and famine; in Japan over 1000 died in floods following a volcanic eruption that blocked the course of a river, which then burst through the dam. In August in Britain, a bright meteor was seen to light up the sky, followed by the sound of a great explosion. To cap it all, that summer England suffered from a plague of wasps.

———

Boy Wonder Becomes PM ❧ (December) William Pitt the Younger became prime minister, aged only 24. A popular ditty of the time commented that it was:

> A sight to make all nations stand and stare:
> A kingdom trusted to a schoolboy's care.

1784

———

A Remarkable Mirage ❧ (20 March) A mirage of Mount Etna in Sicily appeared off the coast of Malta, some 200 km (125 m) distant.

———

Edinburgh Man Takes to the Air ❧ (27 August) James Tytler, an impoverished eccentric and the editor of the second edition of the *Encyclopaedia Britannica*, made what is thought to have been the first balloon flight in Britain. As he could not find a means of taking the burner with him, his hot-air flight over Edinburgh was of necessity short: he rose to no more than 90 m (300 ft), and travelled only about 0.8 km (½ mile). In 1792 he published what was deemed to be a seditious handbill and was obliged to leave for the USA, where he set up as a newspaperman in Salem, Massachusetts.

But Flashy Italian Makes More of a Splash ❧ (15 September)
Vincent Lunardi, a young attaché at the embassy of Naples in London, made the first balloon flight in England, taking off from the artillery ground at Moorfields, London. Such was the public interest (at least according to Lunardi's own account) that a jury trying a highwayman rapidly returned a verdict of not guilty so that they could go outside to witness his flight.

Riding One's Cow to Market ❧ (27 November) In defiance of the
government's tax on horses, Jonathan Thatcher rode his cow to market at Stockport.

1785

An Embittered Will ❧ The following will was published:

> I, Charles Parker, of New Bond Street, Middlesex, bookseller, give to Elizabeth Parker, the sum of £50, whom, through my foolish fondness, I made my wife, without regard to family, fame, or fortune; and who, in return, has not spared, most unjustly, to accuse me of every crime regarding human nature, save highway robbery.

Duke of Norfolk Revealed as Filthy Old Drunk ❧
Anonymous publication of *The Heraldry of Nature*, in which, in his preface, the author says he has 'rejected the common and patented bearings already

painted on the carriages of our nobility, and instituted what he judges a wiser delineation of the honours they deserve'. Among the book's targets was Charles Howard, 10th Duke of Norfolk, a noted 'six-bottle man' who at any public banquet would drink himself insensible. The book suggested that his arms should include three quart bottles, a broken flagon and a naked arm holding a corkscrew. The Duke's blinders were not all bad news for his servants, however, as once he was unconscious at the dinner table they could carry him off to bed, and, before tucking him up, give him a thorough wash – something that the Duke singularly failed ever to do himself, 'for his repugnance to soap and water was equal to his love of wine'.

———

Acquainted with Seven Generations &ambient; Horace Walpole wrote to his friend Horace Mann, observing that he was acquainted with seven generations of the one family:

> There is a circumstance which makes me think myself an antediluvian. I have literally seen seven descents in one family . . . I was school-fellow of the two last Earls of Waldegrave, and used to go to play with them in the holidays, when I was about twelve years old. They lived with their grandmother, natural daughter of James II. One evening when I was there, came in her mother Mrs Godfrey, that king's mistress, ancient in truth, and so superannuated, that she scarce seemed to know where she was. I saw her another time in her chair in St James's Park, and have a perfect idea of her face, which was pale, round, and sleek. Begin with her; then count her daughter, Lady Waldegrave; then the latter's son the ambassador; his daughter Lady Harriet Beard; her daughter, the present Countess Dowager of Powis, and her daughter Lady Clive; there are six, and the seventh now lies in of a son, and might have done so six or seven years ago, had she married at fourteen. When one has beheld such a pedigree; one may say, 'And yet I am not sixty-seven!'

———

A Startling Apparition &ambient; (15 October) The day that a young lieutenant, John Otway Wynard of the 3rd Regiment of Foot Guards, died in England, his likeness appeared to his brother George and a fellow officer,

John (later Sir John) Cope Sherbrooke, in their barrack room on Cape Breton Island, Canada. Some years later, Sherbrooke was walking along Piccadilly, London, when he was shocked to see a man closely resembling the apparition he had seen on Cape Breton Island. Taking his courage in his hands, he accosted the man, and found that it was John Wynward's twin brother.

1786

The Cretins of the Alps &. Horace Bénédict de Saussure published *Voyages dans les Alpes*, in which he describes arriving at a village afflicted by cretinism and goitres. At that time it was not known that these conditions – common in various parts of the Alps, in Derbyshire and the Isle of Wight – were caused by an absence of natural iodine in the water supply. Saussure recounts his experience thus:

> I asked the first person I met what the name of the village was, and when he did not reply I asked a second, and then a third; but a dismal silence, or a few inarticulate noises were the only response I received. The stupid amazement with which they looked at me, their enormous goitres, their fat, parted lips, their heavy, drooping eyelids, their hanging jaws, their doltish expressions, were quite terrifying. It was as if an evil spirit had transformed every inhabitant into a dumb animal, leaving only the human form to show that they had once been men. I left with an impression of fear and sadness which will never be erased from my memory.

By the following century, when the remedy was discovered, sufferers of goitre often refused the proffered iodine tablets, in the knowledge that their affliction excused them from military service. Edward Whymper, the first man up the Matterhorn and no indulger of weakness in his fellow men, had little patience with such excuses: 'Let them be formed into regiments by themselves, brigaded together, and commanded by cretins. Think what *esprit de corps* they would have! Who could stand against them? Who would understand their tactics?' (*Scrambles Amongst the Alps*, 1871)

———

An Irish Hellraiser ❧ The noted Irish duellist George Robert Fitzgerald was hanged on the second attempt for murder. On the first attempt the rope had broken, and Fitzgerald found himself earthbound. 'You see I am once more among you unexpectedly,' he said to an appreciative crowd. So addicted had Fitzgerald been to duelling that he would annoy people in the street with the hope of starting a quarrel (on one occasion shooting a man's wig off). Fitzgerald's relations with his father were poor, and when the latter refused to change his will, Fitzgerald chained him to a bear for a day, then confined him in a cave. He was arrested and sentenced to two years in prison for this lack of filial piety, but was released by his own private militia, which he had raised to resist the French. It was this militia that undertook the murder for which Fitzgerald was eventually hanged.

1787

Financial Prudence ❧ William Stevenson, a Scotsman, separated from his wife, both agreeing that whoever of them should first propose a reconciliation should forfeit the sum of £100 to the other. They never met again.

———

Dining with Rats ❧ Death of Susanna Kennedy, Countess of Eglintoune, one of many among the upper classes to have preferred animals to her fellow human beings. Her particular weakness was for rats, dozens of whom she would daily invite to share her table.

———

Duke Dies in Theatre in Unseemly Circumstances ❧ The Duke of Leinster impaled himself while storming the stage of a theatre in Cork. Such was the riotous disposition of audiences in those days that spikes had been arranged along the front of the stage.

Maggoty Soup ❧ (27 November) The poet William Cowper wrote to Lady Hesketh describing how a beggar had rejected a bowl of vermicelli soup on the grounds that he was not so hungry that he would 'eat broth with maggots in it'.

1788

Some Pointed Bequests ❧ A certain David Davis left the following will: 'I, David Davis, of Clapham, Surrey, do give and bequeath to Mary Davis, daughter of Peter Delaport, the sum of 5 shillings, which is sufficient to enable her to get drunk for the last time at my expense.' Another will from six years earlier reads: 'I, William Blackett, governor of Plymouth, desire that my body may be kept as long as it may not be offensive; and that one or more of my toes or fingers may be cut off, to secure a certainty of my being dead. I also make this request to my dear wife, that as she has been troubled with one old fool, she will not think of marrying a second.'

Two Edinburgh Characters ❧ There occurred the deaths of two Edinburgh characters. Firstly, that of Deacon William Brodie, the respectable burgess who had pursued a second, nocturnal career as a burglar. He was obliged to employ his skills as a cabinet maker to build the gallows from which he was subsequently hanged. Secondly, James Duff, a noted eccentric who attended every society funeral, and who in his youth had entered himself in a horse race on Leith Links. He came last.

The Vicar and the Anatomist's Wife ❧ The Revd Henry Bate was accused of seducing and conducting a criminal conversation (i.e. adultery) with a Mrs Dodwell. In his defence, Bate claimed that it was quite excusable for Mrs Dodwell to seek solace in the arms of another, as Mr Dodwell, a keen amateur anatomist, was in the habit of dissecting cadavers in the matrimonial chamber. Bate was acquitted.

The Demanding Miss Corbett

The Demanding Miss Corbett ❧ The 1788 edition of *Harris's List of Covent Garden Ladies* – a directory of prostitutes in London's West End – listed a Miss Corbett of Goodge Street, who 'always measures a gentleman's *maypole* by a standard of *nine inches*, and expects a guinea for every inch it is short of full measure'.

Barrels of Lard Provide Relief

Barrels of Lard Provide Relief ❧ (8 December) Death of the great French admiral Pierre André de Suffren de Saint Tropez, who saw to the amatory needs of his sailors by providing them with three lard-filled barrels, each with a hole of a different diameter, labelled, respectively, 'Grandmère', 'Fille' and 'Nymphette'.

When Dwarfs Fall Out

When Dwarfs Fall Out ❧ The Polish dwarf, Joseph Boruwlaski, who had been fêted in the courts of Europe, published his memoirs. Among his adventures was a close escape from death when the French dwarf Bébé, taller than Boruwlaski by four inches, had flown into a jealous rage and attempted to push his rival into a fire. Boruwlaski suffered a number of rejections from young ladies who thought him too small, but eventually married and settled down in Durham, England, fathering a number of children and living to nearly 100. When his wife was annoyed with him she would pick him up and place him on the mantelpiece.

1789

On the Importance of Good Diction

On the Importance of Good Diction ❧ During an argument between different sectors of the audience at Sadler's Wells Theatre, London, a woman called Elizabeth Luker shouted 'Fight, fight!' in the hope of warming up the proceedings. Unfortunately many took this as a shout of 'Fire, fire!' and 18 people were killed in the stampede for the exits. Luker served 14 days in prison.

Playing Ball Against the Wailing Wall ❧ For a bet of £10,000 the Anglo-Irish hell-raiser, Buck Whaley, travelled to Jerusalem and played handball against the Wailing Wall.

Fall of Bastille of No Account ❧ (14 July) Louis XVI, after a day's hunting at Versailles, noted in his diary, 'Nothing'. That day the Bastille had been stormed, and the French Revolution had begun.

1790

Barry Bested by Bullock the Butcher ❧ Richard Barry, Earl of Barrymore, was one the rakes in the Prince of Wales's circle at Brighton. A great gambling man, he unwisely accepted a bet from a fat butcher called Bullock that he could not beat him in a 100-yard race, if Bullock were given a 35-yard start and the choice of course. Although Barry was a fit young man, Bullock had chosen to race down Black Lion Lane in Brighton, one of the narrowest streets in Britain – in places no more than 100 cm (40 in) wide. When the gun went off, Barry quickly caught up with the rotund butcher – but it proved quite impossible to pass him, and Bullock won the bet.

1791

Unseen Hand Fails to Pull Sect Heavenward ❧ Death of Elspeth Buchan, founder of a Scottish millenarian sect known as the Buchanites. Encouraged by the Revd Hugh Whyte of Irvine, she believed that she was the woman described in Revelation 12: 'clothed with the sun, and the moon under her feet, and upon her head a crown of twelve stars'. In 1784 the Buchanites settled near Dumfries, and, convinced that they would shortly be translated to heaven without the inconvenience of dying, they built a platform on Templand Hill. Here they sang and waited throughout the night, expecting to be pulled upward at daybreak by the topknots of their hair (the rest of their heads were shaved). Unfortunately, a wind blew up and caused the platform to collapse, and Buchan and her followers found themselves flung in a earthbound rather than a celestial direction. At her death seven years later, the Revd Whyte tried to convince her adherents that she was merely in a trance; she herself had told them she would be back in six months to lead them to heaven. The last surviving Buchanite, Andrew Innes, died in 1848.

1792

A Peruvian Giant (May) Huaylas, a native of Peru, was exhibited in Lima on account of his height (2.18 m / 7 ft 2 in), the monstrous size of his head, and the fact that his arms extended down to his knees.

Welsh-Speaking Indians Beyond the Missouri
Wales was gripped by a nationalistic fervour when it was reported that Welsh-speaking Indians had been discovered beyond the Missouri. It was presumed that these were descendants of the Welsh prince, Madoc, who had reputedly discovered America in 1170. A young Methodist preacher, John Evans, determined to find these lost Welshmen, and boldly explored all the way to the headwaters of the Missouri, but found no trace of Welsh Indians. In his disappointment he took to drink, and died in 1798. However, both President Thomas Jefferson and Meriwether Lewis (leader of the famous transcontinental expedition of 1803–6) continued to believe in the idea of a lost tribe of Welshmen in the wilds of the West.

1793

Milton's Teeth Knocked Out
The grave of the poet John Milton at St Giles without Cripplegate in the City of London was opened. One of the parish overseers, Mr Fountain, failed in his efforts to extract the poet's teeth

from his skull, but a bystander knocked out a handful with a stone, and shared them out among those present. Someone else took a rib, while others grabbed handfuls of hair. The caretaker, Elizabeth Grant, then assumed possession of the coffin, and charged visitors sixpence to view it. The charge was later reduced to threepence, and then tuppence.

1794

Warm Trout and Cow Dung &ampe; Death of Daniel Dancer, the notorious miser, who was wont to roam the countryside collecting cow dung, which he turned into a hiding place for his money. On one occasion his neighbour, Lady Tempest, presented him with some trout. Dancer was too mean to light a fire to cook them, so warmed up the fish by sitting on them.

Experiments as to Whether a Severed Head Maintains Consciousness &ampe; (8 May) The great French chemist, Antoine Lavoisier, was guillotined during the Terror. A dedicated scientist to the last, he wished the world to know for how long one is conscious following decapitation, so determined to see how often he could blink following the fall of the blade. Acting according to his master's instructions, Lavoisier's manservant promptly picked up the severed head, and counted between 15 and 20 blinks. This, at least, is the story, but it seems that it originates with Jean-Josephe Sue, a French physician who believed the guillotine was a far from painless and instantaneous instrument of execution, and regretted that he had not suggested this last experiment to the great scientist. It appears that the experiment *was* suggested to a condemned murderer called Lacenaire in 1836. But he did not even blink once after decapitation.

'Female' Preacher Seduces Young Ladies &ampe; In Alnwick, Northumberland, a Mr Thomas Heppel, posing as a Methodist preacher called Jane Davison, managed to inseminate both daughters of another Methodist minister, a Mr Hastings. He then absconded with their wardrobes,

but was later arrested in York for wearing a dress, and sentenced to transportation.

———

Failed by His False Heart 🐌 (1 June) At the battle of the Glorious First of June, Captain Molloy of HMS *Caesar* failed to bring his ship into action, and was subsequently found guilty of this charge (effectively one of cowardice) and dismissed from his command (his bravery on previous occasions had mitigated against the more usual death sentence). It was said that Captain Molloy had, prior to the battle, behaved less than honourably towards a young lady, and that she, rather than bringing a suit of breach of promise against him, had confronted him with the following words: 'Captain Molloy, you are a bad man. I wish you the greatest curse that can befall a British officer. When the day of battle comes, may your false heart fail you!'

———

A Nudist Beach in North Wales 🐌 (July) Samuel Taylor Coleridge was taken aback by what he saw on the shore at Abergele, as he reported in a letter to Henry Martin:

> Walking on the sea sands, I was surprised to sea a number of fine women bathing promiscuously with men and boys – *perfectly* naked! Doubtless, the citadels of their chastity are so impregnably strong, that they need not the ornamental outworks of modesty.

———

Captain Courageous 🐌 (20 August) At the Battle of Fallen Timbers, Captain Asa Hartshorn found himself isolated from his men, and surrounded by Indians. He defended himself fiercely, until felled by a fatal arrow. So impressed were they by his courage that the Indians cut an incision in his chest and inserted two leather hearts, to signify that he was as brave as two men.

1795

Dutch Fleet Surrenders to Cavalry ❧ (January) It was such a harsh winter in the Netherlands that the Dutch fleet found itself frozen fast in the Texel – enabling the French cavalry to surround the ships and demand their surrender.

A Match Made in Hell ❧ (5 April) Caroline of Brunswick, betrothed to her cousin, the Prince of Wales, arrived in London. The couple had never before met, and on first being introduced to her at St James's Palace, the Prince is said to have turned to a courtier and whispered a request for a glass of brandy. She for her part loudly declared how surprised she was at how fat and unattractive her fiancé was. The two married three days later – George's friends had to get him inebriated in order to get him through the ceremony – and within the year they were separated. They apparently only had sex on three occasions, George complaining that his wife stank. When he was crowned king as George IV in 1821, Caroline – who had in the meantime taken numerous lovers and spent much of the intervening period abroad – was physically prevented from entering Westminster Abbey, where the coronation was taking place. That night she fell ill, and died three weeks later.

A Nephew of the Almighty ❧ Lieutenant Richard Brothers RN (retired) declared himself the Nephew of the Almighty, the Prince of True Hebrews and Ruler of the World. The latter claim was thought to be disrespectful to His Majesty King George III, and as a consequence Brothers was charged with high treason. He was sentenced to 11 years' imprisonment.

1796

A Solemn Mockery ❧ (2 April) *Vortigern and Rowena*, supposedly a lost play by Shakespeare, was presented at Drury Lane by R.B. Sheridan.

During the rehearsals, some of the actors, including Mrs Siddons, had withdrawn their services, smelling a fish. At the first (and last) night, the audience became increasingly boisterous, and when one of the characters uttered the line 'When this solemn mockery is o'er', the house collapsed into uproar. Later that year a 19-year-old youth called William Henry Ireland confessed that he had forged this and other Shakespeariana, including a love poem to 'Anna Hatherrawaye' and a historical drama, *Henry II*.

Salacious Rumours Regarding the Death of Catherine the Great

&♣ (5 November) Death of Catherine the Great of Russia from a stroke, suffered while in the room containing her water closet. Her enemies at court circulated a number of unsalubrious stories about the circumstances of her death. One stated that the water closet collapsed under her weight, fatally injuring her; another alleged that she died while attempting sexual intercourse with a stallion.

1797

Monsieur Sawbones &♣ Dominique Jean Larrey became Napoleon's surgeon-in-chief, a post he held until the Battle of Waterloo. He was reputed to be able to amputate a man's leg in 13 seconds.

1798

Death on Stage &♣ (2 August) The actor John Palmer, his spirits diminished by the recent deaths of his wife and a favourite son, appeared at Liverpool in the title role of Kotzebue's drama *The Stranger*. At the very point of the Stranger's on-stage death, accompanied by the scripted lines 'Oh God, oh God! There is another and a better world!', Palmer collapsed on stage and, in fact, himself expired. His last words, as quoted above, are inscribed on his gravestone in Walton churchyard.

A Poor Anatomist 🐚 (12 November) Wolfe Tone, the Irish rebel, cheated the hangman by slitting his own throat with a penknife. Unfortunately, he cut his windpipe rather than his jugular, and died a slow death, eventually expiring on 19 November. 'I find I am a poor anatomist,' he said.

1799

An Errant Husband 🐚 The painter George Romney returned to his wife in Lancashire, having left her 37 years earlier to make his fortune in London. There was, apparently, no ruction: Romney kept her in funds throughout his absence, and spent his last few years happily living with his long-deserted spouse.

Dispatched by Leeches 🐚 As Napoleon's army marched across the Sinai Desert en route for Syria, they slaked their thirst on any water they could find. It transpired that one pool they drank from was full of leeches, and many of the soldiers suffered horrible ends when the leeches, engorged with their blood, swelled up inside their noses and throats and suffocated them.

Earth-Eating Tribes in South America 🐚 Alexander von Humboldt set out upon his travels in Venezuela and Brazil, during which he came upon a man who claimed to breastfeed his children, a tribe that ate earth, and another whose favourite dish was palm of human hand.

SERPENT
is Egede.)

Various detailed descriptions of sea serpents have come down to us from the 19th century (see, for example, 1817 and 1857). This illustration, c. 1860, is based on an account by Hans Egede, a Norwegian missionary known as the 'Apostle of Greenland'.

The 19th Century

Murder of a Ghost ❧ A Russian Amazon ❧ Peculiar Phenomena Blamed on Comet ❧ Second Messiah Fails to Appear ❧ Sea Serpent Recognized by Science ❧ Gregor MacGregor, the Cazique of Poyais ❧ On the Dangers of Hot-Buttered Toast ❧ Dancing on the Dead ❧ Book Bound in Human Skin ❧ The Enigma of Kaspar Hauser ❧ Lost Tribes of Israel Found in Mexico ❧ Snakes Return to Ireland ❧ Dining on Roast Infant ❧ Shooting Stars Herald Apocalypse ❧ Spontaneous Generation by Means of Electricity ❧ The Last Battle in England ❧ The Abode of Love ❧ Doktor Kuckenmeister's Gruesome Experiment ❧ The Mad Maids of Morzine ❧ The Empress's Little Problem ❧

1800

—

Castles of Ice ❧ The Austrians defended the Tonale Pass between Lombardy and Trentino against the French by building fortifications out of solid ice – which the French found too slithery to scale, and too solid to batter down.

1801

—

Rossmore No More ❧ (6 August) Death of Lord Rossmore, commander of British forces in Ireland. His exit was unexpected and sudden, his lordship never having suffered a day's indisposition in his life. However, his neighbour, Sir Jonah Barrington, who was staying at Rossmore's house at Mount Kennedy, Co. Wicklow, was awakened in the early hours of the morning of 6 August . . .

> . . . by a sound of a very extraordinary nature. I listened: it occurred first at short intervals; it resembled neither a voice nor an instrument; it was softer than any voice, and wilder than any music, and seemed to float in the air. I don't know wherefore, but my heart beat forcibly; the sound became still more plaintive, till it almost died away in the air; when a sudden change, as if excited by a pang, altered its tone: it seemed descending. I felt every nerve tremble: it was not a natural sound, nor could I make out the point whence it came . . . The sounds lasted for more than half an hour. At last a deep, heavy, throbbing sigh seemed to issue from the spot, and was as shortly succeeded by a sharp but low cry, and by the distinct exclamation, thrice repeated, of 'Rossmore! Rossmore! Rossmore!' I will not attempt to describe my own sensations; indeed I cannot. The maid fled in terror from the window, and it was with difficulty I prevailed on Lady Barrington to return to bed: in about a minute after, the sound died gradually away, until all was silent.

The next morning Barrington discovered that the triple repetition of his host's name coincided with the very moment of Rossmore's death.

An Illegitimate Descent 🙣 Birth of Elizabeth Fitzclarence, illegitimate daughter of William, Duke of Clarence – the future King William IV – and great-great-great-great-grandmother of David Cameron, who, 204 years after her birth, became leader of the Conservative Party. Genealogists have thus calculated that Cameron is fifth cousin twice removed to Queen Elizabeth II.

The Life, Adventures and Opinions of Col. George Hanger 🙣 Publication of *The Life, Adventures and Opinions of Col. George Hanger*. Hanger had as a young man married a gypsy, who had in turn run off with a tinker. He served with distinction in the American War of Independence, and later became an associate of the Prince Regent. On one occasion, it is said, the latter hurled a glass of wine in Hanger's face; Hanger promptly threw the contents of his own glass in the face of the man on his other side, and bid him pass it round the table. On another occasion, while accompanying the Prince on a tour in Plymouth, having pushed a fishwife out of the way, she took her revenge by giving him such a punch he was knocked into a kennel. An inveterate gambler, Hanger once organized a cross-country race between a flock of turkeys and a flock of geese, and lost £500 on his bet. Eventually imprisoned for debt, Hanger, once released, took up a career as a coal merchant, and refused to take up his seat as Lord Coleraine in the House of Lords, to the horror of his society friends.

Hanger's *Life, Adventures and Opinions* contains chapters with such headings as 'Advice to the lovely Cyprians, and Fair Sex in general, how to conduct themselves in future, and to practise with greater satisfaction the three cardinal virtues, namely, Drinking, Gambling and Intriguing'. Examples of his advice to the Fair Sex include a cod reading list, mocking the pious tracts of the time. Among the volumes he recommends are:

Crumbs of Comfort to a Repentant Sinner
Hooks and Eyes for Believers Breeches

High-heeled Shoes for Dwarfs in Holiness
A Shot Aimed at the Devil's Headquarters, through the Tube of a Cannon of
    the Covenant
Heaven Ravished by a Repentant Sinner
Little in Stature, but Exalted on the Stilts of Faith

As far as choosing a lover is concerned, the stupider (and better-endowed) he is the better: 'the more stupid ass you have to deal with, with greater ease and facility will you be able to play upon him, and use him as an instrument for your wants and pleasures. In the choice of a lover you should be attentive in particular to his features, as they are a great ornament to the *outward* man, and a type of grace in the inward. For it is held by naturalists, that if there be a protuberancy of parts in the superior region of the body, as in the ears or nose, there must be a parity also in the inferior. This evidently accounts for the predilection which some women have had for long noses.'

———

The Value of a Classical Education   Sir George Murray, while serving in the campaign against the French in Egypt, found himself and the men under his command in desperate need of water. He was near Alexandria, and realized he was in the same place where Julius Caesar had found himself in similar difficulties nearly two millennia before. He flicked through the copy of the Roman general's writings that he always had with him, and discovered that Caesar's men had found water at a particular depth underground. Murray set his men to digging, and sure enough they struck water.

1802

———

Poet Surprised by Flying Dog   While writing a letter in the White Hart Inn in Narberth, Pembrokeshire, the poet Coleridge was surprised when a large sheepdog crashed through a closed window and landed on his back.

Crossing the Line could be a humiliating experience,
as Lieutenant Shaw found out in 1802.

An Ordeal at Sea ❧ Lieutenant Shaw, a passenger on a ship bound for
Bombay, was unwilling to be the subject of the sailor's traditional rite of
passage for neophytes 'crossing the line' (i.e. the Equator) for the first time,
which in those days could be both a rough and a humiliating experience. Shaw
barricaded himself in his cabin, and offered money to the sailors should he be
spared the indignity. The sailors – and the first and third mates of the ship –
declined his offer, and the captain, whose cabin door was shut, seemed deaf to
Shaw's entreaties. The sailors eventually broke in and seized the lieutenant,
plunged him into a boat filled with 'noisome liquid', covered his face in tar,
scraped it off with 'Neptune's razor' (a rusty hoop), then plunged his head

under the filthy liquid, holding it there for several seconds. On reaching Bombay, Shaw instituted legal proceedings against the first and third mates, and was awarded 400 rupees damages.

———

A Poke in the Eye for Miss Truss 🙦 Publication of *A Pickle for the Knowing Ones* by the American eccentric Timothy Dexter. The book entirely eschewed the use of punctuation, although in the second edition Dexter supplied an appendix of full stops, commas and other marks, in order that the reader could season his work to their own taste.

———

The Patagonian Sampson 🙦 A strongman known as The Patagonian Sampson appeared on the stage at Sadler's Wells, London, and demonstrated his ability to carry up to ten men at once. The strongman was Giovanni Battista Belzoni, the son of a barber from Padua, who had learnt his father's trade, then become a monk in Rome, until his monastery was closed by Napoleon's troops. Belzoni went on to have considerable success on the stages of Europe over the next decade, and subsequently went to Egypt, where he made a small fortune by exporting Egyptian antiquities. He subsequently set himself up in London as a gentleman, and cared not to disclose his theatrical past. But his wanderlust returned, and in 1823 he contracted a fatal dose of dysentery in Benin, while travelling to Timbuktu.

———

A Clutch of Eccentrics 🙦 A number of Notable Characters went to meet their Maker.

Firstly, Beauchamp Bagenal, the Irish hell-raiser who suffered from a limp and who was therefore obliged to fight his duels leaning upon a tombstone. He fought his last duel, at the age of 60, sitting in a chair, but nevertheless managed to wound his opponent, while he himself survived uninjured.

Secondly, Jemmy Hirst, gentleman-farmer, who used to ride with Lord Beaumont's hunt mounted on a bull. His efforts to train piglets as foxhounds proved fruitless.

Thirdly, Dr George Fordyce, a bibulous but popular physician. Before going on his rounds he would consume, with a meal of steak, chicken and fish, a tankard of ale, a bottle of port, and several glasses of brandy. On one occasion he was too inebriated to take the pulse of one of his more aristocratic female patients, and muttered to himself, 'Drunk, by Jove!' Nervous on his next visit that he would be scolded for his behaviour, he was relieved when the lady apologized for her condition the last time he had visited, and swore never to touch strong drink again.

1803

A Happy Accident 🖎 (21 June) During the British assault on French-held St Lucia, Captain Edward Packenham received a neck injury from a spent bullet, which obliged him to carry his head at a peculiar angle for several years – until, while engaging the enemy on Martinique, he was hit on the other side of his neck by another spent bullet, with the result that his head was restored to a more conventional position.

1804

Murder of a Ghost 🖎 (13 January) Francis Smith, an excise officer, was condemned to death for the murder of the 'Hammersmith Ghost'. An apparition had made several terrifying appearances in what was then the quiet village of Hammersmith, west of London. In one instance, a pregnant woman had been passing the churchyard when a tall, white figure had arisen from the tombstones, and taken her in its arms. The poor woman had retired to her bed and died two days later. A number of men, including Smith, determined to avenge themselves on the spectre, and when one night Smith spotted a white figure approaching him, which failed to respond to his inquiries, he drew his pistol and shot it. It turned out that he had killed a bricklayer, one Thomas Millwood, who, according to the *Newgate Calendar*, 'was in a white dress, the usual habiliment of his occupation'. Smith was convicted of murder, but his sentence was commuted to a year in prison.

———

A Plague of Frogs 🐸 Professor Pontus of Cahors, near Toulouse, reported to the Académie Française that after a thunderstorm he found the road and fields covered with young frogs, to a depth of three of four deep. The hoofs of the horses pulling the carriage he was travelling in must, he estimated, have killed thousands of the creatures.

———

Hysteria at the Theatre 🐸 (1 December) After a tumultuously successful provincial tour, the 13-year-old Irish acting prodigy, William Henry West Betty, dubbed 'The Young Roscius', made his debut on the London stage. Such was the hysterical anticipation of his appearance at Drury Lane that Bow Street Runners were positioned inside the theatre, and Foot Guards without. Men fought for seats and even standing room in the theatre, and such was the uproar that no one could hear a word of the first act, and the audience did not quieten until The Young Roscius himself appeared in the second. The other Theatre Royal, at Covent Garden, clamoured for his services, and the two theatres agreed to divide the prodigy between them. Betty himself made a fabulous £1000 per week. Soon afterwards the boy retired from the stage. An attempted comeback as an adult was not a success.

1805

———

A Faithful Hound 🐸 (18 April) Charles Gough, a Quaker from Kendal, fell from crags on Helvellyn and was killed, while walking from Patterdale to Wythburn in the Lake District. His loyal dog Foxie stayed by his body for three months, and was in a pitiable state of starvation when found on 20 July. This example of surpassing canine fidelity inspired poems by Wordsworth and Walter Scott, and a painting by Landseer.

1806

A Trespass on Nature 🙚 A man of unusual size exhibited himself in London, advertising his charms thus:

EXHIBITION

MR DANIEL LAMBERT, OF LEICESTER, THE HEAVIEST MAN THAT EVER LIVED; WHO, AT THE AGE OF THIRTY-SIX YEARS, WEIGHS UPWARDS OF FIFTY STONE (FOURTEEN POUNDS TO THE STONE), OR EIGHTY-SEVEN STONES FOUR POUNDS, LONDON WEIGHT, WHICH IS NINETY-ONE POUNDS MORE THAN THE GREAT MR BRIGHT WEIGHED. MR LAMBERT WILL SEE COMPANY AT HIS HOUSE, NO 53 PICCADILLY, NEXT ALBANY, NEARLY OPPOSITE ST JAMES'S CHURCH, FROM ELEVEN TO FIVE O'CLOCK. TICKETS OF ADMISSION, ONE SHILLING EACH.

Among Lambert's audience in London was another noted fat man, Mr Palmer of Brompton, Kent, within whose waistcoat five men could be buttoned. But Palmer was a mere 25 stone (159 kg), and it was said that he was so distressed by the superior size of his rival that it hastened his death, which took place three weeks later. Lambert himself went on growing, and by the time of his own death in Stamford on 21 July 1809, the local newspaper reported his weight as 336 kg (739 lb), and commented that 'Nature had endured all the trespass she could admit.' His coffin measured 1.92 m (6 ft 4 in) long by 1.32 m (4 ft 4 in) wide by 0.7 m (2 ft 4 in) deep.

1807

A Russian Amazon 🙚 A young Russian woman called Nadezhda Durova left her husband and son to become a soldier. She served so bravely in the wars against Napoleon that the tsar made her an officer – the first female officer in the Russian army. She later had to change regiments after the colonel's daughter fell in love with her.

1808

—

Duelling Balloons

Duelling Balloons 🐝 Two men, a M. de Grandpré and a M. le Pique, fought a duel in balloons above Paris over the favours of Mlle Tirevit of the Imperial Opera. The idea was that each man should in turn fire at the other's balloon with a blunderbuss. As the two balloons, some 80 metres apart, rose above the Tuilleries Gardens, watched by a massive crowd, the signal was given to commence the fight. M. le Pique fired first, but missed. Then it was M. de Grandpré's turn. He hit his mark, and the other balloon instantly deflated, plunging the unfortunate M. le Pique and his second to their deaths. M. de Grandpré landed with less haste some kilometres away from the scene, and claimed the hand of Mlle Tirevit.

—

A Shameless Bonaparte

A Shameless Bonaparte 🐝 Pauline, the Princess Borghese, sister of the Emperor Napoleon, caused a scandal by posing partly nude for Canova's sculpture of Venus. Asked if she did not feel a little uncomfortable, she replied, 'No, there was a fire in the room.'

—

Lamp Fuel Taken for Finest Gin

Lamp Fuel Taken for Finest Gin 🐝 (25 September) Death of Richard Porson, classical scholar and professor of Greek at Cambridge. Porson, a noted eccentric, cared little for his state of dress, and was on more than one occasion refused entrance by the servants when he called on his friends. He was also over fond of the bottle – his contemporary Horn Tooke said he would rather drink ink than nothing at all, and on one occasion, at his friend Hoppner's house, in want of a tipple, he uncovered a hidden bottle and drank its contents, declaring it to be the finest gin he had had in years. It turned out to be spirits of wine for the lamp.

—

Skewered

Skewered 🐝 At Valladolid, General Jean Malher was inspecting some raw recruits as they undertook musket practice. They were supposed to be firing blanks, but several men forgot to remove their ramrods before pulling their triggers, and the unfortunate general was killed when one of these shot through his body.

1809

___

The Great Pedestrian 🐾 (1 June–12 July) Captain Barclay (Robert Barclay Allardice of Ury, in Kincardineshire), known also as The Great Pedestrian, walked 1600 km (1000 miles) at Newmarket in 1000 hours for a wager of 1000 guineas. During the course of his walk Captain Barclay lost 14.5 kg (2 stone 4 lb).

___

The O.P. Riots 🐾 (17 September) Opening of the new Theatre Royal, Covent Garden, following the destruction by fire of the previous building. The re-opening saw the beginning of the so-called 'O.P. Riots', provoked by the management increasing the prices of tickets to cover the cost of the rebuilding. The public, however, demanded the return of the old prices (O.P. in their slogans), claiming that as the two Theatre Royals (the other was at Drury Lane) had virtually exclusive rights to present spoken drama in London, the management were exploiting their monopoly. For weeks, the crowds would disrupt performances, stamping their feet followed by a shout of 'O.P.', again and again. Speeches were made by both sides from the pit and the stage, reports were commissioned into the fairness or otherwise of the price rises, and in the end the management brought in professional pugilists to take on the more disruptive elements among the audiences. Eventually a 'Treaty of Peace' was agreed, the management giving in to many demands, and dropping prosecutions against the rioters.

___

Mysterious Disappearance of Our Man in Vienna 🐾 (25 November) While returning to Britain, Sir Benjamin Bathurst, the country's ambassador in Vienna, stopped off at the German town of

Perleberg, in Brandenburg. As he inspected the horses drawing his coach prior to his onward journey, he walked around to the side opposite to the inn, and was never seen again. On 23 January 1810 a brief notice appeared in a Hamburg newspaper stating that Bathurst's friends had received a letter from him stating that he was safe and well. However, when inquiries were made, his friends denied ever having received such a letter. There were suggestions that Napoleon had had the diplomat abducted, but the French emperor went out of his way to deny this.

1810

King Converses with Angelic Host 🦚 George III entered his final madness, in which he believed he talked to angels, and on one occasion mistook an oak tree for the king of Prussia.

The Origin of Eonism 🦚 (21 May) Death of the Chevalier d'Eon, the French soldier, diplomat and secret agent. According to his unreliable memoirs of 1779, he was born a woman, but he claimed his parents brought him up as a boy, believing this would further his chances in life. He fought for Louis XV as a captain of dragoons, and served him as a diplomat in London. In 1771 he wrote to the French government, requesting that they recognize his true gender; this they duly did, and the king even provided d'Eon with money to purchase a suitable wardrobe. For the rest of his life, d'Eon lived as a lady, in 1792 volunteering to lead a division of French revolutionary women against the Austrians. His last years were spent in cohabitation in London with a Mrs Cole, a widow. At his death, the doctors who examined his corpse identified him as anatomically male. His name gave rise to the term eonism, denoting the adoption of female dress and behaviour by a male.

Napoleon's Sole Virtue 🦚 At a public dinner, during the period of the Napoleonic Wars, the Scottish poet Thomas Campbell astonished his

fellow diners by proposing a toast to Napoleon. On being asked to account for himself, Campbell explained, 'He once shot a bookseller.'

1811

Bride Bathed in Whisky &

The poet Percy Bysshe Shelley eloped with Harriet Westbrook. The night they arrived at their lodgings in Edinburgh, the landlord knocked on the door and insisted that it was an old Scottish custom that new brides should be washed by the wedding guests in whisky. Shelley took this impudence amiss, and ushered the fellow out at pistol point.

Peculiar Phenomena Blamed on Comet &

The appearance of a comet in the sky was given as the reason for the number of twins born that year. Other phenomena attributed to the comet included the fine vintage, the plenteous harvest, the dearth of wasps and the fact that flies that year appeared to be sightless.

1812

A Double Life &

Death in Berlin of Herr Dandon, who was a professor of languages by day, but by night spent his time begging on the streets. After his death 20,000 crowns were found under the floorboards in his room. For nearly four decades he had been alienated from his brother, because the latter had once failed to pay the postage on a letter he had sent.

Vessels of Heavenly Medicine &

(June) Shelley and his wife Harriet stayed in a rented cottage in Lynmouth, Devon, where they delighted in dispersing radical documents such as *The Declaration of Rights* via waxed-paper boats ('vessels of heavenly medicine') set loose upon the sea. They also tried miniature hot-air 'balloons of knowledge', but these frequently ignited. The Home Office kept a close eye on these subversive goings-on, and arrested the Shelleys' Irish servant, Dan Healy.

Baby Raised by Goat 🐐 (July)

In a sea fight off Majorca a sailor called Phelan was fatally injured. His wife, whom he had on board with him, rushed to his side, only to have her head blown off by a cannonball. The shock was too much for the husband, who promptly expired. They left behind them on the ship their three-week-old baby, and the crew were at a loss what to do with it. Then one of the officers produced a nanny goat and introduced the infant to its teat. The baby duly suckled, and in time the goat happily lay down to allow the hungry mite to feed. The child, called Tommy, thrived.

(For another notable nautical goat, *see* 1772.)

A Controversial New Dance 🐐 (July)

General Thornton, a fan of the *Waltz*, a novel dance called then sweeping Europe, issued a challenge to Theodore Hook, who had, according to *The Times*, 'bitterly reprobated it as leading to the most licentious consequences'. The duellists exchanged one shot each, with no harm done, and the affair was settled amicably – although, as a consequence, Thornton was obliged to resign his commission.

The First Deserter 🐐 (October)

As the French retreat from Moscow began, Napoleon rushed ahead of his army, leaving them to make their own way back through the gathering Russian winter. When he reached the River Neman, Napoleon asked the ferryman if many deserters had passed through. 'No,' replied the ferryman, 'you are the first.' Only 40,000 men from Napoleon's 650,000-strong army returned from Russia.

1813

Postman Will 🐐

The poet William Wordsworth obtained the post of Distributor of Stamps for the County of Westmorland, a sinecure that brought him £400 per annum. (*See also* 1924.)

Lese-Majesty ❧ Leigh Hunt and his brother were fined £1000 and jailed for two years for publishing an article in the *Examiner* critical of the Prince Regent:

> What person, unacquainted with the true state of the case, would imagine that ... this delightful, blissful, wise, pleasurable, honourable, virtuous, true, and immortal prince, was a violator of his word, a libertine, over head and ears in disgrace, a despiser of domestic ties, the companion of gamblers and demireps, a man who has just closed half a century without one single claim on the gratitude of his country, or the respect of posterity?

By the time of George's death in 1830, even *The Times* found it hard to say a kind word, concluding, 'there never was an individual less regretted by his fellow creatures'.

1814

Wordsworth Receives Poor Notice ❧ The *Edinburgh Review* greeted the publication of Wordsworth's prolix nine-book poem *The Excursion* with the curt notice, 'This will never do.'

The Last Frost Fair ❧ (1–4 February) The last Frost Fair was held on the Thames, the river never again freezing sufficiently to bear the weight of people and market stalls. On this occasion, for a few days, the ice was strong enough to bear the weight of an elephant, which crossed the frozen river below Blackfriars Bridge.

Second Messiah Fails to Appear ❧ (19 October) A 64-year-old farmer's daughter and former servant from Devon, Joanna Southcott, had announced that on this day she would give birth to the Prince of Peace. She claimed she was the woman mentioned in Revelation 12, 'a woman clothed

The winter of 1814 was the last time a Frost Fair was held on the frozen River Thames.

with the sun, and the moon under her feet, and upon her head a crown of twelve stars', who was to bring forth 'a man child, who was to rule all nations with a rod of iron: and her child was caught up unto God, and to his throne'. When the Second Messiah was not forthcoming, Miss Southcott fell into a coma, and was dead by the end of the year. Her followers, who then numbered some 100,000, asserted she was merely in a trance, and were only persuaded to give up her body for burial when evidence of putrefaction became unignorable.

1815
———

Battle of Waterloo Heard in Sussex ❧ (18 June) The sound of the guns at the Battle of Waterloo was so great that it was heard as far away as Heathfield, in Sussex. In the evening, the body of Sergeant Weir, a pay sergeant of the Scots Greys, was found on the battlefield with his own name painted in blood on his forehead. He had done this while mortally wounded, so that his body might be recognized, and so that no one should think he had absconded with the money of his troop.

1816

The Year Without a Summer ❧ The year 1816 – known as the Year Without a Summer, the Poverty Year, or Eighteen Hundred and Froze to Death – was marked by such poor summer weather conditions – including frosts, snowstorms and exceptionally heavy rains – that crops failed across northern Europe and the American northeast, leading to widespread famine. The harsh conditions were exceptional, even for Europe's 'mini ice age' of the 17th and 18th centuries, and were almost certainly the result of the massive eruption the previous year of the volcano Tambora in the East Indies, which put so much dust into the atmosphere that it blocked out much of the light of the sun, creating the equivalent of a nuclear winter. The dust in the atmosphere led to some spectacular sunsets – as recorded in the paintings of J.M.W. Turner – and Byron wrote the poem 'Darkness', beginning:

> I had a dream, which was not all a dream.
> The bright sun was extinguish'd, and the stars
> Did wander darkling in the eternal space,
> Rayless, and pathless, and the icy earth
> Swung blind and blackening in the moonless air . . .

Another consequence of the cool, wet weather was that Byron and the Shelleys spent much of their summer holiday in Switzerland indoors. Byron suggested they each write a ghost story to while away the time. The others soon gave up, but Mary Shelley persisted, and the result was her masterpiece, the novel *Frankenstein* – which, appropriately enough, ends in the frozen wastes of the Arctic.

The Raft of the *Medusa* ❧ (17 July) The French frigate *Medusa* ran aground off the west coast of Africa, en route to Senegal. The captain, an inexperienced sailor who had only been given the command because he had

opposed the now-defeated Napoleon, decided to abandon ship, but there were not enough lifeboats for all the passengers and crew. While the officers and passengers of higher rank occupied the boats, the remaining 150 or so persons were put on a raft, with negligible supplies. The intention was to tow the raft to shore, but the boats soon gave up, and the raft was cut adrift. Over the next two weeks, murder, suicide and cannibalism took their toll, and when the raft was found, there were only 15 survivors on board, and five of these died shortly afterwards. The remaining men were assisted back to France by the Royal Navy, as the French government appeared unwilling to help. The incident led to a political scandal back in France, and was taken by many as a symbol of the reactionary nature of the Bourbon Restoration. Three years later Théodore Géricault exhibited his huge painting of *The Raft of the Medusa* at the Paris Salon. He employed cadavers from the morgue as models, as well as friends such as the painter Eugène Delacroix.

———

Small Earthquake in Scotland: Few Hurt 🍂 (13 August) In the evening much of northeastern Scotland experienced a minor earthquake, lasting some six seconds. Crockery and kitchen implements rattled, tables and chairs were moved about, and caged birds fell off their perches. In Montrose, two excisemen lying in wait for smugglers jumped up as the Earth trembled, believing that they felt horses' hooves approaching. In Inverness a man swore that 'he was tossed in his bed, as he had never been tossed out at sea, for full five minutes'. No fatalities were reported.

———

A Dandy in Disgrace 🍂 The dandy Beau Brummell fled England to escape his debtors, and his social ostracism following his falling out with the Prince Regent. When the latter had snubbed him at a ball, Brummell had loudly asked his companion, 'Who's your fat friend?' Brummell claimed to take five hours to dress himself, and recommended that one's boots should be polished with champagne. He disdained the eating of vegetables as unfit for gentlemen, although confessed that he had once eaten a pea. Having contracted syphilis, he eventually went mad, and died in exile in France in 1840.

Lateral Thinking 🍂 (30 September) The Ottoman general Ibrahim Pasha began his successful campaign against the Wahhabi rebels in the Nejd, a desert area of Arabia. His father, Muhammad Ali of Egypt, had selected his son to lead the campaign after having set his various generals a test. He placed an apple in the middle of a carpet and asked them to devise a way of retrieving the apple without treading on the carpet. While the other generals scratched their heads, Ibrahim knelt at the edge of the carpet and rolled it up until he could reach the apple.

1817

The Consequences of Failing to Attend Church 🍂 Sir Montague Burgoyne was prosecuted at the Spring Assizes in Bedford for failing to attend his parish church for several months. The charge was dismissed when it was established that the baronet had been unwell. However, in 1830 ten people were still being held in prison for similar offences.

Princess Caraboo of Java 🍂 (3 April) Mary Baker, the daughter of a Devon shoemaker, began her impersonation of Princess Caraboo, supposedly a native of Java. Princess Caraboo became the toast of English society, and many showered expensive gifts upon her, in the hope of future patronage. Eventually exposed, Miss Baker fled with her ill-gotten gains to America.

Sea Serpent Recognized by Science 🍂 (18 August) The Linnaean Society of New England identified a deformed land snake as a juvenile form of a sea serpent. Such a creature had recently been spotted off the coast, and they gave it the name *Scoliophis atlanticus*.

The End of Trial by Combat *&* A man called Abraham Thornton became the last person in England to claim the right of trial by combat. He had been acquitted of murdering one Mary Ashford, but her brother, William Ashford, persisted in accusing Thornton of the crime. The courts allowed Thornton to claim the right of 'wager of battle in front of the king', but Ashford declined the challenge. The following year Parliament abolished trial by combat.

1818

Cleaning Up the Bard *&* Publication of Dr Thomas Bowdler's *Family Shakespeare*, an expurgated (or 'bowdlerized') version of the bard, in which the good doctor 'endeavoured to remove every thing that could give just offence to the religious and virtuous mind'. For example, Ophelia's drowning in *Hamlet* is reported as an accident rather than suicide, and Lady Macbeth cries not 'Out, damned spot' but 'Out, crimson spot'. Bowdler's work was so successful that it went through many editions.

The Hollow Earth Theory *&* An American, John Cleves Symmes, proposed that the Earth was a hollow shell containing four inner spheres, each of which had gaps some 1400 miles wide at both poles. Over the next few decades, various planned expeditions to the North Pole to find the enormous hole were abandoned.

1819

The First Chocolate Bar *&* The first ever bars of chocolate were made by the Swiss confectioner François-Louis Cailler.

1820

Old Soak Leaves Stage ✤ The English actor Edmund Kean was so drunk while playing Macbeth in New York that at the interval it was announced that an understudy would take over his part, as Mr Kean was suffering from malaria. 'I'd like a bottle of that,' jeered a member of the audience.

Gregor MacGregor, the Cazique of Poyais ✤ A man called Gregor MacGregor arrived in London, claiming to be the 'cazique' or prince of a principality called Poyais on the Bay of Honduras, which, according to his own account, had been granted him by King George Frederick of the Mosquito Coast. MacGregor had come to Britain, he said, to encourage people to settle and invest in Poyais, which he depicted as a fertile and pleasant land, replete with rich natural resources and a peaceable population. He was lauded in London society, and even had his ambassador received at the Court of St James. Investors threw money at MacGregor, who claimed to have fought alongside Simón Bolívar against the Spanish, and to be a descendant of Rob Roy MacGregor.

The fraud was exposed when, in 1822–3, two shiploads of immigrants arrived at Poyais (having changed their pounds for Poyais dollars) and found nothing but a disease-ridden, deserted swamp. The survivors were eventually evacuated by the authorities in British Honduras. MacGregor, meanwhile, had left England for France, where in 1825 he attempted to repeat the scam. He was arrested, but acquitted at his trial. Returning to Britain, he faced more charges, but these were dropped, and he attempted to launch yet more Poyais schemes through the 1830s. He retired in 1839 to Venezuela, where he was awarded a pension as a hero of the struggle for independence.

1821

All the News That's Fit to Print ✤ (5 May) The first edition of the *Manchester Guardian* briefly reported the death of Napoleon, and noted that 'a colony of rooks has lately established itself in a garden at the top of King Street'.

1822

—

On the Dangers of Hot-Buttered Toast ❧ (12 August) Lord Castlereagh, the British foreign secretary, killed himself by cutting the carotid artery in his throat. His contemporary, the painter Benjamin Haydon, blamed the suicide on Castlereagh's consumption of hot buttered toast, which, he asserted, caused a fatal rush of blood to the head.

—

The Last Jacobite ❧ A Jacobite survivor of the Battle of Culloden, which had been fought 76 years previously, visited George IV at Holyrood Palace in Edinburgh, and introduced himself as 'the last of his enemies'.

1823

—

Dancing on the Dead ❧ The Revd Marmaduke Rabbett opened Eon Chapel in the Strand, London, and offered the poor cut-price burials under its floor. Thousands of people took up the offer, but by 1838 there was no space left. Then the Revd Rabbett hit upon the idea of turning the chapel into a dance hall. His advertisements read: 'Dancing on the Dead – Admission Three Pence'.

1824

—

Second Messiah Fails to Appear – Again ❧ John Wroe of the Christian Israelite Church, who was subject to visions and trances, declared to a crowd of 30,000 that he would make the waters of the River Aire part. No one seems to have been too disappointed when this failed to materialize. Wroe subsequently had himself circumcised in public, and in 1830 declared that heaven had instructed him 'to take seven virgins to cherish and comfort him'. Some of the Church's followers were outraged when one of the girls became pregnant, while others said that the child would be the new Messiah. But when a baby girl was born, rather than the expected boy, they decided that Wroe was a fraud and turned him out.

1825

Mermaid on Show in London

A 'mermaid' was exhibited at Bartholomew Fair, London. It turned out to consist of the dried head and body of a monkey and the tail of the fish, and was thought to have come from China.

A Demon Barber

(12 March) Several poor women appeared in London's metropolitan police court as witnesses at the trial of a barber, Thomas Rushton. They testified that Rushton had, on the same day, visited each of them in their homes, offered them a guinea for a hank of their hair, and then had swiftly shorn their entire heads, concealed the hair under his hat and fled without leaving them a penny.

An Appalling Scene

The artist William Brockedon visited the hospice run by the monk on the Great St Bernard Pass in the Alps, and discovered the charnel house where the semi-mummified corpses of unfortunates who had died in the nearby mountains were kept 'in the postures in which they had perished':

> Upon some the clothes had remained after eighteen years, though tattered like a gibbet wardrobe. Some of these bodies presented a hideous aspect; part of the bones of the head were exposed and blanched, whilst black integuments were attached to other parts of the face ... A mother and her child were among the latest victims; several bodies were standing against the wall, upon the accumulated heaps of their miserable predecessors, presenting an appalling scene.

Between the 17th and the 19th centuries, the bodies of the wealthier citizens of Palermo, Sicily, were embalmed and placed in the Catacombe dei Cappucini. A similar sight in the charnel house of the hospice on the Great St Bernard Pass gave one English visitor a bit of a turn in 1825.

1826

—

Russian Efficiency 🔖 (25 July) Kondraty Fyodorovich Ryleyev, one of the leaders of the Decembrist revolt in Russia, was hanged. The first attempt failed when the rope broke, and Ryleyev sourly remarked, 'In Russia we cannot even make a rope properly.' In such circumstances it was usual for the tsar to offer a pardon, but when Nicholas I heard what Ryleyev had said about the rope, he refused, saying 'Let us prove him wrong.'

1827

On the Evils of Tea ❧ (8 January) The *Manchester Guardian* condemned tea drinking:

> The tea itself, perhaps, if taken moderately, is an innocent thing. But to take into the stomach, morning and evening, several cups of a very hot liquid – so hot that the drinkers are obliged to sip it, in order to get it down without scalding their throats – is a practice replete with mischief. The stomach is in consequence much relaxed, and the digestive power sadly weakened, to the great promotion of nervous and other never-ending complaints ... and even the heart becomes cold and selfish.

Cooper the Dog Confounds County Players ❧ (21 May) A farmer called Francis Trumper and his dog Cooper challenged two Middlesex county players to a game of cricket. The challengers went in to bat first, Trumper making 31 and Cooper a more modest 3. The county players were confident of victory as they strode to the crease, but the swiftness of Cooper in retrieving their hits made it nigh impossible for them to score at all.

Snow Bugs ❧ (17 October) At Pakroff in Russia, according to the *Journal of St Petersburg*, an early snowfall brought with it a great shower of large black insects, over an inch in length, which seemed to thrive in the low temperature, and which died if brought into the warmth.

Book Bound in Human Skin ❧ After William Corder was hanged for the 'Red Barn' murder of Maria Martin, the record of his trial was bound in his own skin. It can be seen in the museum at Bury St Edmunds, Suffolk. The earliest extant volumes bound in human skin date from the 17th century, and there exist a number of copies of the French constitution of 1793 with what bibliophiles describe as anthropodermic bindings.

1828

Fields Covered in Herring Fry 🐟 (14 April) While walking on

his farm in Ross-shire, Major Forbes Mackenzie of Fodderty found one of his fields covered in herring fry, each between three and four inches in length. His farm was some three miles from the sea.

The Enigma of Kaspar Hauser 🐟 (26 May) A youth of about 16

or 17 years of age, dressed in peasant costume and in a somewhat confused condition, was found in the market-place of Nuremberg, Bavaria. The boy could say little more than '*Weiss nicht*' ('I don't know'). He could write his name, Kaspar Hauser, but nothing else, behaved much like a six-year-old, and seemed unacquainted with the ways of the world. He carried with him a letter from a nameless poor labourer, a father of ten, who said the boy had been left at his door some years previously, and that he had brought him up in secret. The letter was addressed to the captain of the fourth squadron of the Sixth Regiment of Horse, and begged the recipient to either take the boy on or to 'strike him dead or hang him'. Another letter with the boy, purportedly from his mother and dated October 1812, claimed that his dead father had belonged to the same regiment. Subsequent interrogation of the youth by the magistrates revealed that he had been kept in a dark place, with food being brought while he was asleep. His keeper had latterly taught him to read and write, and given him some instruction in the basics of Christianity.

In July 1828 Kaspar was placed in the care of a school teacher, Friedrich Daumer, who undertook his education – a process that, after a promising start, failed to yield any very spectacular results. The following year, on 17 October, Kaspar was found with a slight wound on his forehead, which he said had been given him by a man with a black head – it was thought his attacker was hooded, and wielded an axe. Subsequently the magistrates provided the youth with a constant guard.

Kaspar was taken up by an English nobleman, Lord Stanhope, who secured him a lowly position in the court of appeal at Ansbach. Here the young man made little impact, and gradually faded from notice – until his violent death in 1833. In that year a stranger, claiming to have a message from Lord Stanhope containing information about his birth, arranged to meet him in the palace gardens in the afternoon of 14 December. Kaspar duly met the stranger who, according to Kaspar's own account, after a little conversation, stabbed him in the chest and fled. Kaspar managed to struggle home, but three days later he died of his wound.

Conjectures as to the identity of Kaspar Hauser had already spread like wildfire across Europe: he was the illegitimate son of a priest, or of a lady of high rank, or, most popularly, he was the only son of Karl Ludwig Friedrich, Grand Duke of Baden, abducted as an infant so that Karl's uncle Leopold should succeed to the grand dukedom. It was said that Stanhope was in cahoots with the perpetrators of this latter plot, having tried to gain custody of the young man, and having declared that Kaspar was a Hungarian, and not of noble birth. Most significantly, Stanhope had claimed that Kaspar's death was suicide. Others agreed that Kaspar's death *was* suicide, and claimed that he had been nothing but a conman. In 2002 DNA tests on hair and body cells thought to have belonged to Kaspar Hauser suggested that he was indeed a scion of the House of Baden.

1829

Purse Made from Skin of Murderer &• After his execution for the murder of several people whose cadavers he sold to Edinburgh's Anatomy School, William Burke was handed over to his former clients. A purse made out of his skin can still be seen in the museum of the Royal College of Surgeons of Edinburgh.

One of Our Naughtier Vicars &• The Revd Edward Drax Free, having been found guilty by an ecclesiastical court of immorality and lewdness (at least four of his housekeepers did double duty in his bed), was deprived of his living in Sutton, Bedfordshire. The authorities also disapproved of the fact that he had sold the lead from the church roof, and allowed sheep to urinate in the porch and pigs to dig up newly dug graves. Refusing to submit to the ecclesiastical authorities, Free locked himself up inside the rectory with his latest mistress and fired on the Archdeacon of Bedford when he came to reason with him. Eventually, after a ten-day siege, Free was starved out. In 1843, without a living and reduced to beggary, Free died of his injuries after being run over by a varnish-maker's cart in London.

1830

Silly Billy &❧ William IV, having recently succeeded to the throne at the age of 64, was not prepared to change his ways, and would sometimes walk around the streets of London unaccompanied. To the shock of his stuffier contemporaries, on one such occasion he was embraced and kissed by a prostitute in St James's Street. He had acquired his nickname 'Silly Billy' after visiting an insane asylum, where one of the inmates had pointed at him and shouted, 'Silly Billy! Silly Billy!' William not being the brightest button in the box, the nickname stuck, but after he succeeded to the throne he had the pleasure of asking his privy council, 'Who's the Silly Billy now?'

Lost Tribes of Israel Found in Mexico &❧ Publication of the first of several volumes of *Antiquities of Mexico*, in which the author, Edward King, Viscount Kingsborough, argued that the lost tribes of Israel were to be found in Mexico. Kingsborough spent his entire fortune on funding the printing and binding of his *magnus opus*, and died in 1837 in a debtor's prison in Dublin.

A Cure for Hiccoughs &❧ 'Mad Jack' Mytton, MP, prankster and Olympian toper, having succumbed to an attack of hiccoughs, decided that the only cure was to give himself a fright. He duly set his nightclothes on fire with a candle. Although badly burned, he was happy to report, 'The hiccough is gone, by God!'

1831

Man Conceals Glass of Ale Under Hat

(February) George Cole was charged with the theft of three drinking glasses, each one from a different public house. When arrested he had two in his pockets, while the third glass, still containing some ale, was under his hat. He was sentenced to two months' hard labour.

———

Archbishop Fidget

The notoriously fidgety Richard Whately was appointed as Anglican Archbishop of Dublin. On one occasion, whilst at a meeting of the privy council, Chief Justice Doherty, needing to blow his nose, put his fingers into his pocket to locate a handkerchief, only to find that the Archbishop's foot was already in residence. Whately appears to have treated religion with some circumspection, holding it to be tainted by superstition. His practical approach to this and other matters is demonstrated by his method of testing whether someone had criminal tendencies: if one placed a handful of peas on top of the subject's head, and only some of them rolled off, then 'tell the butler to lock up the plate', for a flat head was a strong indicator of dishonesty. He had, according to one biographer, 'a wholly uncontrollable love of punning', a failing not unknown among men of his period and station.

———

Rebel Slave Flayed

(11 November) In Virginia, Nat Turner was hanged for leading a slave rebellion. His body was skinned and then dismembered, various bits of his anatomy being preserved by triumphal whites as trophies.

———

Snakes Return to Ireland

A certain James Cleland conducted an experiment in County Down, Ireland, to see whether it was the natural environment rather than St Patrick that had made the island inimical to snakes. When some of the half dozen English grass snakes he released were discovered by the locals, they were taken for eels, but when their reptilian nature was established by the distinguished naturalist Dr J.L. Drummond, wild rumours spread that with the return of snakes to Ireland the end of the world was surely nigh.

———

The Last Vatican Jester ❧ Gregory XVI became pope, and went on to prohibit the building of railways in the Papal States, referring to them as *chemins d'enfer* ('roads of hell', punning on the French term for railways, *chemins de fer*, 'road of iron'). He was the last pope to have a court jester, in the person of Cardinal Soglia. When blind man's buff was being played, Soglia was always the one wearing the blindfold, and would lash about him with a stick. On one occasion the Pontiff stooped to rescue a vase from a swipe of Soglia's stick, and only just avoided a blow to the head when his officials roughly pulled him out of harm's way.

1832

———

No News ❧ An old sign on the door of a house in the Fife village of Culross states:

> IN 1832 ON
> THIS SPOT
> NOTHING
> HAPPENED

———

Pickled Philosopher Attends Council Meetings ❧ (6 June) Death of the utilitarian philosopher Jeremy Bentham. In his will he requested that his body be preserved and put on display in a wooden cabinet, which he styled an 'auto-icon', at University College London, an institution with which he was closely associated. The philosopher's corpse is sometimes produced at meetings of the Council of UCL, and is minuted as 'present but not voting'.

———

The Republic of Indian Stream 🐚 Settlers in a small area between Quebec and New Hampshire declared themselves an independent nation, the Republic of Indian Stream (named after a small river in the territory). The area was claimed both by British Canada and the United States, and the settlers objected to visits by tax collectors from both countries. In 1835, after some Streamers (as the settlers were called) had 'invaded' Canada to free a fellow countryman who had been seized for an unpaid debt, the Indian Stream Congress voted that their republic be annexed by the USA. Britain happily relinquished its claim the following year. The area now comprises the township of Pittsburg, New Hampshire.

———

Dining on Roast Infant 🐚 Alexandre Dumas visited the Alps, and ate what he thought was roast infant, but which turned out to be marmot. He also attended a trial at which two live bears were summoned as witnesses.

———

Wife for Sale 🐚 A Cumbrian farmer, Joseph Thomson, put his wife up for sale in Carlisle. There was long a belief among country folk that such sales, if mutually agreed upon by man and wife, provided a legal means of dissolving a marriage. According to the *Annual Register* for 1832, Thomson had a fine line in matrimonial sales pitches, addressing prospective purchasers thus:

> Gentlemen, I have to offer to your notice my wife, Mary Anne Thomson, otherwise Williams, whom I mean to sell to the highest and fairest bidder. Gentlemen, it is her wish as well as mine to part for ever. She has been to me only a born serpent. I took her for my comfort, and the good of my home; but she became my tormentor, a domestic curse, a night invasion, and a daily devil. Gentlemen, I speak truth from my heart when I say – may God deliver us from troublesome wives and frolicsome women! Avoid them as you would a mad dog, a roaring lion, a loaded pistol, cholera morbus, Mount Etna, or any other pestilential thing in nature. Now I have shewn you the dark side of my wife, and told you her faults and failings, I will introduce the bright

and sunny side of her, and explain her qualifications and goodness. She can read novels and milk cows; she can laugh and weep with the same ease that you could take a glass of ale when thirsty. Indeed, gentlemen, she reminds me of what the poet says of women in general:

> Heaven gave to women the peculiar grace,
> To laugh, to weep, to cheat the human race.

She can make butter and scold the maid; she can sing Moore's melodies, and plait her frills and caps; she cannot make rum, gin, or whisky, but she is a good judge of the quality from long experience in tasting them. I therefore offer her with all her perfections and imperfections, for the sum of fifty shillings.

In the end Thomson settled for 20 shillings and a Newfoundland dog, offered by a man called Henry Mears.

1833

An Imaginary Helpmeet 🍀 (6 March) Death of John William Ward, 1st Earl of Dudley, Tory politician and Secretary of State for Foreign Affairs in 1827–8. A studious man, and something of a recluse, Dudley was notoriously absent-minded. On one occasion, having being invited out to dinner, he apologized to the company for the poor food, explaining that his cook was not well. He was a lifelong bachelor, although in his later years he invented a wife, and spoke of her fondly. When he died, having been certified insane, his titles became extinct.

Shooting Stars Herald Apocalypse 🍀 (13 November) A spectacular display of shooting stars was observed across much of North America. Many people were convinced the end of the world was nigh, recalling the words of Revelation regarding the Apocalypse:

> The stars of heaven fell unto the earth, even as a fig tree casteth her untimely figs, when she is shaken of a mighty wind.

Such, however, was not the case.

Justice Delayed – Part II ❦ A suit contesting the distribution of valuable land and property in Calcutta after the death of Rajah Naba Krishna Deb was lodged before an Indian court. The case remained pending for 173 years, until reopened in 2006.

1834

Fracas at Royal Academy Narrowly Avoided ❦ While being guided round an exhibition at the Royal Academy by the president, King William IV stopped in front of a portrait of Admiral Napier – with whom he was furious for intervening on the liberal side in the civil war in Portugal – and exclaimed, 'Captain Napier may be damned, sir. And you may be damned, sir, and if the Queen was not here, sir, I would kick you downstairs.'

1836

Madam's Legacy Spurned ❦ Theresa Berkeley left her not inconsiderable fortune to her brother, a missionary in Australia. However, when he learnt that she had made her money as the proprietor of a brothel in Hallam Street, London, that specialized in flagellation, he declined to accept the legacy.

Spontaneous Generation by Means of Electricity ❦ Andrew Crosse, an amateur scientist and member of Parliament, was surprised to find that out of some chemicals through which he had been passing an electrical current there had appeared first one, then several, then hundreds of insects, identified as belonging to the genus *Acarus*. Word got out, and a furore resulted. Some maintained that this was evidence of spontaneous generation, while others denounced Crosse for usurping the role of God in creating life. He even received death threats, and the local farmers in his native Somerset blamed him for the failure of the wheat harvest, going so far as to commission a priest to perform an exorcism. Crosse himself drew no conclusions, simply reporting what he had observed. He and others repeated the experiment, taking every measure to try to ensure that any insect eggs that might be present would be destroyed – but still the insects emerged. It is now thought that the 'insects' were probably some kind of mite, whose eggs were resistant to decontamination.

1837

A Custard Without Eggs

Alfred Bird invented custard powder. As his wife was allergic to eggs, his powder did without them.

Spring-Heeled Jack

(Autumn) Sightings began in London and its environs of a creature soon dubbed 'Spring-Heeled Jack'. Witnesses described a muscular man in a tight-fitting garb, with pointed nose, ears and chin, and glowing eyes. He was capable of great leaps and bounds, breathed blue flames, and had a habit of grabbing at the clothing of young women with steel-like claws. By January 1838 the Lord Mayor of London, although sceptical that any devil's work was afoot, asked the police to investigate, suspecting one or more pranksters were at play (among the chief suspects was the hellraising, misogynistic Marquess of Waterford, who was known to jump upon passers-by for fun). Sightings continued through that year, then died away. Further clusters of sightings occurred in 1843, and again in the 1870s. In this latter period, Spring-Heeled Jack was transformed into a hero of popular fiction, in which he was portrayed as a nobleman cheated of his inheritance, who used his powers for good. A century later, on 18 June 1953, Spring-Heeled Jack was spotted up a tree in Houston, Texas. He had apparently leapt across the Atlantic.

1838

Leg Buried with Military Honours

At the siege of French-occupied Veracruz, the Mexican general Santa Anna lost a leg to cannon fire. The severed limb was buried with full military honours.

The first sightings of Spring-Heeled Jack were reported in the autumn of 1837. He continued to elude the authorities for many years, and in due course became a hero of the 'penny dreadfuls'.

The Last Battle in England ◆ (31 May) At Bossenden Wood in

Kent there took place 'the last battle in England'. On one side was a 30- or 40-strong group of agricultural workers protesting about their conditions, on the other armed soldiers sent by the government. The workers were led by John Thom, a former wine merchant from Truro who had adopted the name Sir William de Courtenay and who claimed to be the Messiah. Thom told his followers that he could kill 10,000 men by clapping his hands, and that if he was killed, he would rise on the third day. Prior to the battle, a warrant had been put out for Thom, following a complaint by a farmer that he had lured away his workers. Thom shot a constable sent to arrest him, prompting the intervention of the 45th Regiment of Foot. Thom shot an officer, Lieutenant Bennett, and was himself mown down, along with nine of his followers. The survivors were quickly rounded up, and later sentenced to transportation or hard labour.

1839

Slaughter Forbidden in Streets of London ◆ The

Metropolitan Police Act made it illegal to slaughter cattle in the streets of London, unless the slaughtered animal had previously been run over by the slaughterer. The act also banned children from sliding on snow or ice, setting off fireworks or ringing doorbells 'without lawful excuse'.

A Mathematical Prodigy ◆ (3 July) A group of members of the

Academy of Sciences in Paris met to examine a mathematical prodigy called Vito Mangiamele, the son of a Sicilian shepherd. The boy, who was about 11 years old, found the cube root of 3,796,416 in some 30 seconds. The tenth root of 282,475,249 took him a little longer – three minutes. Then his questioners put to him this: 'What number has the following proportions, that if its cube is added to 5 times its square, and then 42 times the number, and the number

40 be subtracted from the result, the remainder is equal to 0?' As the questioner, a M. Arago, was repeating the question, young Vito interrupted him with the answer: 5.

1840

A Poem on Dentistry ❧ Publication of *Dentologia*, a 'poem on the diseases of teeth and their proper remedies' by the US dentist Solyman Brown.

Good Manners ❧ An authority on etiquette offered the following advice: 'Ladies may wipe their lips on the tablecloth, but not blow their noses on it.'

An Enthusiastic Couple ❧ (10 February) Queen Victoria married Prince Albert. Victoria recorded of her wedding night: 'We did not sleep much.'

Fanny's Fervent Following ❧ The Austrian ballerina Fanny Essler began her tour of the USA, where her sensual dancing, involving the exposure of much thigh, caused a sensation. On one occasion, so many Senators went to see her dance that Congress lacked a quorum and had to abandon its session.

1841

Fish Fall from Sky ❧ (30 June) During a thunderstorm in northern Germany many fish, including pike, perch and roach, fell from the sky, some of them still alive.

The First Package Holiday ❧ (5 July) Thomas Cook, the travel agent, organized his first excursion: a day trip for temperance campaigners from Leicester to Loughborough.

1842

A Traffic Accident ❧ A 'gentleman' was fined five shillings in Glasgow after the vehicle he was driving, which 'moved on wheels turned by the hand by means of a crank', knocked down a girl while travelling at 13 kph (8 mph).

An Experiment on Public Credulity ❧ (17 March) The newspapers carried a story about a prophecy from 1203 predicting that on this day London would be destroyed by an earthquake. It was reported that 'a great number of timid persons left the metropolis', until it was revealed the prophecy was the work of a hoaxer, who described it as 'an experiment on public credulity'.

1843

Siamese Twins Marry ❧ (13 April) Chang and Eng, the original Siamese twins, married two sisters, Sarah and Adelaide Yeates, of Wilkes County, North Carolina, where the twins had set up as planters, having originally been brought to America in 1829 by a Captain Coffin. The twins, who were conjoined at the chest and never separated, proceeded to father a total of 21 children.

An Elevated Organ ❧ Charles Dickens began the serial publication of *Martin Chuzzlewit*, which in chapter 24 has the following:

> She touched his organ, and from that bright epoch, even it, the old companion of his happiest hours, incapable as he had thought of elevation, began a new and deified existence.

1844

Industrious Fleas and Other Entertainments ❧ (24 February)

The following advertisement appeared in the *Caledonian Mercury*:

Now Exhibiting at No 63 Princes Street, Edinburgh
ALLART's HAPPY FAMILY

consisting of upwards of 100 ANIMALS, of an Opposite Nature,
All Living and Feeding in One Apartment. The following are a
few of the Collection, namely Rats, Cats, Ferret, Coatimundi,
Squirrel, Hawks, Owls, Pigeons, Crows, Jackdaws, Magpies,
Starlings, Blackbirds, Chickens, Monkeys, Hedgehog, Sea-Gull,
Guinea Pigs, Goose, Parrots, &c, &c too numerous to mention.
Most wonderful to see how they all agree in one large cage.

Also, the INDUSTRIOUS FLEAS will
Perform a Variety of Feats too numerous to mention.

This last is thought to be a reference to Signor Bertolotto's Extraordinary
Exhibition of the Industrious Fleas, one of the earliest known flea circuses.
However, the history and true nature of flea circuses is shrouded in lore and
legend, and whether there were actually any performing fleas in Signor
Bertolotto's entertainment, or whether it was all an illusion, is unknown.

1846

The Abode of Love ❧ In Spaxton, Somerset, the Revd Henry Prince,
formerly of the Church of England and now convinced that he was the
embodiment of the Holy Ghost, established an *Agapemone* (a Greek word
meaning 'abode of love'), coyly defined by *Chambers English Dictionary* as 'a
religious community of men and women whose "spiritual marriages" were in
some cases not strictly spiritual'. In the Abode of Love, or so one of many
rumours had it, Prince would set his female followers on a revolving stage,
and after the stage had been spun, whichever woman should come to rest

where Prince stood would, for that week, serve as his wife. More certainly, on one occasion Prince forcibly deflowered 16-year-old Zoe Patterson in front of his entire congregation, to the accompaniment of organ music and the singing of hymns. When she became pregnant, Prince blamed the Devil.

1847

—

Invention of the Ring Doughnut 🍋 The ring doughnut was invented by accident, when a baker's apprentice called Hanson Gregory pushed out the soggy, uncooked centre of conventional doughnut that he had just pulled out of the deep fryer.

1848

—

I Am the Emperor, and I Want Dumplings! 🍋 During the upheavals in Vienna, the feeble-minded Emperor Ferdinand I of Austria, watching the revolutionaries march past the palace, supposedly asked, 'Are they allowed to do that?' He abdicated shortly afterwards. On an earlier occasion, when advised that he should not eat dumplings because his digestive system could not cope, he said, *'Ich bin der Kaiser und will Knödel!'* ('I am the Emperor, and I want dumplings!')

—

Widow McCormick's Cabbage Patch 🍋 (29 July) The Irish contribution to the year of revolutions across Europe comprised a brief skirmish near Kilkenny between a hundred Young Ireland rebels and half that number of men from the Royal Irish Constabulary. The abortive revolt was for ever after known by the piece of ground upon which it was fought – Widow McCormick's Cabbage Patch.

—

An Experiment in Free Love 🍋 The utopian Oneida Community was established in New York state. The Community practised 'complex marriage', in effect free love, and the women on average had 'interviews' with three different partners every week. To avoid unwanted pregnancies and the 'waste' of seed, the men aimed to avoid ejaculation during coitus, which could last for up to an hour. Pubescent boys trained to achieve this degree of control by engaging in intercourse with women who had just passed the menopause. Those who wished to bear children had to appear before a committee, which would determine their spiritual and moral fitness for breeding. All children were raised communally. The community's founder, John Humphrey Noyes, was obliged to flee to Canada in 1879 when he was warned that he was about to be charged with statutory rape. He wrote to advise his followers to abandon complex marriage, and within a year many community members had contracted conventional marriages.

1849

Violent Objections to Macready's Macbeth

Violent Objections to Macready's Macbeth &. At the Astor Opera House, New York, where the English actor William Charles Macready was appearing as Macbeth, a claque sponsored by Edwin Forrest, his American rival, began to pelt him on stage. The disturbance developed into a riot involving a mob of some 20,000 people. Eventually the militia were called in, resulting in 23 deaths.

A Hyperpolyglot &. (15 March) Death of Cardinal Giuseppe Caspar Mezzofanti, keeper of the Vatican Library and, due to his prodigious memory, undoubtedly the greatest linguist of his age. As pilgrims came to Rome from all over the world, his services were often required as confessor, and if he found he did not know the language of those whose confession he took, he set about learning it. It was said that at the time of his death he was fluent in 38 languages (and their various dialects), and proficient in many more – not only those from Europe, but also many from Africa and Asia. The story is told how, when asked what his next project was, he answered, 'To teach the Californians their own language.' When asked how he had learnt Californian, he replied, 'They taught me, but had no grammar. I have now created a grammar, and am going to teach them how to read and write it.'

1850

Rum Ration Slashed 🙰 The Royal Navy reduced its daily rum allowance from one-quarter to one-eighth of a pint.

1851

Sparrows, the Lower Orders, and Nasty Foreigners Talking All Kinds of Gibberish 🙰 The new Crystal Palace, home
to the Great Exhibition, was infested with sparrows, which were defecating everywhere. To shoot them was impractical, because of all the glass. Distraught, Queen Victoria consulted the Duke of Wellington. He tersely delivered his solution: 'Sparrowhawks, ma'am.' Wellington was more worried that the Exhibition would provide an occasion for the lower orders to riot, estimating that 15,000 troops would be required to restore order. Other politicians, such as Colonel Charles de Laet Waldo Sibthorp, MP for Lincoln, were more concerned that the Exhibition would attract 'nasty foreigners who live on brown bread and sauerkraut', and, what is more, 'talking all kinds of gibberish'.

The First Bloomers 🙰 (3 July) Mrs Amelia Bloomer, the American feminist and temperance campaigner, shocked her contemporaries by appearing at a ball in the town of Lowell, Massachusettss, in a dress only extending down to mid-calf. Modesty, in her eyes, was preserved by clothing the legs that would otherwise have been exposed in baggy trousers gathered in at the ankle – a garment forever after known as 'bloomers'. Mrs Bloomer's sartorial innovation was for a short time adopted in certain quarters, but in general met with derision. Writing a decade later, Robert Chambers observed, 'As by a sort of reaction, the monstrosity of cumbrous skirts has since, in all countries, become more monstrous, until men are beginning to ask what over-proportion of the geographical area the ladies mean to occupy.'

———

Life Imitates Art ❧ (October) Shortly after the publication in London of Herman Meville's *Moby-Dick*, news came from the Pacific that the ship *Ann Alexander* had sunk after being rammed by a whale.

———

Provisions for an Alpine Ascent ❧ Murray's guidebook to the Alps averred, regarding those who had climbed Mont Blanc, 'It is a somewhat remarkable fact that a large proportion of those who have made this ascent have been persons of unsound mind.' That same year the showman Albert Smith climbed the mountain with three Oxford undergraduates, each man being accompanied, as local regulations dictated, by four guides. Such a large party required the services of some 20 porters to carry the provisions, comprising:

60 bottles of vin ordinaire
6 bottles of Bordeaux
10 bottles of St George
15 bottles of St Jean
3 bottles of Cognac
1 bottle of syrup of raspberries
6 bottles of lemonade
2 bottles of champagne
20 loaves
10 small cheeses
6 packets of chocolate

6 packets of sugar
4 packets of prunes
4 packets of raisins
2 packets of salt
4 wax candles
6 lemons
4 legs of mutton
6 pieces of veal
1 piece of beef
11 large fowls
35 small fowls

In contrast, when Professor John Tyndall, who suffered from chronic indigestion and insomnia, made the first ascent of another Alpine giant, the Weisshorn, in August 1861, he survived on a diet of 12 meat lozenges, and undertook the climb after 48 hours without sleep.

1852

Ophelia Catches Cold

Ophelia Catches Cold 🍂 Elizabeth Siddal, John Everett Millais's model for his painting *Ophelia*, caught a bad chill while posing for him lying in a bath (Ophelia is depicted having drowned herself in a flower-strewn stream). Her father threatened to sue the artist until he agreed to pay her medical expenses.

Strange Discoveries in Virginia and Massachusetts

Strange Discoveries in Virginia and Massachusetts 🍂 (5 June) The *Scientific American* (Volume 7, issue 38) reported a story in the Fairmont (Va.) *True Virginian* that a landslip had revealed a stretch of Macadamized (i.e. tarmac) road some 16 feet wide where no such road had hitherto been recorded. 'When and by what race of people this road was made,' mused the *True Virginian*, 'is unknown at the present day, but it gives evidence of the existence of a population here at some former age of the world, as far advanced in civilization, or at least in the art of road making, as ourselves.' The more sceptical *Scientific American* observed, 'We have oftentimes seen round stones embedded in what is called "hard pan" stratum, and so thick that they looked like an old Macadamized road; but they were merely hard worn water courses of the olden time, never made by mortal hands.' In the same issue, the magazine carried a report from the *Boston Transcript* that during blasting of puddingstone some 15 feet below the surface of Dorchester, Massachusetts, there was blown out of the ground 'a curious and unknown vessel' made of some kind of metal, carrying floral decorations inlaid with silver. Those prone to credit stories of Atlantis have pointed out that the 'Dorchester pot' (which has subsequently disappeared) is surely another OOPArt (out-of-place artefact) proving the existence of lost civilizations of unimaginable technological advancement. Alternatively, creationists use such tales to 'prove' that the Earth is as young as is suggested in the Bible. The *Scientific American* suggested that the Dorchester pot was 'perhaps made by Tubal Cain, the first inhabitant of Dorchester' (an ironic reference to the first metalworker, Genesis 4:22).

1853

The Bog That Went for a Walk ❧ (3 January) On a night of teeming rain, a bog around a mile in circumference at Enagh Monmore in Ireland began to move down sloping ground. Twenty-four hours later it came to rest, having shifted about a quarter of a mile.

***

Doktor Kuckenmeister's Gruesome Experiment ❧ Herr Doktor Friedrich Kuckenmeister conducted a pioneering medical experiment on a prisoner awaiting execution. He persuaded the prison authorities to allow him to feed the unfortunate man a soup made from meat laced with cysts. Six weeks later the man was hanged, and when he was cut down, Kuckenmeister performed the autopsy. He found the man's digestive tract riddled with tapeworms, confirming his suspicions that cysts in animal carcases formed part of the lifecycle of these parasites. Had the condemned man been allowed to live, the tapeworms would have grown and grown, feeding on his digested food, and might have reached a length of 30 m (100 ft).

***

A Tedious Maiden Speech ❧ Lord Robert Cecil, later Marquis of Salisbury and three times Conservative prime minister, entered the House of Commons. In the middle of his maiden speech he seemed to tire of his subject, yawned and sat down.

***

The Mad Maids of Morzine ❧ An outbreak of supposed demonic possession began in Morzine, a town in the foothills of the French Alps south of Lake Geneva. The outbreak followed the case of a young girl thought to be possessed by the Devil, who had been taken to Besançon and exorcized by means of the handkerchief of Christ, a relic kept in that city's cathedral. This miraculous outcome seems to have encouraged others in

Morzine to show symptoms of demonic possession, such as speaking in tongues (particularly Arabic), suffering from convulsions, clambering up trees with the speed of a squirrel, and uttering foul obscenities and hideous blasphemies. But as suddenly as the outbreak had started, it stopped.

Shortly afterwards, Professor Tissot, of the school of medicine at Dijon, visited Morzine to investigate. He found that victims of possession had almost all been young women between the ages of 18 and 25, that the holy water used in the exorcisms was only effective in casting out Satan if the subject knew it was being administered, that the witnesses who had sworn the girls were speaking Arabic were entirely ignorant of that language so could not have told Arabic from gobbledegook, and that the outbreak had ended when the government had transferred two of the town's more zealous clerics elsewhere and sent in the police to inform the townspeople that anyone behaving in an irregular manner would be diagnosed as insane and locked up in a lunatic asylum.

The Empress's Little Problem &. (23 March) Karl Marx wrote to Friedrich Engels concerning the Empress Eugénie, the consort of Napoleon III:

> That angel suffers, it seems, from a most indelicate complaint. She is passionately addicted to *farting* and is incapable, even in company, of suppressing it. At one time she resorted to horse-riding as a remedy. But this having now been forbidden by her Bonaparte, she 'vents' herself. It's only a noise, a little murmur, a nothing, but then you know that the French are sensitive to the slightest puff of wind.

1854

Cannibalism in the High Arctic &. The Scottish explorer John Rae, while travelling in Arctic Canada, learnt from the Inuit something of the fate of the expedition of Sir John Franklin, which had set sail to find a way through the Northwest Passage in 1847 but had not been heard of since. The evidence strongly suggested that Franklin's men had resorted to cannibalism, and for this reason, when Rae returned to London, the authorities suppressed his story, and Rae himself was shunned by the Establishment. In the 1990s, examination of the bodies of some of the lost expedition revealed cut marks on the bones consistent with the flesh having been trimmed off with a knife.

1855

The Spending of the First Pennies &c British public lavatories began charging a standard 1d (one old penny) for admission, a charge that remained unchanged until decimalization in 1971. Hence the euphemism 'to spend a penny'.

Liszt Decomposes &c (30 June) The *Musical World* (London) warned its readers against the music of Liszt: 'Composition indeed! – decomposition is the word for such hateful fungi.'

The Ghost Ship of the Davis Strait &c (17 September) An American whaler, the *George Henry*, encountered an unmanned ship in the Davis Strait, near Cape Mercy. This was the *Resolute*, which had been abandoned on 15 May 1854 off Melville Island by her crew, the vessel having become stuck fast in the ice. In the intervening 16 months, the *Resolute* – which had been sent out to search for Sir John Franklin's lost expedition – had made a journey of around a thousand miles, without a soul on board.

1856

Five Minutes in China &c Charles Dickens moved to Gad's Hill, and installed a secret door to his study, concealed by a false bookcase containing the spines of dummy books whose titles he delighted in creating. These included *A Carpenter's Bench of Bishops*, *Shelley's Oysters*, the three-volume *Five Minutes in China* and the nine-volume *Cats' Lives*.

Mount Eve-rest
🙢 Andrew Waugh, Surveyor General of India, proposed that the newly measured Peak XV, thought to be the highest peak in the region, should be named after his predecessor, Sir George Everest. The latter pronounced his name 'Eve-rest' (as in Adam and Eve), but his eponymous mountain has been mispronounced ever since.

On the Undesirability of Brains
🙢 Prince George, Duke of Cambridge, a grandson of George III, became commander-in-chief of the British army. He was known for his resistance to innovation and reform, his motto being 'There is a time for everything, and the time for change is when you can no longer help it.' He promoted officers largely on the basis of their rank in society, once telling a subordinate, 'Brains! I don't believe in brains. You haven't any, I know, sir.' He was eventually eased out of his post in 1895.

1857

Strange Meteorological Phenomena
🙢 (2 May) It was reported from Hungary that a mirage rendered visible the inscriptions on tombstones in a village 5 km (3 miles) distant. The locals confidently predicted the end of the world was nigh. Three weeks later, on 20 May, a dust storm plunged the city of Baghdad into a darkness 'deeper than the darkest night'. People again prepared for the end of the world, but the darkness lifted when large quantities of sand fell from the sky.

The Hills are Alive with Poets and Professors
🙢 Charles Algernon Swinburne, poet of sadomasochism and decadence, made his only appearance in the annals of mountaineering history when, in the company of fellow republican, atheist and drunk, Professor John Nichol, he made the first recorded ascent of Bla Bheinn, a rocky mountain in the Cuillin of Skye.

Tales from the Mutiny ᔥ (23 September) Death of General John Nicholson, from wounds sustained during the recapture of Delhi from the Indian mutineers. Earlier in his career, while serving as a district commissioner, Nicholson had been worshipped as the god 'Nikal Seyn', supposedly an avatar of Vishnu (he had some his worshippers imprisoned and whipped). In response to the massacre of British civilians during the Mutiny, Nicholson had proposed 'a bill for the flaying alive, impalement or burning of the murderers of the women and children of Delhi'. In fact the British came up with an even more brutal vengeance: many of the sepoys were punished by being tied across the muzzles of cannon, which were then fired. At Barrackpore two Englishwomen dressed in white rode up to view such an execution at close quarters, and rode away covered with blood, apparently well pleased that justice had been done.

After the suppression of the Indian Mutiny, some of the rebellious sepoys were, by way of retribution, blown from the mouths of cannon.

The Sea Serpent of St Helena ❧ (12 December) The ship *Castilian*, en route to Liverpool from Bombay, encountered an unusual creature in the seas near St Helena, in the south Atlantic. The master, Captain G.H. Harrington, lodged the following report with the Board of Trade:

> While myself and officers were standing on the lee-side of the poop, looking towards the island, we were startled by the sight of a huge marine animal, which reared its head out of the water, within twenty yards of the ship; when it suddenly disappeared for about half a minute, and then made its appearance in the same manner again – showing us distinctly its neck and head, about ten or twelve feet out of the water. Its head was shaped like a long nun-buoy; and I suppose the diameter to have been seven or eight feet in the largest part, with a kind of scroll, or tuft of loose skin, encircling it about two feet from the top.
>
> The water was discoloured for several hundred feet from its head: so much so, that on its first appearance my impression was that the ship was in broken water, produced, as I supposed, by some volcanic agency since the last time I passed the island; but the second appearance completely dispelled those fears, and assured us that it was a monster of extraordinary length, which appeared to be moving slowly towards the land. The ship was going too fast, to enable us to reach the mast-head in time to form a correct estimate of its extreme length; but from what we saw from the deck, we conclude that it must have been over two hundred feet long. The boatswain and several of the crew who observed it from the top-gallant fore-castle, state that it was more than double the length of the ship, in which case it must have been five hundred feet. Be that as it may, I am convinced that it belonged to the serpent tribe; it was of a dark colour about the head, and was covered with several white spots.

1858

Pope Seizes Child from Parents ❧ (23 July) In the Jewish ghetto of Bologna, then part of the Papal States, the police called at the house of the Mortara family to take away their six-year-old son Edgardo. They had been

informed that Edgardo had been baptized by a Christian servant of the family, and it was against the laws of the Papal States for a Christian child to be raised by Jews. Pope Pius IX regarded Edgardo as his spiritual child, and refused requests from various European governments and heads of state to return the boy to his parents. The pope himself blamed the case for the lack of support he received in his failed attempt to maintain his temporal power against the encroachments of the new Italian state. Pope John Paul II beatified Pius in 2000, placing him on the fast track for canonization.

1859

A Treatise on Root Vegetables &. Publication of *On the Composition of a Mangold-Wurzel Kept for Two Years* by Dr Augustus Voelcker.

Remember, Remember ... &. Repeal of the law requiring everybody in England and Wales to attend church every 5 November to celebrate the foiling of the Gunpowder Plot in 1605.

A Whiff of Sulphur &. (19 March) Premier of the opera *Faust* by Charles Gounod. Because *Faust* was so much more successful than Gounod's other operas, one contemporary critic suggested that Gounod could not have written it – but withdrew this accusation after the composer challenged him to a duel. After Gounod's death there re-emerged rumours about the opera's authorship, some suggesting that Gounod had stolen the score from a mad but brilliant composer locked up in a mental institution.

The Emperor of the United States &. Joshua A. Norton, a citizen of San Francisco who had lost a fortune speculating in rice, proclaimed himself 'Emperor of these United States and Protector of Mexico', and shortly afterwards dissolved the United States Congress. The people of San Francisco humoured the Emperor Norton I for more than twenty years, until his death in 1880, and helped to subsidize his very modest lifestyle (he lodged in a boarding house). He issued his own currency, which was honoured in the establishments he patronized, and his decree that a bridge be built across San Francisco Bay was eventually obeyed when the Bay Bridge began construction in 1933. Among his other decrees was that strife between religions and sects should cease, and that the nations of the world should come together in a league. He himself stopped an anti-Chinese riot by standing, head bowed, in front of the rioters, repeating the Lord's Prayer again and again until, shamed, they dispersed. When in 1867 the police attempted to incarcerate Norton in a mental institution there was public outrage. Norton was released, and the Chief of Police issued an apology. Tens of thousands of citizens lined the streets on the day of Norton's funeral, and the day afterwards the skies went dark as the sun entered a total eclipse.

Across Niagara on a Tightrope

Across Niagara on a Tightrope ❧ Charles Blondin made the first of several tightrope walks across Niagara Falls. The wire was 335 m (1100 ft) long, suspended 50 m (160 ft) above the water. On the various occasions that he undertook this feat, he would add little touches, such as walking backwards or blindfolded or with a man on his back. In the middle of one crossing he stopped to make himself an omelette.

The Pig War ❧ (15 June) Lyman Cutler, an American settler on San Juan Island, a territory in the Pacific northwest claimed by both the USA and Britain, shot a pig belonging to Charles Griffin, an employee of the Hudson Bay Company, and almost precipitated a war. Prior to the shooting (the only fatality of the so-called Pig War), it is said that Cutler had yelled at Griffin, 'Keep your pigs out of my potatoes,' to which Griffin had replied, 'Keep your potatoes out of my pigs!' Griffin demanded $100 compensation, but was refused, and when the British authorities threatened to arrest Cutler, the American settlers on the island called for military protection. Both sides sent contingents of troops to San Juan, and the situation began to escalate, although Admiral Baynes of the Royal Navy refused the order of the governor of Vancouver Island to engage the enemy, opining that 'a squabble about a pig' was not justification enough for a war between two great nations. Eventually, it was agreed that both sides should maintain a military presence on the island, and in 1872 a commission of arbitration under Kaiser Wilhelm I of Germany allocated the territory to the USA. Nevertheless, park rangers still fly the Union Jack above the 'British Camp' at the north end of San Juan Island.

1860

An April Fool in London (1 April) An April Fool was successfully perpetrated upon a large number of people in London, who received a card with an official-looking seal and the following message:

TOWER OF LONDON
Admit the Bearer and Friend to view the Annual
Ceremony of Washing the White Lions
on Sunday, April 1st, 1860.
Admitted only at the White Gate.
It is particularly requested that no gratuities be given
to the Wardens or their Assistants.

On the morning appointed, a Sunday, there were said to be crowds of people vainly attempting to find the White Gate of the Tower.

Hanged from the Yardarm (13 July) Private John Dalinger of the Royal Marines became the last man to be hanged from the yardarm when he swung from the spars of HMS *Leven* off China. He had tried to kill the ship's captain.

A Fickle Twist of Fate (August) Otto von Bismarck, Prussian ambassador to Paris, was swept out to sea with his mistress, Katharina Orloff, while swimming off Biarritz. The couple were rescued with some difficulty by a French lifeguard, Pierre Lafleur, who had to revive the unconscious Bismarck. Lafleur was drowned four weeks later, while Bismarck went on to mastermind the creation of the German Empire and the defeat of France in the Franco-Prussian War. However, he did become godfather to Lafleur's orphan son.

———

Experimental Zoophagy ❧ Francis Buckland, the naturalist, presided over the first dinner of the Acclimatization Society, whose purpose was to see which exotic animals might suitably be bred in Britain for the table. The menu included sea slug, kangaroo and curassow, and on other occasions Buckland enthusiastically subjected his taste buds, in the interests of science and progress, to squirrel, hedgehog, frog, snail, roasted fieldmouse, elephant trunk, rhinoceros pie, porpoise, barbequed giraffe (there had been a fire in their quarters at London Zoo) and disinterred panther (having heard that the specimen at the Surrey Zoological Gardens had died, he wrote to ask whether he might have the corpse). His father, William Buckland, a distinguished geologist, claimed to have eaten the embalmed heart of Louis XIV.

———

The Kingdom of Araucania and Patagonia ❧ (17 November) Foundation in southern South America of the independent Kingdom of Araucania and Patagonia, also called Nouvelle France. The first king was a French lawyer and adventurer, Orélie-Antoine de Tounens, who sympathized with the efforts of the local Mapuche people to resist encroachments on their land by Chile and Argentina. The Mapuche, believing that having a European such as Tounens as their leader would aid their cause, duly elected him king. He was arrested in 1862 by the Chilean authorities, but the French consul managed to persuade them that Tounens was insane, and arranged for his repatriation. Tounens subsequently made a number of unsuccessful attempts to repossess his kingdom, and died in poverty in France in 1878. Various of his relatives continued to claim the throne of Nouvelle France, although the current pretender, Prince Felipe, has renounced his claim.

1861

Cold Baths with Mrs Beeton ✒ Mrs Beeton published her *Book of Household Management*, in which she decried the use of garlic and recommended a cold or tepid bath be taken every morning.

1862

The Footless Duke ✒ At the death of Alexander Douglas, 10th Duke of Hamilton, it was discovered that the ancient Egyptian sarcophagus that the duke had purchased ten years earlier as his final resting place was too short for his embalmed corpse. To solve the problem, his feet were cut off and buried beside him.

1863

Farmer Reads Shakespeare to Labourers ✒ Death of John Alington, a philanthropic farmer from Letchworth, who would read his labourers extracts from Shakespeare as they worked, and who liked to be transported round his garden in an open coffin.

Strange and Cruel Punishments ✒ An old law passed under Henry VIII in 1530 was eventually repealed. It required that those convicted of wilful poisoning should be boiled alive. It was not until 1870 that hanging, drawing and quartering, the traditional punishment for traitors, was abolished.

1864

Famous Last Words ✒ (May) At the Battle of Spotsylvania Court House during the American Civil War, the Confederate general 'Uncle John'

Sedgewick berated his men for taking cover. 'They couldn't hit an elephant at this distance,' he shouted. They could – moments later Sedgewick took a fatal bullet.

1865

Head of Army Medical Services Proves to be Female 🦶

Death of Dr James Barrie, the distinguished army physician who rose to become medical superintendent general, and whose career was punctuated by the fighting of a number of duels. Post-mortem examination revealed Barry to have been a woman.

Cows on the White House Lawn 🦶

(15 April) Andrew Johnson became president on the assassination of Abraham Lincoln. After the former vice-president moved into the White House, his daughter, who ran the household, installed two Jersey cows on the lawns, to keep the family in milk and butter.

1866

Treated Worse than Dogs 🦶

(10 April) Henry Bergh founded the American Society for the Prevention of Cruelty to Animals. One of his chief concerns was the use of dogs to turn roasting spits in restaurants. After legislation was passed to outlaw this practice, Bergh would drop into restaurants to check that dogs were no longer being used for this monotonous and cruelly hot work. He found that the dogs had been replaced by black children.

The Mercy of Slaves 🦶

(May) After the Civil War, the former Confederate president Jefferson Davis was indicted for treason, a charge that attracted the death penalty. Among those who petitioned for mercy were former slaves on Jefferson's own plantation. The case against Jefferson was dropped in February 1869.

———

Brotherly Love 🐝 (June) Near the start of the Seven Weeks' War between Prussia and Austria, Bismarck, the Prussian chancellor ordered General Manteuffel to advance into Austrian territory. 'Treat them like fellow Germans,' he advised the general. 'Homicidally if necessary.'

1867

———

Cannibals Eat Missionary 🐝 A missionary to Fiji, the Revd Thomas Baker, was cooked and eaten, having offended the chief by removing a comb from the headman's hair. In 2003 the chief's descendant issued an apology to the Baker family.

Another missionary heads for the pot, this time in the New Hebrides, c. 1905.

1868

—

Hara-Kiri 🍂 A British diplomat in Japan, Algernon Bertram Freeman-Mitford (later Lord Redesdale), witnessed the seppuku or hara-kiri (ritual suicide) of a samurai who had ordered an attack upon foreigners in Kobe. He recounted his experience in *Tales of Old Japan* (1871):

> Bowing once more, the speaker allowed his upper garments to slip down to his girdle, and remained naked to the waist. Carefully, according to custom, he tucked his sleeves under his knees to prevent himself from falling backwards; for a noble Japanese gentleman should die falling forwards. Deliberately, with a steady hand, he took the dirk that lay before him; he looked at it wistfully, almost affectionately; for a moment he seemed to collect his thoughts for the last time, and then stabbing himself deeply below the waist on the left-hand side, he drew the dirk slowly across to the right side, and, turning it in the wound, gave a slight cut upwards. During this sickeningly painful operation he never moved a muscle of his face. When he drew out the dirk, he leaned forward and stretched out his neck; an expression of pain for the first time crossed his face, but he uttered no sound. At that moment the kaishaku, who, still crouching by his side, had been keenly watching his every movement, sprang to his feet, poised his sword for a second in the air; there was a flash, a heavy, ugly thud, a crashing fall; with one blow the head had been severed from the body.
>
> A dead silence followed, broken only by the hideous noise of the blood throbbing out of the inert heap before us, which but a moment before had been a brave and chivalrous man. It was horrible.

—

The Last Public Hanging in Britain 🍂 (26 May) Michael Barrett became the last man to be hanged in public in Britain.

—

Fear of Being Buried Alive 🍂 (22 July) Miss Hannah Beswick, who had died in 90 years previously, was at last buried. Because she had had a fear of being buried alive, she left £25,000 to her physician, Charles White, with

orders that he was to examine her regularly for signs of life. Dr White had her embalmed and kept her in the case of a grandfather clock in his attic, where he duly attended her on an annual basis, accompanied by a witness. After White's death, Miss Beswick's body eventually came into the custody of the Manchester Museum of Natural History, whose trustees agreed that she was indeed dead, and had her interred in the city's general cemetery.

The same year that Miss Beswick was finally laid to rest, the US inventor Franz Vester came up with an idea for a coffin with an escape hatch and a ladder, 'should a person be interred ere life is extinct'. If the prospect of ascending the ladder was too daunting, the prematurely buried person could pull a cord attached to a bell on the surface to draw attention to their plight.

An Eccentric Vicar ֍ The Revd Sabine Baring-Gould, author of 'Onward, Christian Soldiers', married Grace Taylor, an illiterate 16-year-old mill girl. The marriage, which lasted for 48 years, inspired George Bernard Shaw's *Pygmalion*. Baring-Gould was said to teach with a pet bat sitting on his shoulder, and at a party for his own children he asked one child present, 'And whose little girl are you?' The girl burst into tears and sobbed, 'I'm yours, Daddy.'

1869

For the Sake of His Art ֍ The painter Dante Gabriel Rossetti, wishing to resume his second career as a poet, had the corpse of his wife Elizabeth Siddal dug up so he could retrieve the manuscript of poems he had buried with her in 1862.

One Can't Get the Staff ֍ Death of James Carr-Boyle, 5th Earl of Glasgow, a racehorse owner of uncertain temper. On one occasion he dropped in on the Doncaster Club in the middle of the night, only to find there was no one up to serve him a whisky. Incensed, the Earl sought out the steward's room and set fire to his bed.

1870

The Romance of Chastisement ❧ Publication of *The Romance of Chastisement: or, Revelations of the School and Bedroom*, by Lieutenant St George H. Stock of the Queen's Royal Regiment.

Tit for Tat ❧ Alfred, Lord Tennyson was taken aback when, having asked for an opinion of his latest, not yet published poem, Benjamin Jowett, Master of Balliol College, Oxford, replied, 'I shouldn't publish that, if I were you, Tennyson.' Quick as a flash, Tennyson responded, 'If it comes to that, Master, the sherry you gave us at lunch was downright filthy.'

1871

Roast Cat and Carpaccio of Spaniel ❧ During the Prussian siege of Paris, the starving inhabitants were wont to resort to such dishes as donkey steak, rat salami, carpaccio of spaniel, roast cat, and kittens served in an onion ragout.

1872

The *Marie Celeste* Found Unharmed and Crewless ❧ (5 December) The *Marie Celeste* was found drifting west of Gibraltar. It had set sail from New York the previous month with a crew of ten. When it was found, the ship was intact, but no one was on board.

1873

When Poets Fall Out 🙚 The poet Paul Verlaine shot his lover, the poet Arthur Rimbaud, in a hotel room in Brussels.

1874

Bertie the Brothel Creeper 🙚 The Prince of Wales (the future Edward VII, and known to his family as 'Bertie') made the first visit to Paris of any member of the British royal family since the Revolution. He began an enthusiastic patronage of the brothels of the French capital that was to last a lifetime. He even had his own room in the most exclusive of Parisian bordellos, 12 rue Chabanais, where he would bathe in champagne and devised *la chaise Edouard*, also known *as la siège d'amour*, a complex and adaptable contraption on which, for example, he could comfortably perform cunnilingus on one woman while being fellated by another.

1875

A Deadly Souvenir 🙚 The King of Fiji brought back measles from a state visit to Australia and wiped out a quarter of his own people.

———

A Cad and a Bounder 🙚 (17 June) Colonel Valentine Baker (49), a friend of the Prince of Wales, indecently assaulted Rebecca Dickenson (21) on the Portsmouth-to-London train. To escape the unwanted attentions of the married father of two, Miss Dickenson was obliged to scramble out of the door, perch herself precariously on the running board and hang on for dear life as the train sped past Walton. Her plight was observed, and the train was stopped at Esher. Baker was later sentenced to one year in jail and cashiered from the army.

The Victorians did not believe in sparing the rod, and flagellation for grown men blossomed into a flourishing, albeit secret, sub-culture. The 'Romance of Chastisement', as Lieutenant St George H. Stock termed it (*see* 1870), is here captured by Aubrey Beardsley.

1876

Taking a Turkey to be One's Father ❧ Death of Adolphus Cooke, one of many eccentric Anglo-Irish landowners. Cooke's weakness was that he took a turkey on his estate near Mullingar to be the reincarnation of his dead father, and ordered that his servants show it due deference.

—

Amazon Warriors at Little Big Horn ❧ (25–6 June) Among the Native Americans who participated at the Battle of Little Big Horn, in which Custer and his 7th Cavalry were massacred, were the women warriors known as Buffalo Calf Road Woman, Little Hollow Wood, Moving Robe Woman and One Who Walks With the Stars. The last named fighter clubbed and slashed two cavalrymen to death on the banks of the Little Big Horn River.

1877

Pro and Contra Onan 🐚 Publication of *Pathology and Treatment of Spermatorrhoea*, in which Dr J.L. Milton argued against the practice of onanism, which, he held, wastes the body's precious fluids and results in madness and death. The same year saw the publication of Henry Spencer Ashbee's *Index Librorum Prohibitorum* ('index of forbidden books'), an extensive bibliography of erotic and pornographic literature. Ashbee was the model of Christopher Lilly in Sarah Waters's novel *Fingersmith* (2002).

1878

Swedish Withdrawal from the Americas 🐚 The Swedes sold their sole Caribbean possession, the island of Saint-Barthélemy, back to the French, from whom whey had bought it in 1785. The island is now part of the French *département* of Guadeloupe, but the main town is still known as Gustavia – named after the Swedish king, Gustav III.

Married Life in the Army 🐚 Death of Mrs Nash, company laundress of the 7th Cavalry at Fort Meade, and 'wife' to a succession of US cavalrymen. It was discovered as her body was prepared for burial that Mrs Nash had, in fact, been a man. When her latest 'husband', a corporal, returned from campaign, he shot himself.

1879

Biscuits not Bullets 🐚 (22 January) As the Zulus attacked at the Battle of Isandlwana the British redcoats turned to their ammunition boxes, only to find they were filled with biscuits, not bullets. Out of a force of 1400 men, fewer than 100 survived the Zulu onslaught.

———

Wonders in the Skies ❧ (7 June) A brilliant meteor, moving in a serpentine path, was seen in the skies above Switzerland. Around the same time, a shower of objects fell into Lake Lugano, causing a series of large waves that almost swamped a number of fishing boats.

1880

———

Dog Awarded Medal ❧ (27 July) One of the few survivors from the British force wiped out by Afghans at Maiwand was a dog called Bobbie, whose master, Sergeant Kelly of the 66th Foot, had been killed. Bobbie found his own way back to regimental headquarters, 80 km (50 miles) away at Kandahar, and was later presented with the Afghan Medal by Queen Victoria.

1881

———

Loving Talk with Soldiers ❧ Publication of *Hurrah! A Bit of Loving Talk with Soldiers* by Samuel Gillespie Prout.

———

World Fails to End ❧ The end of the world failed to manifest itself, despite the prediction of Mother Shipton (1488–1561):

> The world to an end will come
> In Eighteen Hundred and Eighty-One.

In fact most of Mother Shipton's predictions were made up by a man called Hindley in 1871.

———

Darwin's Musical Worms ❧ Charles Darwin published his much overlooked work, *The Formation of Vegetable Mould through the Action of*

Worms with Observation of their Habits. Regarding the latter, Darwin was interested in the degree to which worms might be said to display musicality, and concluded:

> Worms do not possess any sense of hearing. They took not the least notice of the shrill notes from a metal whistle, which was repeatedly sounded near them; nor did they of the deepest and loudest tones of a bassoon. They were indifferent to shouts, if care was taken that the breath did not strike them. When placed on a table close to the keys of a piano, which was played as loudly as possible, they remained perfectly quiet. Although they are indifferent to undulations in the air audible by us, they are extremely sensitive to vibrations in any solid object. When the pots containing two worms which had remained quite indifferent to the sound of the piano, were placed on this instrument, and the note C in the bass clef was struck, both instantly retreated into their burrows. After a time they emerged, and when G above the line in the treble clef was struck they again retreated. Under similar circumstances on another night one worm dashed into its burrow on a very high note being struck only once, and the other worm when C in the treble clef was struck.

———

Man-Eating Trees in Madagascar &. The traveller Carl Liche published an eyewitness account of the sacrifice of a young woman of the Mkodo tribe of Madagascar to a man-eating tree, which, 'as if instinct with demoniac intelligence, fastened upon her in sudden coils round and round her neck and arms ... here trickled down the stalk of the tree great streams of the viscid honey-like fluid, mingled horribly with the blood and oozing viscera of the victim ... May I never see such a sight again.' However, it later transpired that not only was the man-eating tree a hoax, so were the Mkodo tribe and Carl Liche himself. It is possible that the tall tale was inspired by the island's agy tree, which has stinging hairs reportedly many times more painful than a nettle.

1882

—

Mass Fish Death 🐟 (Spring) The surface of an area of sea some 480 km (300 miles) in extent off the east coast of America was covered with the corpses of an estimated 1400 million fish. It was thought that the fish might have been killed by an incursion of a cold-water current following severe storms.

The Sleeper of Paris 🐟 In Paris a young woman, presumed to be drunk, was picked up by police. As the woman failed to recover consciousness, she was committed to the Hôpital Beaujon, where she remained in a 'lethargic sleep' for 74 days, baffling the medical authorities, until eventually aroused with douches of cold water.

1883

—

The Cultivation of Personal Perfection 🐟 Establishment in Britain of the Fellowship of the New Life, whose aim was 'the cultivation of a perfect character in each and all'.

1884

—

Cremating Jesu Grist 🐟 (13 January) The druid and former Chartist agitator Dr William Price attempted to cremate his son Jesu Grist on Caerlan Fields, Llantrisant, in a barrel of paraffin. He was stopped by the police and brought before the courts, but was able to satisfy the judge that cremation breached no laws. In March Price made a second, and this time successful, attempt to cremate his son on Caerlan Fields, with the aid of half a ton of coal. Cremation was formally legalized in 1902.

———

The Great Colchester Earthquake 🐚 (22 April) Colchester and surrounding villages were rocked by an earthquake measuring 6.9 on the Richter Scale. Over a thousand buildings were destroyed.

1885

———

Thos. Cook and Gordon of Khartoum 🐚 (28 January) A huge relief force arrived in Khartoum, two days after General Gordon, had been killed by the Mahdi's forces. The relief force sent up the Nile to Khartoum involved 18,000 soldiers, 40,000 tonnes of supplies, 800 whaleboats, 650 luggers, 7000 railway trucks, 27 steamers and 40,000 tonnes of coal. The relief force may have arrived too late to save Gordon, but no one blamed the travel arrangements – organized by Thomas Cook & Son.

Gordon himself had earlier attempted to establish the site of the Crucifixion, the location of the Garden of Eden, and precisely where Noah's Ark had come to rest after the Flood had subsided.

1886

———

The End of a Fairy-Tale King 🐚 (13 June) Death of 'Mad' King Ludwig II of Bavaria, known as the *Märchenkönig* ('fairy-tale king') in German on account of his construction of such fantastic edifices as Neuschwanstein, the famous 'fairy-tale' castle, and his extravagant patronage of the composer Richard Wagner, for whom he funded the construction of the opera house at Bayreuth. Ludwig had been declared insane on 10 June by Professor Bernhard von Gudden (possibly at the behest of his political enemies, aghast at the king's spendthrift ways), and was held at Schloss Berg, south of Munich. On the day of his death he asked the professor to accompany him – alone – along the shores of Lake Starnberg. They set off at 6.30 pm, and when they did not return a search party was sent out. At 11.30 that night both men were found dead in shallow water near the shore. The inquest declared that

Ludwig had committed suicide by drowning, although he was a good swimmer and the autopsy report suggests there was no water found in his lungs.

———

Brahms a 'Giftless Bastard' ❧ (9 October) Tchaikovsky noted in his diary: 'I played over the music of that scoundrel Brahms. What a giftless bastard!'

———

A Disreputable Prime Minister ❧ Lord Salisbury, the British prime minister at the time, was refused entry to the casino at Monte Carlo on the grounds that he was dressed like a tramp.

1887

———

Fifteen-Year-Old Wins Wimbledon ❧ The ladies' singles championship at Wimbledon was won by a 15-year-old English girl called Lottie Dod.

———

Sculptor Shoots Pet Python ❧ *Dryope Fascinated by Apollo in the Form of a Serpent*, a sculpture by Robert 'Pen' Barrett Browning, son of the poet, was rejected by the Royal Academy. The creation of the work had caused the sculptor no little upset, for the pet python that he used threatened to strangle his naked Italian model, Adelia Abbruzzesi, and, even though he was an animal lover, he was obliged to shoot the unfortunate reptile.

1888

———

An Indecent Act with a Duck ❧ James Brown, a young man of the county of Essex, was found guilty at Chelmsford assizes of an indecent act with a duck, despite a legal argument that a duck was not an animal within the meaning of the act prohibiting bestiality.

———

Marie the First, King of the Sedang 🔔 (3 June) In the remote village of Kon Gung in the Central Highlands of what is now Vietnam, a French adventurer and alleged fraudster called Charles-Marie David de Mayréna declared himself Marie the First, King of the Sedang. He had established his small kingdom in the territory of a number of tribes, between the fiefdoms of the king of Siam and the emperor of Annam. King Marie issued stamps and awarded honours – including aristocratic titles and knighthoods – to his supporters. He offered his kingdom to the French in exchange for a trading monopoly, and then to the British, but neither appeared to be enthusiastic. He then travelled to Belgium to stir up interest and support, but when he returned to the Orient he found that the French would not allow him to enter any port in Indochina. He died on 11 November 1890 in Malaya. The circumstances of his death remain a mystery. Sedang was subsequently annexed by the French.

On 2 November 1995, in Montreal, some of the descendants of those on whom King Marie had bestowed honours formed the Assembly for the Restoration of the Sedang Nobility. In the absence of any known heir of King Marie, the Assembly adopted a 'Constitution of the Regency', elected Colonel Derwin J.K.W. Mak as 'Prince Regent et Duc de Sédang', and renounced any territorial claims over Sedang, which it recognizes as the sovereign territory of Vietnam. The following year they established diplomatic relations with the leader of the Melkite Catholics of the Levant, His Beatitude Maximos V Hakim, Patriarch of Antioch and all the East, of Alexandria and of Jerusalem. The same year also saw a treaty of friendship with the Order of the Holy Western Empire, based in Belgium. Colonel Mak resigned as Regent in 1997, and was succeeded as Regent Pro Tempore by the Marshal of the Assembly, the Comtesse Capucine Plourde de Kasara. In 1998 the Assembly became the Sedang Royalist Assembly, and in 1999 a descendant of King Marie's brother was found by genealogists working on the Assembly's behalf, but this descendant demonstrated little interest in his patrimony. Among its several aims, the Assembly seeks 'to re-establish and promote the social institutions of monarchy and nobility and practise their principles in a world which has largely forgotten them: chivalry, honour, duty, loyalty, respect, enlightenment, tolerance'. The Sedang Chancellery is currently located at 711 Bay Street, suite 517, Toronto, Ontario, M5G 2J8, Canada.

———

Ear Floors Whore ❧ (23 December) Vincent Van Gogh cut off part of his left hear, wrapped it up in newspaper and presented it to a woman called Rachel, who worked in the local brothel in Arles. The painter asked her to look after it carefully, but when curiosity got the better of her she opened the package, and promptly fainted.

1889
———

On the Psychic Life of Micro-Organisms ❧ Publication of
The Psychic Life of Micro-Organisms, by Alfred Binet, better known as the originator of the IQ test.

———

Man Falls Over Niagara in Barrel ❧ Carlisle Graham, an
English-born cooper, survived the descent of the Niagara Falls in a barrel of his own devising, although he was unconscious when rescued by his associates at the foot of the falls. The *Manchester Guardian* commented that 'His workmanship is evidently better than his wits.'

———

Bovril, Food of the Master Race ❧ Formation of the Bovril
Company. The beef extract had its origins in Johnston's Fluid Beef, supplied to Napoleon III's armies in the Franco-Prussian War of 1870–1 by a Scottish grocer called John Lawson Johnston. The name Bovril was a combination of 'bovine' and 'vril', the latter word deriving from Edward Bulwer-Lytton's 1870 science fiction novel *Vril: The Power of the Coming Race*, in which vril was a fluid that gave superhuman powers to a subterranean master race (many readers believed the story was true; *see* 1938). In 2004 Bovril denied its name

An 1892 advertisement for Bovril, the beef extract that began production in 1889, taking its name from an early work of science fiction.

and became vegetarian, replacing beef stock with yeast mix in the wake of the ban on the export of British beef, but in 2006 it was announced that beef stock would once again be the main ingredient.

1890
—

Old Sparky ❧ New York State introduced the electric chair, supposedly as a humane alternative to hanging. Experience indicates otherwise: in 1997, during the execution of Pedro Medina on Florida's electric chair – known as Old Sparky or the Florida Flambée – flames were seen to shoot from the victim's head. The state's attorney general, Bob Butterworth, told the press: 'People who wish to commit murder, they'd better not do it in the state of Florida because we may have a problem with the electric chair.' It turned out that prison officers had not moistened the sponge on the electrode attached to the victim's head.

Problems such as this led Florida in 2000 to switch to lethal injection as the favoured mode of execution, but this method is not without its unpleasant aspects. In 2006, 27 years after the crime for which he was sentenced to death, Angel Nieves Diaz took more than half an hour to die. Witnesses said that he was still moving and grimacing with pain 20 minutes after the first injection. The director of Floridians for Alternatives to the Death Penalty said, 'He was still conscious when they put in the chemicals that burn the internal organs. It's exactly like being burned at the stake from the inside.'

1891
—

The Slander of Women Act ❧ By the Slander of Women Act, it became illegal in England and Wales to impute that a women had committed adultery or otherwise behaved in an 'unchaste' fashion. The law is still in force.

The Man Who Broke the Bank at Monte Carlo ❧ (July)

Charles Wells became 'the man who broke the bank at Monte Carlo', when, during a roulette session lasting 11 hours, he won some £16,000 from an initial purse of £4000. He had originally made his money as a confidence trickster, soliciting the wealthy to invest in such devices as a musical skipping rope. He continued in this career after his spectacular win at Monte Carlo, and his downfall came about when he lost his investors' money on the gaming tables. He subsequently served a number of sentences for fraud.

1892

The Lambeth Poisoner ❧ (3 June) Dr Thomas Neill Cream, a cross-eyed physician, was arrested for the murder of four prostitutes in south London. An inveterate self-publicist, he had previously offered a reward of £30,000 for the capture of the 'Lambeth Poisoner'. He was hanged on 15 November.

1893

The First Striptease ❧ (9 February) At the Bal des Quatre Arts, Paris, students witnessed the world's first striptease, when an artist's model called Mona, apparently under the influence of champagne, disrobed to music. She was subsequently arrested and fined 100 francs, causing the students to demonstrate in front of the Prefecture of Police, in turn necessitating intervention by the army. Some claim that the world's first striptease was in fact performed by Salome, nearly 2000 years previously. The striptease as an act developed in the burlesque theatres of the 1890s, and a popular early theme was that the woman shed her clothes one by one in search of a flea.

1896

Horror Film 🐚 (6 January) In Paris the Lumière brothers showed their pioneering 50-second film for the first time to a paying audience. The film, *The Arrival of a Train in a Station*, was said to have caused the audience to panic and flee to the back of the hall, believing they were about to be run down by the locomotive, but it has been suggested that this story may be an urban legend.

First Fatal Car Accident 🐚 (17 August) Britain's first fatal car accident takes place when Bridget Driscoll is hit by a car travelling at a reckless 4 mph at Crystal Palace, South London. The coroner expresses the hope that such a an unfortunate accident would be a unique occurrence.

The Thirty-Eight-Minute War 🐚 (27 August) Between 9.02 and 9.40 a.m. Britain was at war with Zanzibar, the shortest conflict in history. Sultan Hamad bin Thuwaini had objected to the Royal Navy sailing into his harbour, and opened fire. The Royal Navy replied in kind, destroying his palace. The sultan fled, and was replaced by the more pliant Hamoud bin Mohammed.

1897

Gentlemen and Players – Part I 🐚 The 80-year-old cricketer Charles Absolon took 101 wickets for his club, Osterley Park. In the same season, the Yorkshire and England bowler, Bobby Peel, turned up drunk for a match against Middlesex. He started bowling at a sight screen – and even, so rumour had it, relieved himself on the pitch. 'Lord Hawke put his arm round me,' Peel recalled, 'and helped me off the ground – and out of first-class cricket. What a gentleman!'

1898

A Massive Waterspout 🐾 (16 May) Possibly the highest waterspout ever recorded appeared off the coast off Eden, New South Wales, Australia. It was estimated to be over 1500 m (5000 ft) high.

———

Flying Wombats 🐾 A series of articles began to appear in *Wide World Magazine* by Louis de Rougemont, recounting his explorations in New Guinea and his 30 years living with Australian Aboriginals. Among the experiences he recounted were rides on the back of a turtle, and the unforgettable sight of wombats flying overhead. When his claims were queried by the Royal Geographical Society, de Rougemont stated that he was unable to pinpoint where he had been on the map, because he had signed a confidentiality agreement with a gold-mining syndicate. He was eventually exposed as a certain Henri Louis Grin, a Swiss-born servant who had at one time been footman to the actress Fanny Kemble. He had concocted his travels in the Reading Room of the British Museum.

1899

Pompe Funèbre 🐾 (16 February) The President of France, Félix Faure, died of apoplexy, apparently while being fellated by his mistress, Marguerite Steinheil. It is said that Georges Clemenceau joked, '*Il voulait être César, hélas, il ne fut que Pompée*' ('He wanted to be Caesar, but, alas, he was only Pompey'; in French, *pompé* means 'sucked'). Mlle Steinheil, who was romantically linked to a number of other gentlemen, including King Sisowath of Cambodia, became known as *Pompe Funèbre*.

The Phantom Ship &. Captain William A. Andrews attempted to cross the Atlantic in the smallest vessel ever to make the voyage, a canvas-covered folding boat 12 feet in length, dubbed 'the Phantom Ship' by the press, and by him named the *Doree*. He already held the record for the smallest vessel to cross the Atlantic, following his successful voyage in 1892 aboard the 14ft 6in *Sapolio* (a record that was to stand for 73 years). His intention on this voyage was to visit the Paris Exhibition the following year, and he was to have been accompanied by Miss Belle Shane (22), who unaccountably abandoned the expedition before it set sail. Andrews himself seems to have suffered from some kind of nervous collapse once he embarked, and almost collided with a number of vessels without realizing they were nearby. 'Whilst sleeping I believe I was asphyxiated,' he told reporters, 'I think by carbonic gas from the mineral water I had on board. Sometimes,' he added, 'I was actually unaware of my existence.' He was eventually picked up by the SS *Holbein*. Two years later, Williams was lost at sea with his new bride while attempting another Atlantic crossing aboard the unfortunately named *Flying Dutchman*.

The Lost Ark &. The British–Israel Association – who believed that the Anglo-Saxon race was descended from the Lost Tribes of Israel – began to excavate the Hill of Tara in Ireland, believing that the Ark of the Covenant was buried beneath it. Irish Nationalists were outraged at this desecration of the seat of the ancient High Kings.

Five Afternoons in June &. In a junior house match between Clarke's House and North Town House at Clifton College in Bristol, the 13-year-old Arthur Edward Jeune Collins scored 628 not out, the highest individual score recorded in any form of cricket. The innings was spread over five afternoons (22, 23, 26, 27, 28 June). Collins, who carried his bat in his team's total of 836 all out, was dropped seven times – on 80, 100, 140, 400, 556, 605 and 619. The scorer described his final tally thus: '628 – plus or minus 20, shall we say'. Collins also took 11 wickets for 63 runs in the match, which Clarke's

House won by the not inconsiderable margin of an innings and 688 runs.

The Irish playwright George Bernard Shaw once remarked: 'The English are not very spiritual people, so they invented cricket to give them some conception of eternity.'

After leaving Clifton, Collins opted for an army career. He was killed in action at the First Battle of Ypres in 1914.

The inventor Rotwang with his greatest creation – a gynoid or female robot – in a scene from Fritz Lang's 1927 science-fiction classic *Metropolis*. Brilliant, excitable and amoral, Rotwang is a prototype of the mad scientist of 20th-century film and fiction.

From 1900 to the Present

The Mystery of the Flannan Isles 🐾 Clever
Hans, the Calculating Horse 🐾 On the
Therapeutic Value of Bovine Flatulence 🐾
Queen Victoria Seduced by Poet Laureate 🐾
The Last Castrato 🐾 Curse of the White
Bambi 🐾 The Nationalization of Women 🐾
Battleships in Space 🐾 The Wolf Girls of
Midnapore 🐾 Birth of the Abominable
Snowman 🐾 Beastly Manners and
Promiscuous Fornication 🐾 Big Ben Toppled
by Revolutionists 🐾 Transplantation of
Monkey Glands 🐾 Garden of Eden located in
Bedford 🐾 A Women's Outfitter on Everest 🐾
Decapitation as a Competitive Sport 🐾 Nazis
Seek Subterranean Superhumans in Tibet 🐾
Grass as a Source of Human Nutrition 🐾

1900

—

Prince Swears 🦨 In Brussels, a young anarchist made an assassination attempt on the Prince of Wales (the future Edward VII). His Royal Highness reputedly exclaimed, 'Fuck it, I've taken a bullet', although he was in fact untouched.

—

Commander Takes a Bath during Battle 🦨 (12 February) At the Battle of Hussar Hill during the Boer War, the British second-in-command, Sir Charles Warren, decided it was an opportune moment to take a bath, which he preferred to do in public.

—

The Mystery of the Flannan Isles 🦨 Ships passing the Flannan Isles – a remote group of seven little islands to the west of Lewis in the Outer Hebrides – noticed that since 15 December 1900, no light shone from the lighthouse on the largest of the islands, Eilean Mór. The weather was bad, and it was not until Boxing Day that the Northern Lights tender *Hesperus* called with a new set of keepers, but found no sign of those they were meant to replace. Within the lighthouse, all seemed to be in good order. The table was laid for a meal, the lamp had been made ready for lighting and the log was complete up to the morning of 15 December. The only signs of anything untoward was the absence of two sets of oilskins, and a knocked-over chair. The official inquiry into the disappearance concluded that the three men had gone down to the landing site in a storm to secure equipment when a freakishly big wave broke over them and swept them away. However, this does not explain why one of the men would have ventured out in such inclement weather without his oilskins. A famous poem about the incident by Wilfred Wilson Gibson (1878–1962), told from the point of view of one of the relief keepers, concludes:

We seemed to stand for an endless while,
Though still no word was said,
Three men alive on Flannan Isle,
Who thought on three men dead.

1901

A Strange New Creature 🍂 A bizarre-looking mammal, hitherto unknown to Western science, was found in the rainforests of the Congo. The natives called this shy nocturnal creature, which stands up to 2 m high at the shoulder, 'okapi'. At first it was thought to be a cross between a giraffe and a zebra, although it turned out to be unrelated to the latter.

1902

The King's Mistresses 🍂 (9 August) So numerous were the mistresses of Edward VII that at his coronation a special pew, known as 'the Loose Box', was reserved for them.

1903

Three Pieces in the Shape of a Pear 🍂 Erik Satie composed his set of piano pieces entitled *Trois Morceaux en forme de poire* – 'Three pieces in the shape of a pear'. His sister Olga later remarked of her brother, 'He doesn't seem to have been quite normal.'

1904

A Female Freemason 🍂 The French physician and psychiatrist, Madeleine Pelletier, a cross-dressing celibate feminist, became a Freemason, joining La Nouvelle Jérusalem lodge.

1905

'Fatty' Foulkes of Chelsea FC

The 25-stone Chelsea goalkeeper, William 'Fatty' Foulkes, lifted a Port Vale forward off the ground and hurled him into his own goal. A penalty was awarded against Chelsea.

Crowley on Kanchenjunga

Aleister Crowley, later renowned as a Satanist and 'the wickedest man alive', led an expedition to climb Kanchenjunga, the world's third highest mountain. After the others in the team revolted against his autocratic leadership and sadistic treatment of the porters, Crowley continued alone. When an avalanche buried the rest of the party below him, Crowley declined to descend to aid them. He later wrote, 'A mountain accident of this kind is one of the things for which I have no sympathy whatever.'

The Cullinan Diamond

(25 June) Discovery of the Cullinan Diamond by Frederick Wells of the Premier Diamond Mining Company in South Africa. It weighed 621.35 g (3106.75 carats), the largest rough diamond ever found. It was presented to Edward VII and was sent to England on a ship, accompanied by a number of detectives. That, at least, was what was given out to the press. The stone on the ship was in fact a fake, intended as a decoy, while the real stone was sent in a plain box by parcel post. The stone was cut in Amsterdam by Joseph Asscher, who, as he prepared to strike the diamond, had a doctor and nurse standing by, such was his state of nerves. As it happened, the stone broke cleanly in two – at which point Asscher fainted. The largest two polished diamonds that resulted – the Great Star of Africa, and the Lesser Star of Africa – now form part of the British crown jewels.

Letting the Train Take the Strain

Maurice Garin won the Tour de France, but four months later it was shown that he had travelled some of the route by train rather than by bicycle.

———

A Haul of Pilchards 🎣 (November) In a single night, 13 million pilchards were caught off the coast of Cornwall.

1906

———

The Captain of Köpenick 🎣 (16 October) Wilhelm Voigt, a poor shoemaker who had been expelled by the police from Berlin as an undesirable, dressed himself up as an army officer, took a train to the town of Köpenick, and there commanded ten soldiers from the town barracks to accompany him. So used were they to obeying orders that they followed him unquestioningly to the town hall, where Voigt ordered them to guard the doors while he arrested the mayor and town secretary on suspicion of dodgy accounting. He gave them a receipt for the 4000 marks and 70 pfennigs he confiscated, and told some of the soldiers to take them to Berlin for questioning. The other soldiers he ordered to remain in place for half an hour, during which time Voigt caught a train and changed back into civvies. Voigt was arrested ten days later and sentenced to four years' imprisonment. However, perhaps because the public was so amused by the incident, the Kaiser pardoned Voigt in August 1908. The town hall where he perpetrated his deceit now has a statue to the 'Hauptmann von Köpenick'.

1907

———

Clever Hans, the Calculating Horse 🎣 Clever Hans, the calculating horse, was shown to be an imposter. *Der Kluge Hans*, as he was known in his native Germany, had caused a sensation by apparently showing human-like intelligence: if asked a question, for example a simple arithmetic problem, he would tap out the answer with his hoof. Then in 1907 a psychologist called Oskar Pfungst demonstrated that Hans kept an eye on his questioner to detect a slight relaxation in posture when he had achieved the requisite number of taps, upon which he would stop. Pfungst showed that if the questioner did not know the answer, Hans was stumped.

1908

On the Therapeutic Value of Bovine Flatulence ❧ Death of Helena, Comtesse de Noailles. She was a firm believer in the therapeutic value of methane, and kept a herd of cows in her garden so that the vapours resulting from their flatulence could permeate the house. Her other eccentricities included sleeping with a bag of dead squirrels wrapped round her head.

The Tunguska Event ❧ (30 June) Nearly a thousand square miles of forest in the remote and sparsely populated Siberian region of Tunguska were devasted by a massive explosion. It is thought that this was caused by an asteroid or comet exploding some 5000 m above the Earth's surface, with an energy equivalent to the most powerful hydrogen bomb ever tested by the USA. One eyewitness, who had been 64 kilometres north of the explosion, recalled:

> ... the sky split in two and fire appeared high and wide over the forest. The split in the sky grew larger, and the entire Northern side was covered with fire. At that moment I became so hot that I couldn't bear it, as if my shirt was on fire; from the northern side, where the fire was, came strong heat. I wanted to tear off my shirt and throw it down, but then the sky shut closed, and a strong thump sounded, and I was thrown a few yards. I lost my senses for a moment, but then my wife ran out and led me to the house. After that such noise came, as if rocks were falling or cannons were firing, the earth shook, and when I was on the ground, I pressed my head down, fearing rocks would smash it. When the sky opened up, hot wind raced between the houses, like from cannons, which left traces in the ground like pathways, and it damaged some crops. Later we saw that many windows were shattered, and in the barn a part of the iron lock snapped.

A Bad Review ❧ (22 October) The *Times Literary Supplement* dismissed *The Wind in the Willows* thus: 'As a contribution to natural history, the work is negligible.'

1909

Queen Victoria Seduced by Poet Laureate &. (10 April) Death

of the poet Algernon Charles Swinburne. Among his lesser known works is a play (in French) entitled *La Soeur de la reine*, in which Queen Victoria is a cruel and debauched tyrant, whose twin sister becomes a prostitute. Among the queen's lovers is the diminutive Liberal prime minister Lord John Russell, whom she threatens to have beheaded when he seems on the point of revealing her scandalous private life (the headmaster of Eton has met with a similar fate). At one point Victoria confesses to having surrendered her virtue to a philandering William Wordsworth, who seduces her after delivering a particularly sultry reading of *The Excursion*.

Chief Buffalo Child Long Lance &. Sylvester Clark Long, born

the son of former slaves in North Carolina, having noticed that whites treated Native Americans somewhat better than they did blacks, began to pass himself off as a half-Cherokee, calling himself Long Lance. He served with the Canadians in France during the First World War, then, back in the USA, campaigned for Native American rights, becoming something of a celebrity. By the late 1920s he was claiming to be a Blackfoot from Montana, and used the name Chief Buffalo Child Long Lance. He was eventually exposed as an impostor by the Native American adviser to a film in which he was starring. He took to drink, and shot himself in 1932.

King Marries Prostitute &. (12 December) King Leopold II of the

Belgians married Caroline Lacroix, a prostitute who had borne him two sons. He died five days later.

The Emperor of Abyssinia and his court about to inspect HMS *Dreadnought*. In fact, the emperor turned out to be Horace de Vere Cole, an English prankster (on the right), while among his courtiers was Virginia Woolf (on the left).

1910

—

Virginia Woolf and the Emperor of Abyssinia ❧ Horace de Vere Cole undertook his most successful practical joke when he dressed up as the Emperor of Abyssinia and was received as such on board HMS *Dreadnought*, flagship of the Royal Navy's Home Fleet. Accompanying him were various courtiers, including, suitably disguised, Virginia Stephen, later to find fame as the novelist Virginia Woolf.

1911

Against the Advancement of the Sons of Pork Butchers 🙚

(29 March) A public schoolboy from Kensington wrote to *The Guardian* to decry the award of scholarships for poor children to attend secondary schools (there was no universal free provision until after the 1944 Education Act). 'Is it not more probable,' the youth argued, 'that the sons of gentlemen will be levelled down rather than the sons of Pork Butchers levelled up by continual daily contact. The lessons of the gutter are more easily learnt than the traditions of caste. The fact that by keeping particular secondary and Public Schools a reserve for a particular class keeps the higher walks of life in the professions and public services a preserve for the same class, is surely a great argument in its favour. The lower classes never were a Governing class and why should the master sit side by side with the servant?'

An Automobile on Ben Nevis 🙚

A Mr Henry Alexander Jnr of Edinburgh drove his Model-T Ford to the summit of Ben Nevis. It took him five days.

A Noble Descent 🙚

Birth of William Francis Brinsley Le Poer Trench, who became 8th Earl of Clancarty in 1975 and claimed to be able to trace his ancestry to 63,000 BC. His origins, he averred, were extraterrestrial, his forefathers having arrived on Earth from spaceships. Clancarty founded the UFO Study Group in the House of Lords, and was married four times. He died in 1975.

1912

A Caring Employer 🙚

(15 April) As soon as the *Titanic* went down, the White Star Line, the ship's owners, stopped the wages of the crew.

Piltdown Man 🐚 Charles Dawson, an amateur archaeologist, announced the discovery at Piltdown in Sussex of some ancient bones that scientists at the British Museum declared to be 'missing link' between apes and humans. Although doubts were almost immediately expressed, it was not until 1953 that *Eoanthropus dawsonii* – popularly known as 'Piltdown Man' – was conclusively shown to be a hoax, comprising a human cranium some 50,000 years old and the much younger jawbone of an orang-utan; both had been stained with potassium bichromate to make them appear the same age, and the teeth of the orang-utan filed to make them look more human. Among various suggestions as to the identity of the hoaxer, the most likely plausible is that it was Dawson himself. Just prior to the exposure of the hoax, L. Ron Hubbard, in *Scientology: A History of Man*, listed Piltdown Man as an ancestor of modern humans.

1913

The First Cuckoo 🐚 (6 February) A Mr R. Lydekker FRS wrote to *The Times* to report that he had just heard the song of the cuckoo, which would surely be a record. Six days later, however, he was obliged to write again to confess that he had been taken in by a clever imitation made by a bricklayer's labourer.

The Last Castrato 🐚 The last remaining castrato in the Sistine Chapel choir, Alessandro Moreschi, gave his final performance. Over the previous 300 years, thousands of boys had been castrated to preserve their fine treble voices. They were first 'loosened up' in a hot bath, then dosed with alcohol or opium, or pressure was applied to their carotid arteries to render them temporarily senseless. The operation either involved opening the scrotum and cutting certain tubes, or cutting the whole lot off in a single stroke. Many parts in opera (including those by Handel and Mozart) were originally written for castrato voices, and the last eunuch to sing on stage was Giovanni

Battista Velluti, who appeared in an opera by Meyerbeer in 1828. The practice was largely unknown in England, although in 1764 a Methodist preacher from Wiltshire called Henry Timbrell was found guilty of castrating two apprentices with the intent of selling them to the opera. He was sentenced to two years in prison, and fined 13s 4d for each lad. His method was to 'wicker them after the manner in which poor rams are treated'.

A Plutocratic Proboscis ❧ (31 March) Death of J.P. Morgan, the American tycoon, who, among other attributes, was the possessor of a strikingly colourful and bulbous nose (he suffered from the skin condition called rosacea, and was the butt of a popular rhyme beginning 'Johnny Morgan's nasal organ has a purple hue ...'). On one occasion the society hostess Mrs Dwight Morrow was expecting Morgan to tea, and warned her young daughters not to pass comment on anything unusual they might see, particularly regarding the appearance of their guest. The children behaved themselves perfectly, and after they had curtsied and left, Mrs Morrow turned to her guest, and inquired, 'Now, Mr Morgan, do you like one or two lumps of sugar in your nose?'

1914

Curse of the White Bambi ❧ (28 June) Archduke Franz Ferdinand was assassinated in Sarajevo, with consequences that are all too familiar. It was said that he had fallen victim of the curse that traditionally befalls anyone who kills a white deer: in the previous autumn Franz Ferdinand had shot an albino stag. Fear of the curse still reigns in the German-speaking world: in the autumn of 2006 hunters in the Erzgebirge mountains of eastern Germany resisted calls by the president of the Saxony Hunting Federation that they should shoot an albino deer. 'The white deer is a mutation,' President Günter Giese had said. 'It does not belong in the wild; it should be shot.' However, local hunters with a less eugenic attitude said they enjoyed seeing 'White Bambi', and would not kill it – 'because it is pretty'.

On the Profligacy of Failing to Eat One's Enemies &ed; As
Europe combusted into all-out war, the anthropologist Bronislaw
Malinowski was carrying out fieldwork in Papua:

> I once talked to an old cannibal who, hearing of the Great War raging in
> Europe, was most curious to know how we Europeans managed to eat such
> huge quantities of human flesh. When I told him the Europeans did not eat
> their slain foes he looked at me with shocked horror and asked what sort of
> barbarians we were, to kill without any real object.

On the Excellence of Elysium Soap &ed; (10 September) The
German raider *Emden* captured the British merchantman *Indus* in the Indian
Ocean. All it had on board was ballast and soap, but the latter was much
appreciated by the crew, who had run out of supplies. On 25 September the
following advertisement appeared in *The Empire*, a Calcutta newspaper:

> There is no doubt that the German cruiser *Emden* had knowledge that the
> *Indus* was carrying 150 cases of North-West Soap Company's celebrated
> ELYSIUM Soap, and hence the pursuit. The men on the *Emden* and their
> clothes are now clean and sweet, thanks to ELYSIUM Soap. Try it!

Repelled by Bees &ed; (4 November) A British attempt to capture the
port of Tanga in German East Africa was repelled when the invaders were
attacked by swarms of bees, and were obliged to retreat into the sea.

1915

Exhibition of a Urinal &ed; In New York, the French artist Marcel
Duchamp submitted a work entitled *Fountain* to the Salon des Indépendents,
which rejected it. The work comprised a porcelain urinal, signed 'R. Mutt'.

Gentlemen and Players – Part II ❧ (23 October) Death of the cricketer Dr W.G. Grace. In its obituary, *The Times* pointed out that, even though in cricketing terms Grace was a 'gentleman' rather than a 'player' (i.e. an amateur rather than a professional), he could not be considered a true gentleman, because, as a physician, he worked for his living.

1916

The Distinguished Thing ❧ (28 February) Death of the novelist Henry James. His last words were said to have been: 'Here it is at last – the Distinguished Thing.'

War Stymies Games ❧ The Olympic Games, scheduled to be held in Berlin, were cancelled due to the global unpleasantness.

1917

Camouflaged by a Mirage ❧ (11 April) Fighting between Turkish and British forces in Mesopotamia was suspended for a while, as the Turks, who had no cover, were entirely concealed by a mirage.

1918

Condemned Men Encouraged to Smoke ❧ The medical officer at Birmingham prison recommended that condemned men be supplied 'with at least a dozen cigarettes daily'.

The Nationalization of Women ❧ (March) In the southern Russian town of Saratov, an anti-revolutionary café owner posted a notice, in the name of a group of local anarchists, declaring that all women were now the property of the state. The rumour that this was official Bolshevik policy spread across the country, and in some places was taken as a sanction for rape. When Lenin heard about what was going on, he sent in the Cheka, his secret police, to put a stop to the matter in the way they knew best.

1919

English Not Spoken in Illinois ✒ H.L. Mencken successfully lobbied for the revision of a statute in Illinois, by which 'English' was replaced by 'American' as the official language of the state.

———

Battleships in Space ✒ (21 June) The German fleet interned at Scapa Flow, in the Orkneys, was scuttled on the orders of Rear Admiral Ludwig Reuter, to prevent the ships falling into British hands. In all, 51 ships lie on the bottom. The steel from these submerged wrecks is used in satellites, as all steel made since 1945 is contaminated with radiation from nuclear tests, which would upset the delicate instrumentation needed in space.

———

Peg Leg Bates, the One-legged Tap Dancer ✒ A 12-year-old black boy called Clayton Bates lost his left leg after it was mangled by a conveyor belt in a cotton mill in his native South Carolina. Undeterred, 'Peg Leg' Bates had, by the age of 15, become 'the undisputed king of one-legged dancers' (according to the Tap Dance Hall of Fame), bringing new life to such steps as the Shim Sham Shimmy and Susie Q by exploiting the tonal contrast between the high-pitched metallic tap of his right shoe and the deeper wooden note of his peg leg. He was still pursuing a successful international career in vaudeville in the 1960s, and died in 1998. 'Life means, do the best with what you've got,' he used to say.

Peg Leg Bates at the height of his career as a one-legged tap dancer.

1920

King Killed by Monkey &. (25 October) King Alexander of Greece, uncle of the Duke of Edinburgh, died after being bitten by a pet monkey.

The Wolf Girls of Midnapore &. A missionary working near Midnapore, India, spotted two young girls living with a pack of wolves. He managed to capture them, with the aim of integrating them into human society. The younger one, no more than a toddler, began to learn to speak quite readily, although she died within a year. The older one, about seven or

eight at the time of her capture, had much greater difficulty with language, and had only mastered a few dozen words before her death from typhoid in 1929. Both girls had calluses on their knees and the palms of their hands, from walking on all fours, their favoured form of locomotion. They had acute senses of smell and hearing, enjoyed raw meat, and preferred to be active at night. The only emotion they expressed was fear.

Seventh Sons Suspected of Lycanthropy

Seventh Sons Suspected of Lycanthropy ❧ A law was passed in Argentina by which the president became the godfather of every seventh son. Seventh sons were also to be awarded gold medals on their baptisms, and scholarships until they reached the age of 21. The aim was to end the practice, common especially in the north of the country, of abandoning seventh sons, on account of their alleged tendency to grow up into werewolves (a belief derived from a tradition of the native Guaraní people).

1921

Operating on Oneself

Operating on Oneself ❧ (15 February) Dr Evan O'Neill Kane (60), a pioneer of local anaesthesia, which he held to be much safer than the use of ether, demonstrated the efficacy of his approach by performing an appendectomy – on himself. Eleven years later, in 1932, Dr Kane, then aged 70, operated on his own inguinal hernia – a hazardous procedure, as the suture needle has to be inserted within an eighth of an inch (3 mm) of the femoral artery.

Birth of the Abominable Snowman

Birth of the Abominable Snowman ❧ A reconnaissance expedition to Mount Everest led by Lieutenant-Colonel C.K. Howard-Bury found many large footprints at an altitude of 6100 m (20,000 ft) on the Lhakpa La. When Howard-Bury gave his account to a reporter, Henry Newman of the *Calcutta Statesman*, Newman mistook the Sherpa words *meh-the* ('thing like a man that is not a man') for *metoh-kagmi* ('abominable snowman').

Cooking with Horse Dung 🍃 (October) Reporting on the famine in Russia – which cost three million lives – Arthur Ransome found an old woman so desperate for food that she was reduced to cooking horse dung in a broken saucepan.

1922

A Conductorless Orchestra 🍃 The Pervyi Simfonicheskii Ansambl (or Persimfans) was founded in the Soviet Union. This orchestra was unusual in that, in accordance with Marxist ideology, it had no conductor, decisions on interpretation being made by a number of elected committees.

1923

Suntans become Fashionable 🍃 Coco Chanel supposedly set the trend for tanning when, on a Mediterranean cruise, she inadvertently allowed herself to go brown in the sun. The fashion world immediately assumed it was the chic thing to do, such was Chanel's influence. Previously women had sought to protect their skin from the sun, as a tan indicated one was an outdoor manual labourer.

Death of Six Balloonists 🍃 (23 December) Six aeronauts were killed when their balloons were struck by lightning during a race starting from Brussels.

1924

Novelist Fired from Post Office 🍃 The novelist William Faulkner proved himself less able as a literary postmaster than his namesake William Wordsworth (*see* 1813), when he was sacked from his job running the post office at the University of Mississippi.

1925

Ampersand ☙ The US poet e.e. cummings published a volume with the curt title *&*.

A Cross-Dressing Boxer ☙ When Colonel Leslie Barker, pugilist and cricketer, was arrested on bankruptcy charges he was found, on medical examination by the prison physician, to be a woman. She had been born Lillias Valerie Barker, but her sporty father had always wanted a son. Barker was charged with a number of further offences through the 1920s and 1930s, but redeemed her/himself in the eyes of many when, during the Second World War, she/he served in the Home Guard under the name Geoffrey Norton.

Hachiko, the Faithful Hound ☙ Death of Professor Eisaburo Ueno of Tokyo University. For some years his pet dog Hachiko, an akita, had met his train every day. Hachiko continued this daily routine for another nine years, until he himself died in 1934.

Ladies Not Known to Make Love in Broad Daylight, Claims Judge ☙ In a celebrated divorce case, Alexander vs. Alexander and Amos, the judge, Sir Cresswell Cresswell, declined to believe the testimony of a witness, a farm labourer called Sullivan, on the grounds that he could not have seen Mrs Alexander in flagrante with the butler, Amos, as no lady would make love in broad daylight.

Beastly Manners and Promiscuous Fornication ☙ The Whiteway Colony, a commune in the Cotswolds near Stroud, which had long attracted anarchists, socialists, pacifics and believers in free love, came under the scrutiny of the Home Office. 'Manners had they none and their customs are beastly,' wrote one official, while the police paid a couple £400 to infiltrate the commune to come up with evidence that would lead to the closure of the commune. Although they reported that 'promiscuous fornication' was the norm, the couple came up with nothing that would persuade the locals that the communards were anything other than harmless cranks. Whiteway continues to thrive.

The Colonel Vanishes 🦋 Disappearance of Colonel Percy Fawcett in the jungles of the Mato Grosso, Brazil. Fawcett, a friend of H. Rider Haggard and Arthur Conan Doyle, was in search of a lost city he referred to as 'Z'. He was accompanied by his son Jack and Jack's friend Raleigh Rimmell, and after he sent a telegram to his wife on 29 May 1925, saying they were about to enter unexplored territory, no more was heard of Fawcett or his companions. He left a note to say that if they did not return, no one should come looking for them, lest they suffer the same fate. In fact, over the years, several expeditions have attempted, in vain, to find their remains. In 2004 it was suggested that Fawcett had intended to set up a theosophical community in the jungle, and never intended to return to England.

1926

Big Ben Toppled by Revolutionists 🦋 (16 January) A BBC radio talk on 18th-century literature was interrupted by a report that rioters in London had knocked down Big Ben with trench mortars, set the Savoy Hotel on fire, and lynched a government minister. It turned out to be a hoax perpetrated by Father Ronald Knox, but in the remoter parts of the country those who had missed the BBC's assurances that the broadcast was merely fiction were confirmed in their belief, when the next day's papers failed to arrive, that London had been overwhelmed by revolutionists. In fact, delivery had been disrupted by bad weather.

—

Transplantation of Monkey Glands 🙦 Dr Serge Voronoff, a Russian-born physician practising in France, published a book describing his procedure for restoring male potency by transplanting pieces of monkey testicle into the scrotums of his human subjects. A similar procedure was undertaken by Dr John Romulus Brinkley in the USA, using goat glands, and charging $750 per operation. His medical licence was revoked in 1930. Less celebrated than either of these gentlemen, but undoubtedly taking precedence, was Dr Horace Emmett, who in 1889 announced in a lecture at Magdalene College, Cambridge, that by injecting himself with the ground-up testicles of squirrels, he was enabled to 'visit' his wife on a daily basis. Emmett, then aged 79, was shortly afterwards deserted by his spouse, who ran off with a younger man.

—

Plane Landed on Helvellyn 🙦 John Leeming and Bert Hinkler landed an aeroplane, an Avro 585 Gosport, on the narrow ridge near the summit of Helvellyn in the Lake District, and successfully took off again.

—

The Bluest of Blue Bloods 🙦 (28 March) Birth of Doña Maria del Rosario Cayetana Fitz-James Stuart y Silva, the Eighteenth Duchess of Alba in her own right and the most titled noble in the world. She has eight other ducal titles, is 15 times a marchioness, 19 times a countess, 20 times a grandee of Spain, once a viscountess and once a baroness.

1927
—

Fainting at the Theatre 🙦 During a London run at the Little Theatre of a stage adaptation of Bram Stoker's *Dracula*, 29 people fainted, and a nurse was placed on permanent standby at the theatre. Some of those who 'fainted' were in fact planted by the management.

1928

Ireland Defeats West Indies at Cricket ᔥ Ireland defeated the West Indies at cricket by 60 runs in a three-day game. (*See also* 1969.)

1929

Garden of Eden located in Bedford ᔥ The Panacea Society was founded by Mrs Mabel Barltrop. The organization maintains a large Victorian house near Bedford for the use of Jesus Christ, whose second coming they expect shortly. Mrs Barltrop explained that Bedford had been chosen because it was the site of the Garden of Eden.

1930

Scouts in Bondage ᔥ Publication of *Scouts in Bondage*, an adventure story by Geoffrey Prout.

Vile Voltaire, Rude Rousseau ᔥ US Customs seized copies of Voltaire's *Candide* on the grounds of obscenity. The previous year they had seized Jean-Jacques Rousseau's *Confessions*, alleging that it was 'injurious to public morality'.

Suicide Not for Everyone ᔥ (14 April) The Russian poet Vladimir Mayakovsky shot himself. In his funeral note he said, 'I do not recommend it for others.'

1931

Culottes at Wimbledon &

The Spanish player Lili de Alvarez shocked the tennis world when she appeared at Wimbledon wearing a divided skirt – the forerunner of shorts.

Weird Worms &

Publication of *The Supernatural History of Worms*, by Marion C. Fox.

1932

Here Lies Johnny Penis Buried in the Mound of Venus &

Private publication of a book of verse entitled *Here Lies Johnny Penis*, by Count Geoffrey Wladislaw Vaile Potoi Montalk, a polyglot of Polish ancestry who believed that the Maori were the master race, and who had achieved fame as the fastest milker in his native New Zealand. The printer of the Count's slim volume reported the content to the police, and the Count consequently found himself in the Central Criminal Court on a charge of obscenity. Montalk failed to impress Sir Ernest Wild, Recorder of London, when he appeared in a red robe in the medieval style and with his hair trailing over his shoulders (so usurping the judge's monopoly on fancy dress and long hair). Matters did not improve when the Count swore on the collected works of Shakespeare rather than on the Bible. At the end of the trial, Sir Ernest summed up thus:

> A man must not say he is a poet and be filthy. He has to obey the law the same as ordinary citizens, and the sooner the highbrow school learns that, the better for the morality of the country.

The jury agreed with the judge that literature must be protected from 'offal of this kind', and returned a guilty verdict. Montalk was sentenced to six months in Wormwood Scrubs. In 1936 he declared himself to be King Wladislaw V of Poland, Hungary and Bohemia. It was said that when he subsequently hit a London policeman over the head with his own truncheon, he claimed diplomatic immunity.

———

Death of a Hangman 🙢 (20 September) Suicide of John Ellis, public executioner. After he retired from the hanging business in 1924, Ellis opened a pub called The Jolly Butcher. Business was not brisk. 'Conversation ceases suddenly when I'm about,' he confided. 'Socially it's a bad business being a hangman.' He subsequently tried his hand as a barber, with a similar lack of success. He ended his own life, not, as one might have expected, by hanging himself, but by cutting his throat with a razor. It was said that he had never recovered from the execution in 1923 of Edith Thomson, who had been found guilty – unjustly in the eyes of many – of the murder of her husband. Mrs Thomson had been hysterical at the time of her hanging, and had had to be held upright as the noose was slipped over her head. As she dropped, she suffered a massive haemorrhage, suggesting that she might have been pregnant at the time of her execution. After this, all women hanged in Britain were required to wear a special garment to stop such a grisly occurrence from happening again.

John Ellis was not related to Ruth Ellis (d.1955), the last woman to hang in Britain, nor is he to be confused with the John Ellis (b.1952) who was a founding member of the punk band called The Vibrators.

1933

Von Schirach of the Hitler Youth 🙢 Baldur von Schirach was appointed head of the Hitler Youth. Many years later, in an interview with David Frost, he told his interlocutor, 'I haff been reading about you, Mr Frost, und did you know I became ze head of ze Hitler Youth at ze same age you did *Zat Vas Ze Veek Zat Vas*? So ve haff a great deal in common, Mr Frost.' Frost recalled, 'I was appalled. As quickly as I could, I said, "No, we haven't."'

Darkness at Noon ✒ (23 October) A temperature inversion trapped fog and smoke over London, obliterating the sun and causing total darkness at midday. From the air, all that could be seen, according to a pilot with Imperial Airways, was 'a huge black mushroom completely shrouding the city'.

1934

Some Books on Poultry ✒ Publication of *The Art of Faking Exhibition Poultry* by George Ryley Scott, author of *The Truth About Poultry*.

———

A Women's Outfitter on Everest ✒ Maurice Wilson, the son of a Bradford mill worker with no mountaineering experience, died while attempting to climb Mount Everest alone. Wilson, who had been wounded during the First World War and who had then run a ladies' clothes shop in New Zealand, had planned (with divine aid) to crash land an aeroplane on the upper slopes of the mountain, then walk to the summit. Having flown his Gypsy Moth from England to India (no mean feat for a man with only two months' flying experience), he was then forced to sell the plane and proceed on foot, making his way to Everest via Tibet. The following year his body was found inside his tent on the north face of the mountain, at around 6400 m (21,000 ft). There were reports that he was wearing women's underwear. The 1960 Chinese expedition, the first to successfully climb Everest from the north side, found a lady's shoe at 6400 m.

Following in the spirit of Wilson, on 18 May 2006 Martyna Wojciechowska became the first *Playboy* cover girl to reach the summit of Everest. The following week Sherpa Lakpa Tharke reached the summit, where he posed naked for three minutes, claiming a record. His fellow Nepalis regarded this as a defilement of the sacred mountain.

1935

OUP Publishes Biggles ❧ Oxford University Press, better known for its scholarly monographs, began to publish the Biggles books written by Captain W.E. Johns.

Composer Killed by Insect Bite ❧ (24 December) Death of the avant-garde Austrian composer Alban Berg from an insect bite that became septic.

1936

King Jumps From Window ❧ During his brief period as king, Edward VIII once avoided what he thought might be an awkward interview with his private secretary by jumping out of a window of Buckingham Palace and running away to hide in the garden.

Anarchist Soldiers Keep Out of Step ❧ As the Spanish Civil War got underway, the anarchists formed their own militias in defence of the Republic. They elected their officers, arrived at important decisions by vote, and no one had to obey an order they disagreed with. While marching, they made every effort to keep out of step.

United States vs. One Package of Japanese Pessaries ❧ The sending of contraceptive devices or advice through the US mail was ruled to be legal in the case known as 'United States vs. One Package of Japanese Pessaries'. Margaret Sanger, the birth-control campaigner, had ordered the pessaries from a physician in Tokyo, with the intention of provoking a test case.

1937

Policeman's Feet Deemed Clean by Court *&* A policeman successfully sued the manufacturer of Jeyes' fluid footbath for using a photograph of him wiping his brow in an advertisement, accompanied by the words 'Phew, I'm going to get my feet into a Jeyes' fluid footbath.' He asserted that the advertisement implied he had smelly feet, and was awarded £100 damages.

Cheetah Racing at White City Not a Success *&* Kenneth Gandar-Dower, the poet, explorer and international tennis and squash player who had earlier sought in vain for Kenya's fabled *marozi* or spotted lion, attempted to introduce cheetah racing to Britain. Experiments at the greyhound track at White City proved disappointing, the cheetahs being unwilling to exert themselves in such undignified circumstances.

Radio Silence *&* (21 July) At six o'clock in the evening, all BBC transmitters and Post Office wireless telegraph and wireless telephone stations in the British Isles closed down for two minutes, to coincide with the funeral of Guglielmo Marconi, the inventor of radio.

Cleric Killed by Performing Lion *&* (30 July) Harold Davidson, formerly Rector of Stiffkey, was fatally mauled by his performing lion, Freddy. Davidson had taken to a career in variety after he had been defrocked in 1932 for his over-enthusiastic efforts to save fallen women in the West End of London.

Decapitation as a Competitive Sport *&* (December) During the so-called Rape of Nanking, it was reported that two Japanese officers,

Mr Guy Harben about to dine with his cheetah at St Regis, Cork Street, Mayfair, in 1939. He had brought the animal over to England to race against greyhounds, but cheetah racing, initiated at White City in 1937, but did not prove an enduring success.

Toshiaki Mukai and Tsuyoshi Noda, held a competition to see which of them would be first to cut off one hundred Chinese heads. Some doubt has subsequently been cast as to whether this event ever took place, although it was covered in Japanese newspapers at the time.

———

A Pioneering Marital Aid ✌ (17 December) Jake Street, an American inventor, patented a 'Device for promoting marital accord . . . comprising an elongated flat member having a penis receiving opening adjacent one end thereof and a clitoris engaging projection on one face thereof, terminating adjacent the other end.'

1938

A Field Guide to Roadkill ❧ Publication of *Feathers and Fur on the Turnpike*, James Simmons's guide to identifying animals and birds flattened on the highways of America.

———

The Hangman's Fee ❧ The fee for conducting a hanging in Britain was fixed at £1 11s 6d. This was to be doubled should the hangman carry out the job satisfactorily.

———

Nazis Seek Subterranean Superhumans in Tibet ❧ The SS leader Heinrich Himmler sent an expedition to Tibet to find traces of a subterranean race of superhumans, possessed of an occult power called *vril*. *Vril* was in fact a creation of the English novelist Edward Bulwer-Lytton, who published *Vril: The Power of the Coming Race* in 1870, but many had forgotten it was science fiction, and various mystical Vril societies were formed. (The word was also incorporated into the name of the bovinely based savoury spread Bovril.) Himmler and his colleagues believed that the Aryans were descended from these subterranean beings, although other Nazis held that the Aryans had their origins in the lost land of Thule, a kind of Atlantis that had once existed between Greenland and Iceland.

———

Fear of Lightning Justified ❧ (1 June) The Hungarian playwright Ödön von Horváth, who had lived in fear of being struck by lightning all his life, was killed in Paris when a branch fell on his head during a thunderstorm. Despite his fear of lightning, Horváth had loved to walk in the mountains, and once, in a remote spot in the Bavarian Alps, had come across the skeleton of a long-dead walker. In the dead man's rucksack Horváth found an unposted postcard reading 'Having a wonderful time.' Asked by his friends what he did with it, he replied, 'I posted it.'

———

Prime Minister Demands Report on Tits ❧ (30 September)

Having just returned from Munich bringing 'peace for our time', Prime Minister Neville Chamberlain requested an update on the long-tailed tits nesting in the Treasury.

———

America Panics ❧ (Halloween)

Orson Welles broadcast his radio version of H.G. Wells's *War of the Worlds* on CBS, in the form of a live newscast. The programme began with a newsflash interrupting a piece of music to tell listeners that astronomers at Princeton University had just witnessed violent flashes on the surface of Mars. The music resumed, only to be interrupted by another newsflash, announcing that New Jersey had been hit by a meteor. A reporter supposedly at the scene then recounted how Martian warriors had emerged from the 'meteor', and begun to kill the local citizens with death rays. People who had tuned in after the start of the programme were unaware that they were listening to a fictional drama, and the roads leading to the supposed meteor site were clogged with men determined to take on the invaders; some apparently opened fire on a water tower, believing it to be an alien spacecraft. Other rumours swirled around the country: New Jersey had been hit by a gas attack, New York City had been destroyed. People reported smelling poison gas, or seeing the fighting. Hospitals had to treat many people for shock.

In the wake of the broadcast, the Federal Communications Commission expressed its lack of amusement, and CBS was obliged to promise never again to use the 'We interrupt this programme' device in a fictional context. Conspiracy theorists have suggested that the whole affair was a government-sponsored exercise in psychological warfare, and that the panic caused by the broadcast encouraged the authorities to cover up subsequent reports of UFOs. Adaptations of the drama broadcast in Chile in 1944 and Ecuador in 1949 also caused mass panic; in the latter case, some listeners, outraged that they had been deceived, set fire to the radio station.

1939

Fiddling While Rome Burns 🐾 Publication of *Gadsby*, a novel by
E.V. Wright that entirely eschews the letter 'e'. Thirty years later the French writer Georges Perec published *La Disparition*, a novel that achieves a similar feat.

A Remedy for Flatulence 🐾 A patent application was lodged for the
'Wind Bag', designed 'for the receiving and storing of gas formed by the digestion of foods'. A tube linked the rectum to a collection chamber, while the device was held in place under one's clothes by a belt.

The First British Casualty of the War 🐾 (September) The first
British casualty of the war was a police constable who had climbed up a drainpipe of a house in Harley Street, London, to put out a light, there having been no answer to his knock at the door. The unfortunate policeman fell from the fourth storey, and was killed.

Bird Watching and Fox Hunting Disrupted by War 🐾
A contributor to the Country Diary in the *Manchester Guardian* opined, 'I cannot help thinking that if only Hitler had been an ornithologist he would have put off the war until the autumn migration was over.'

Meanwhile, some officers with the British Expeditionary Force in France were not best pleased when the French authorities refused them permission to import foxes, or to use the French countryside for hunting.

Absence of Backbone at Eton 🐾 Lord Hugh Cecil, provost of
Eton College, wrote to the headmaster, Claude Elliott, to complain that the building of air-raid shelters was tantamount to hysteria: 'May I remind you

that under the statutes of the school the headmaster is responsible only for the studies and disciplines of the school – from which a right to protect the boys from bombs cannot be inferred.' Not to be outsmarted, Elliott replied that it would be difficult to either teach or discipline the boys if they were dead.

———

The Colonel in the Tower 🦚 (September) Lieutenant-Colonel A.D. Wintle, frustrated that his superiors would not send him to France, commandeered an aeroplane at gunpoint in order 'to take the war to the Hun', for which he was sent to the Tower of London. Wintle had had a spectacularly 'good' war the previous time round, after a somewhat shaky start. Arriving in the trenches he was promptly splashed with the entrails of his sergeant, to whom he had only just been introduced, and as the bombardment continued he dealt with his nerves by standing at attention and saluting. It worked: 'Within thirty seconds,' he later recalled, 'I was able to become again an Englishman of action and to carry out calmly the duties I had been trained to perform.' He ended the war with a monocle and a Military Cross, having captured 35 Germans single-handedly. The interwar period he found 'intensely boring', but his confinement in the Tower at the beginning of the Second World War was not too irksome:

> My life in the Tower had begun. How different it was from what I had expected. Officers at first cut me dead, thinking that I was some kind of traitor; but when news of my doings leaked out they could not do enough for me. My cell became the most popular meeting place in the garrison and I was as well cared for as if I had been at the Ritz. I would have a stroll in the moat after breakfast for exercise. Then sharp at eleven Guardsman McKie, detailed as my servant, would arrive from the officers' mess with a large whisky and ginger ale. He would find me already spick and span, for though I have a great regard for the Guards, they have not the gift to look after a cavalry officer's equipment. The morning would pass pleasantly. By noon visitors would begin to arrive. One or two always stayed to lunch. They always brought something with them. I remember one particularly succulent duck in aspic – it gave me indigestion – and a fine box of cigars brought by my family

doctor. Tea time was elastic and informal. Visitors dropped in at intervals, usually bringing along bottles which were uncorked on the spot. I don't recall that any of them contained any tea. Dinner, on the other hand, was strictly formal. I dined sharp at eight and entertained only such guests as had been invited beforehand. After a few days of settling in. I was surprised to find that – as a way of life – being a prisoner in the Tower of London had its points.

Wintle was let off with a reprimand, and subsequently went to France as a secret agent. Captured by the Vichy French, he was imprisoned in a fortress near Toulon, from where he escaped, having persuaded the 200-strong garrison to defect to the Resistance. Wintle, who died in 1966, once wrote to the editor of *The Times*:

> Sir,
>
> I have just written you a long letter.
> On reading it over, I have thrown it into the waste paper basket.
> Hoping this will meet with your approval,
>> I am, Sir,
>> Your obedient Servant,
>> A.D. Wintle

Wintle always carried an umbrella with him, but opined that 'No true gentleman would ever unfurl one.'

1940

A Zippy Title &. In the USA Ozzie Nelson published a song that became something of a hit, despite its title: 'I'm Looking for a Guy Who Plays Alto and Baritone and Doubles on a Clarinet and Wears a Size-37 Suit'.

Run, Rabbit, Run &. (16 March) After an air raid on the British naval base at Scapa Flow, Orkney, the Germans claimed to have caused massive casualties. In fact, the only fatality was a rabbit, and it was to this that Flanagan and Allen referred when they sang 'Run, Rabbit, Run' (the song itself dates from the previous year) to wartime audiences, apparently accompanied by the unfortunate creature's corpse.

Grass as a Source of Human Nutrition ᨠ (2 May) A Mr J.R.B. Branson wrote to *The Times* to recommend the nutritional benefits to humans of grass mowings. He had, he said, eaten them regularly for over three years, and off many lawns, and was presently enjoying the cuttings from a golf green on Mitcham Common.

Suspicious Behaviour ᨠ During the height of the German spy scare, a vicar's daughter in Winchester reported the British officer billeted with them to the authorities on the grounds of his suspiciously foreign behaviour. The man had failed to flush the lavatory.

The Spy Who Never Was ᨠ In Lisbon, a Catalan refugee from Franco's fascist Spain called Juan Pujol offered his services to the British as an agent. They declined, so Pujol decided to offer his services to the Germans, so that he could then offer the British something more valuable – a double-agent. Pujol – codenamed Garbo – pretended to the Germans that he was in Britain, and sent them many reports based on information he gleaned from libraries and newsreels in Lisbon. The British eventually invited Pujol to come to England in 1942, and Pujol convinced the Germans that he had successfully recruited a large network of agents, for which he received large sums of money. The Germans were so pleased with Pujol's reports that after 1942 they did not send any new agents to Britain. Pujol played an important part in deceiving the Germans that the Allied invasion of France would occur at the Pas de Calais, and not in Normandy; the Germans were so impressed that they kept 18 divisions in reserve in the Pas, convinced that the D-Day landings were a diversion. Pujol was awarded an Iron Cross by the Germans (who codenamed him Arabel), and an MBE by the British.

———

The Baghdad Battery ⁊ The German archaeologist Wilhelm König, formerly director of the National Museum of Iraq, published a paper speculating that a number of terracotta jars containing copper cylinders and iron rods, found near Baghdad and dating from the Parthian period (250 BC to AD 224), comprised an electrical battery, perhaps used for electroplating. The artefacts have subsequently been dated to the later Sassanid period (224 to 640), and most archaeologists are sceptical that people of this period had sufficient knowledge of electricity to make such an apparatus.

1941

In Case of Gas Attack ⁊ An English vicar reported on what he had officially been advised to do in case of a gas attack: 'I was recommended to put both my hands in my pockets and if I carried an umbrella to put it up.'

———

Band Leader Loses Head at Café de Paris ⁊ (spring) The Café de Paris, a basement nightclub in London's West End, took a direct hit from a German bomb. Rescuers found the bandleader, Snakehips Johnson, decapitated, while at the tables elegantly dressed men and women still sat, without a mark on them, but utterly lifeless. Looters mingled with firemen and the police, cutting off the ring fingers of the dead. Ironically, the previous August the Nazi propagandist Lord Haw-Haw (William Joyce) had made a broadcast contrasting the sufferings of the poor of the East End in the Blitz, while 'the plutocrats and the favoured lords of creation were making the raid an excuse for their drunken orgies and debaucheries in the saloons of Piccadilly and in the Café de Paris. Spending on champagne in one night what they would consider enough for a soldier's wife for a month these moneyed fools shouted and sang in the streets, crying, as the son of a profiteer baron put it, "They won't bomb this part of the town! They want the docks! Fill up boys!"'

Glamour Puss Devises Guidance System
≈ Hedy Lamarr, better known as a goddess of the silver screen, patented a radio-controlled guidance device for torpedoes, which was subsequently taken up by the US Navy, and which contains a frequency-hopping device that is the basis of modern mobile phone and wireless technology. Miss Lamarr never made a penny out of her invention.

Soil Served Up as Custard
≈ (August) The Germans began to besiege Leningrad. The Soviets managed to hold out until they were relieved in January 1944, but over a million of the inhabitants died from bombing, cold, and, above all, famine. So hungry were they that factory workers ate the grease from their machines, and drank engine oil from tins. When a sugar warehouse was burnt to the ground, helpings of the earth beneath it, into which the molten sugar had seeped, were served up as 'candy' or 'custard'. Eventually things got so bad that even the graves of the newly dead were disturbed, as the desperate dug up and ate the corpses.

1942

Bat Bombs
≈ (January) A dentist called Lytle S. Adams submitted an ingenious weapon idea to the White House. It consisted of attaching tiny incendiary devices to large numbers of bats and releasing them via bombers over Japanese cities, where the bats would roost undetected and set buildings alight. President Roosevelt approved the plan. Despite a number of setbacks, testing proved reasonably successful, but the project was cancelled in the summer of 1944.

Deadlier Than the Male
≈ (May) The Soviet sniper Ludmilla Pavlichenko was cited by the Southern Army Council for having killed 257 Germans. By the end of the war her total had reached 309. Later in 1942 she

became the first Soviet citizen to be received at the White House, when she was sent to the USA on a publicity tour.

1943

Sliced Bread Banned 🍂 (18 January) The US government banned the sale of sliced bread until the end of hostilities.

A Diplomatic Gaffe 🍂 (4 February) A US military policeman in Casablanca stopped a car and began to question the driver. 'Name?' asked the MP. 'Sidi Mohammed ben Youssef.' 'Occupation?' '*Fonctionnaire.*' 'What function?' 'Sultan of Morocco.'

Blowing Up One's Father 🍂 (23 July) Eric Brown blew up his paralysed father by attaching a landmine to his wheelchair. He later explained to the court that he had not liked his father's attitude. Brown was declared insane.

An Experiment to Create Siamese Twins 🍂 (24 May) Dr Josef Mengele started work at Auschwitz. Among his many scientifically valueless and sadistic experiments was one in which he attempted to create conjoined twins by sewing the veins in their backs and wrists together. The wounds became badly infected.

1944

Publisher Rejects 'Animal Story' 🍂 The American publishers, Dial Press, rejected George Orwell's political allegory *Animal Farm* on the grounds that it was 'impossible to sell animal stories in the USA'.

The crack Soviet sniper Ludmilla Pavlichenko – responsible for dispatching over 300 Germans – visited Britain and the USA in 1942. She is here seen inspecting a rifle issued to a member of the British Home Guard.

The Last Prosecution under the Witchcraft Act 🙿 (March)

The well-known medium Helen Duncan was found guilty at the Old Bailey under the 1735 Witchcraft Act. At the end of November 1941 she had held a séance in Plymouth at which there reputedly appeared the spirit of a sailor who said, 'My ship is sunk.' On his hatband could be seen the name 'HMS *Barham*', a battleship that had just been sunk in the Mediterranean, and whose loss was being kept a heavily guarded secret by the Admiralty. It was only at the beginning of 1944 that some superstitious members of the intelligence community became anxious that Mrs Duncan might use her powers to leak advance warning of the forthcoming invasion of Normandy, and so decided to bring a prosecution. Mrs Duncan was sentenced to nine months in prison. Prime Minister Churchill poured scorn on this 'tomfoolery', and even paid Mrs Duncan a visit in jail. The Witchcraft Act was repealed in 1951.

Surviving an 18,000-Foot Fall 🙿 (23 March)

Sergeant Nicholas Alkemade was the rear gunner in a Lancaster bomber that was hit by a night-fighter 5500 m (18,000 ft) above Germany. As he watched his parachute go up in flames along with the rest of the plane, he chose to jump rather than burn. As he fell he blacked out, but, remarkably, he survived his fall, having crashed through young pine trees into a deep snow drift. Alkemade lived on for another four decades, dying on 22 June 1987.

The Darkening Ecliptic 🙿 (May)

The Australian avant-garde journal *Angry Penguins* published *The Darkening Ecliptic*, a collection of modernist poems by a hitherto unknown poet, Ern Malley, who had worked as an insurance salesman until his premature death in 1943. That, at least, was what the editor of the journal, Max Harris, was led to believe, until a month later it transpired that the poems had been concocted as a hoax by two young poets, James McAuley and Harold Stewart, who despised the pretensions of later modernism. They had put together the poems in an afternoon: 'We opened books at random, choosing a word or phrase haphazardly. We made lists of these and wove them in nonsensical sentences. We misquoted and made false allusions. We deliberately perpetrated bad verse, and selected awkward rhymes from a *Ripman's Rhyming Dictionary*.' The result included such lines as:

> I am still
> The black swan of trespass on alien waters.

Undeterred by the humiliation he had been subjected to, in the 1950s Max Harris published another literary periodical, with the title *Ern Malley's Journal*. Malley has since become something of a literary celebrity in Australia.

———

Tipping the Doodlebug ᷤ (4 August) Flying Officer Dean, at the controls of a Meteor jet fighter, intercepted a German V1 'doodlebug' over Kent, but found that his guns were jammed. Undeterred, he manoeuvred his plane alongside the flying bomb until his wing was under its wing. He then suddenly banked, upsetting the bomb's steering mechanism, and the bomb fell harmlessly on the countryside south of Tonbridge.

1945

Return to Verdun ᷤ On the walls of one of the fortresses at Verdun, an American GI added to the graffito he had left there two decades before:

> Austin White – Chicago, Ill – 1918
> Austin White – Chicago, Ill – 1945
> This is the last time I want to write my name here.

———

The Crocodiles of Ramree ᷤ (19 February) Japanese troops trapped by Allied forces in the swamps of Ramree Island suffered numerous attacks by crocodiles. One of the Royal Marines guarding the perimeter recalled: 'The scattered rifle shots in the pitch black swamp punctured by the screams of wounded men crushed in the jaws of huge reptiles, and the blurred worrying sound of spinning crocodiles made a cacophony of hell that has rarely been duplicated on earth. At dawn the vultures arrived to clean up what the crocodiles had left .... Of about 1000 Japanese soldiers that entered the swamps of Ramree, only about 20 were found alive.' (In fact, it is thought that about 500 troops had managed to escape, and the number of casualties attributable to crocodile attacks has been debated.)

—

Croix de Guerre for Beckett and Baker &

(March) The playwright and future Nobel laureate Samuel Beckett was awarded the Croix de Guerre by General de Gaulle for performing what Beckett later called 'Boy Scout stuff' on behalf of the French Resistance. Others who received the medal for their underground work in France during the war include the exotic dancer and chanteuse, Josephine Baker.

—

Killed by Balloons &

(5 May) The Revd Archi Mitchell, from Bly, Oregon, and his wife Elsie took some local children on an outing that ended in tragedy, when Mrs Mitchell and five of the children were killed by an unmanned Japanese balloon bomb. From late 1944 the Japanese had launched hundreds of these *fusen bakudan* ('wind ship bombs'), which rose up into the jet stream and were carried across the Pacific to western North America. Elsie Mitchell and the five children were the only victims of enemy action to die in the contiguous United States.

—

Faking Vermeer &

(29 May) Han van Meegeren was arrested by the Dutch authorities as a collaborator, after it transpired that during the German occupation he had, via a dealer, sold a painting by Vermeer – regarded as a Dutch national treasure – to the Nazi leader Hermann Goering. Faced with the death penalty, van Meegeren explained that he had forged the Vermeer, along with several others that he had sold since 1937. To prove his innocence

Josephine Baker, a surprise winner of the Croix de Guerre in 1945.

of collaboration, if not of forgery, he proceeded to paint another 'Vermeer' in prison. He was lauded by the Dutch public as the man who had put one over on the Nazis, and was sentenced to the minimum one year in jail for falsification and fraud. He died of a heart attack on 30 December 1947, before he could serve his sentence.

———

City Saved by Sentimental Attachment &. US Secretary of
War Henry S. Stimson vetoed the choice of Kyoto as the preferred target

for the first atomic bomb as he had spent his honeymoon there and thus had a sentimental attachment to the ancient Japanese capital.

———

On the Cruelty of Karma ❧ (29 July) The USS *Indianapolis*, the cruiser that took components of the atomic bombs later dropped on Japan across the Pacific, was torpedoed and sank. Out of a crew of 800, only 318 survived, the rest dying of thirst, drowning or shark attacks. It was the worst disaster at sea suffered by the US Navy.

———

On the Dangers of Postprandial Cigars ❧ (15 September) The avant-garde composer Anton Webern was shot dead by a US army cook during the Allied occupation of Austria. Webern had stepped outside his house after dinner to enjoy a cigar when the soldier fired three times into the dark. 'I have been shot,' exclaimed the composer. 'It is over.' The cook who killed him was overcome with remorse, declined into alcoholism, and died a decade later.

———

Disappearance of US Planes Spawns Decades of Balderdash ❧ (5 December) A squadron of five US Navy Avenger torpedo bombers piloted by trainees took off from Fort Lauderdale, Florida. They were never heard of again, until they reappeared in a desert in Mexico in Steven Spielberg's film, *Close Encounters of the Third Kind* (1977), a work of fiction that nevertheless reinforced the belief of many Americans in the Bermuda Triangle and alien abductions. In all likelihood the inexperienced pilots became lost, ran out of fuel and were forced to ditch into the sea on a dark and stormy night.

1946

———

Nazi Legacy in Bournemouth ❧ The *Bournemouth Evening Echo* carried the following story:

Mrs Irene Graham of Thorpe Avenue, Boscombe, delighted the audience with her reminiscence of the German prisoner of war who was sent each week to do her garden. He was repatriated at the end of 1945, she recalled. 'He'd always seemed a nice friendly chap, but when the crocuses came up in the middle of our lawn in February 1946, they spelt out Heil Hitler.'

Ghost Rockets Over Scandinavia &ent; (May–December) Some 2000 sightings of unidentified 'ghost rockets' were made across Scandinavia, mostly over Sweden. Intelligence officials at the time concluded that they were almost certainly test flights of German V-1 and V-2 rockets captured by the Soviets, although over the years the usual UFO conspiracy theories have arisen.

A Case of Poor Judgement &ent; The Irish confidence trickster 'Major' Michael Corrigan (not to be confused with Archbishop Michael Corrigan of New York, 1839–1902) hanged himself in Brixton Prison with his Guards tie. He had been arrested in the bar of the Ritz Hotel while trying to sell a pension policy to Sir Richard Jackson, the director of public prosecutions.

1947

Hokum in New Mexico &ent; (early July) The Roswell Army Air Base in New Mexico issued a press release stating that wreckage in the form of a 'flying disk' had been found on a nearby ranch. This inspired great interest in the media, but a few hours later the original statement was revised, stating that it was a weather balloon that had crashed. That might have been that, but in the 1970s the story was revisited by conspiracy theorists, who were convinced that the US government had covered up a UFO landing, and stories (and even a purportedly genuine film) circulated of dead aliens being subjected to autopsies.

The Last Pants of the Raj &ent; Earl Mountbatten of Burma was appointed Viceroy of India. While Mountbatten's relations with Jawaharlal Nehru were diplomatic, those of his wife Edwina with the leader of the Indian independence movement were carnal – or so it was widely believed. Among other affairs rumoured to have been enjoyed by the countess was one with Paul Robeson, although she denied ever having met him.

The Wedding of Mrs Betty Glucksburg &⁕ (20 November)
Princess Elizabeth married Philip Mountbatten, né Schleswig-Holstein-Sonderburg-Glücksburg. Thus to republicans she became known as Mrs Betty Glucksburg.

Legislation Regarding Nuts &⁕ The British government enacted
legislation setting up a scheme to plant vast quantities of groundnuts (peanuts) in the East African colony of Tanganyika. Among the provision of the act was the following:

> In the Nuts (unground) (other than ground-nuts) Order, the expression nuts shall have reference to such nuts, other than ground-nuts, as would but for this amending Order not qualify as nuts (unground) (other than ground-nuts) by reason of their being nuts (unground).

Such clarity was perhaps a herald of things to come. The scheme was a complete failure, owing to lack of leadership and the unsuitability of both climate and terrain, and the entire investment of £49 million was lost.

1948

The Man Who Couldn't Spell 'Fuck' &⁕ Publication of Norman
Mailer's war novel, *The Naked and the Dead*, in which he had been persuaded by his publisher to use the euphemism 'fug'. When he was later introduced to the film star Tallulah Bankhead, she declared, 'So you're the young man who can't spell *fuck*.'

———

Theatrical Criticism 🐾 A member of a Liverpool audience was heard to opine at the end of a performance of Chekhov's *The Cherry Orchard*, 'Well, Mildred, that was the worst play I've seen since *King Lear*.' Of the latter, Queen Victoria had opined, 'A strange, horrible business, but I suppose good enough for Shakespeare's day.'

———

Beastliness in the Boondocks 🐾 Publication of *Sexual Behaviour in the Human Male* by Alfred Kinsey. Among other things, the Kinsey Report (as it became known) estimated that 40–60% of rural US teenagers raised on livestock farms had had sex with animals.

1949

The Artichoke Queen 🐾 The career of Marilyn Monroe began to look up when she became the official Artichoke Queen of California.

———

Shag the Caribou 🐾 Publication of *Shag the Caribou*, a children's book by C. Bernard Rutley.

———

The Ararat Anomaly 🐾 A US Air Force reconnaissance flight over Mount Ararat on the Turkish–Soviet border photographed a feature known as the 'Ararat Anomaly'. The feature, situated some 2.2. km from the summit, at a height of 4724 m (15,500 ft), has subsequently been photographed from both aircraft and satellites. Fundamentalist Christians in the United States are convinced it is the remains of Noah's Ark, which Genesis describes as coming to land on the mountain. Genesis states that the Ark had a length-to-width ratio of 6:1, a ratio that is (approximately) shared by the Anomaly. The director of the Boston University Centre for Remote Sensing has looked at the photographs, and believes the 'Anomaly' is nothing but 'a ledge of rock in partial shadow, with varied thickness of snow and ice cover'.

1950

Delayed in the Post for Fifty-Six Years &▲ (3 March) A letter posted in London on this day took 56 years to arrive at its destination – Trinity College, Cambridge. It was eventually delivered in May 2006. The letter, addressed to a Mr George Green, reads, 'George, will meet at Monty's next weekend. Is 2 p.m. acceptable? Love Gwen.' Who knows whether Mr Green ever made this assignation?

President Threatens Music Critic &▲ (5 December) Miss Margaret Truman, an amateur soprano and daughter of the US president Harry S. Truman, gave a public recital in Washington DC. Paul Hume, music critic of the *Washington Post*, penned an unfavourable review: 'There are few moments during her recital when one can relax and feel confident that she will make her goal, which is the end of the song.' Infuriated, Margaret's father scribbled off an angry note to Hume: 'I have never met you, but if I do you'll need a new nose and plenty of beefsteak and perhaps a supporter below.'

1951

The Smoking Full-Back &▲ The French rugby league team beat Australia in a test series, despite the fact that their full-back, Puig-Albert, was a dedicated smoker who would often nip to the touch line to have a quick drag.

MP Kicks Belgian Ambassador Down Stairs &▲ Lieutenant Colonel Sir Walter Bromley-Davenport MP put paid to his prospects of becoming a high-flyer in government when, as a junior whip in the Conservative Party, he kicked the Belgian ambassador downstairs, in the mistaken belief that the posterior he had aimed at belonged to a colleague who had missed a crucial vote.

1952

Pigeon Suffers Indignity € A Nigerian was fined £50 for committing an act of indecency with a pigeon in Trafalgar Square, and a further £10 for taking it home and eating it.

———

Secret Experiments Over Southwest England € (15–16 August) The Devon seaside village of Lynmouth was devastated by a flash flood as the River Lyn broke its banks, following a rain storm in which 229 mm (9 in) of rain fell within 24 hours on Exmoor. Over 100 buildings were destroyed, 420 people made homeless, and 34 people killed. There have been suggestions that the exceptionally heavy rain may have been caused by secret RAF cloud-seeding experiments being carried out in southwest England.

———

The Sound of Silence € (29 August) First performance of John Cage's piece *4′ 33″*, comprising 4 minutes and 33 seconds of silence. The performer, David Tudor, began by lifting the lid of the piano, and a little later closed it again, without having touched the keyboard.

1953

LSD Administered by MI6 € A group of young national servicemen were taken to Porton Down, the UK's chemical and biological defence research establishment, under the impression that they were to participate in an experiment to test a possible cure for the common cold. However, the experiment, administered by scientists from MI6, involved them unwittingly taking doses of LSD, which MI6 thought might prove effective as a 'truth drug'. One participant recalls seeing the skull beneath his companion's skin, and finding that the floor had turned liquid and was writhing with worm-like forms. In 2006 the Ministry of Defence offered three men compensation.

1954

Sprinkle's Organ ❤ A Pentagon scientist, Leland W. Sprinkle, turned the stalactites in the Luray Caverns, Virginia, into what he called a 'stalacpipe organ'. The stalactites, each carefully tuned, are struck by rubber mallets, controlled electronically from a keyboard.

Haydn's Head ❤ (5 June) The skull of Joseph Haydn was reunited with the rest of his body, 145 years after they had first been separated. On his death in 1809, Haydn's patron, Prince Nikolaus II Esterházy, had given permission to his secretary, Joseph Rosenbaum, to take the composer's head away for a phrenological examination. Rosenbaum had promised to return it in a few weeks, but in 1820, when Prince Nikolaus moved Haydn's body to a specially built mausoleum at Eisenstadt, it was discovered that the corpse was still headless. The skull went through a number of adventures before finally ending up in 1839 on top of a piano in a glass case in the Gesellschaft der Musikfreunde in Vienna. It was from here that it was finally taken to the mausoleum at Eisenstadt in 1954.

The Canvey Island Monster ❤ (November) On the shores of Canvey Island, Essex, a number of residents found the decayed corpse of an apparently bipedal creature some 75 cm (30 in) long, with bulging eyes and hind legs with five toes each. A similar creature was found on Canvey Island the following year. The 'Canvey Island Monster' is thought by ichthyologists to have been an anglerfish, whose fleshy pectoral fins are sometimes taken for short legs and feet.

1955

The Mysterious Paternity of Maurice Utrillo ❤ (5 November) Death of the French painter Maurice Utrillo. His mother had been Suzanne Valadon, the painter and artist's model, but the identity of his father is uncertain. There is a story that after his birth, his mother took him to Renoir, who said the baby could not be his, because the colour was terrible. Then she took him to Degas, who denied paternity on the grounds that the form was terrible. Finally, Mlle Valadon confided her difficulty to a lesser-known artist called Miguel Utrillo, who told her to call the boy Utrillo, declaring 'I would be glad to put my name to the work of either Renoir or Degas.'

1956

Khrushchev Denounces Stalin Shock ♣ (24 February) During Khrushchev's secret speech to the Soviet Communist Party congress denouncing his predecessor Stalin, some in the audience were so shocked that they suffered heart attacks, while others committed suicide shortly afterwards.

Vive la Frangleterre! ♣ (September) The French prime minister, Guy Mollet, proposed to the British premier, Anthony Eden, that France should become part of the United Kingdom. The French economy was then in dire straights, and Mollet regarded that of the UK as a role model. The suggestion of union was rebuffed. Two weeks later Mollet requested that France should become a member of the Commonwealth, with Queen Elizabeth I as the French head of state. This met with no warmer a welcome, and the following year France signed the Treaty of Rome, becoming a founder-member of the Common Market – from which the UK was excluded for another 16 years.

It was not the first proposal for an Anglo-French union. In the darker days of 1940, as the Germans swept over the French defences, Winston Churchill had suggested that the two countries unite. Marshal Pétain responded, 'To make a union with Great Britain would be fusion with a corpse.'

___

Prime Minister's Wife Mascaras His Moustache &

(4 November) A minute before the British prime minister, Sir Anthony Eden, was to make a TV broadcast to the nation on the Suez Crisis, Lady Eden applied mascara to his moustache.

___

A Ruling on Un-Parliamentary Language &

The Speaker of the House of Commons ruled that the word 'twerp' was not un-parliamentary language, as he believed 'it was a sort of technical term of the aviation industry'. However, some years later the republican MP Willie Hamilton was upbraided by the Speaker for referring to Prince Charles as 'that young twerp'.

___

Plumber's Son Possessed by Tibetan Monk &

The distinguished house of Secker & Warburg published *The Third Eye*, a volume of memoirs by a Tibetan lama called Lobsang Rampa. Not everybody was convinced by the book, and Heinrich Harrer, author of *Seven Years in Tibet*, hired a private detective to investigate. It transpired that Rampa was actually Cyril Henry Hoskin, the son of a Devon plumber. When challenged, Hoskin explained that some years previously he had fallen out of a tree onto his head, and that subsequently a Tibetan monk had taken over his body.

1957

An Anthropoid Artist &

A painter called Congo held an exhibition at the Institute of Contemporary Arts in London. Among his admirers were Picasso and Miró. Congo was a chimpanzee.

___

A Bumper Spaghetti Harvest &

(1 April) BBC TV's heavyweight current affairs programme, *Panorama*, carried a report on the bumper spaghetti harvest in Ticino, Switzerland, accompanied by film of spaghetti

being gathered from spaghetti trees. The report was presented by Richard Dimbleby, then the epitome of broadcasting probity, and was thus widely believed, despite the date.

———

Mind-Control Experiments in Montreal

Dr Ewan Cameron began a series of mind-control experiments at the Allan Memorial Institute in Montreal on behalf of the CIA. His experiments – often conducted on patients who has been admitted for relatively minor problems such as anxiety or postnatal depression – included the application of electroconvulsive therapy at up to 40 times the usual power. Dr Cameron would also put patients into drug-induced comas for up to three months, while playing them looped tapes of simple statements or noise.

———

Lord Wharncliffe Joins Beat Combo

Release of the album *Shake, Rattle and Roll* by the Johnny Lenniz band. On drums was Alan James Montagu-Wortley-Mackenzie, 4th Earl of Wharncliffe, whose other careers included able seaman, pub landlord and garage mechanic.

———

The Inventor of the Orgone Box

(3 November) Death of the German-born psychoanalyst Wilhelm Reich in the federal penitentiary in Lewisburg, Pennsylvania. Reich had been imprisoned for promoting, in defiance of the US Food and Drug Act, his orgone boxes, which he declared could cure maladies from common colds and impotence to cancer. He held that orgone energy was a form of 'primordial cosmic energy' responsible for everything from orgasms to gravity and the formation of galaxies. The Food and Drug Administration took Reich – a former communist – to court in 1954. The judge issued an injunction prohibiting the movement of any orgone-therapy equipment across state lines, and ordered that all of Reich's publications that included the words 'orgone energy' be destroyed. Reich was arrested in May 1956 for a technical violation of the injunction, and sentenced to two years in prison.

1958

The Intergalactic Walrus and the Bishop from Mars 🦌
Publication of *Have You Lived Before This Life* by L. Ron Hubbard, the founder of Scientology. The book describes the traumatic past-life experiences remembered by some of Hubbard's followers, including falling in love with a robot disguised as a red-haired beauty, being metamorphosed into an intergalactic walrus, and suffering a literal steamrollering by a bishop from Mars.

The Last of the Red-Hot Debs 🦌 This year saw the last official
season at which debutantes were presented to the Queen. Among those coming out that season was Rose Dugdale, who later described her coming-out ball as 'one of those pornographic affairs which cost about what sixty old-age pensioners receive in six months'. In the 1970s Ms Dugdale was imprisoned for her activities in support of the IRA, including a daring art heist in 1974. Other debs of the class of '58 included Teresa Hayter, later a member of the International Marxist Group, and Nicolette Powell, who left her husband, the Marquis of Londonderry, and ran off with musician Georgie Fame.

1959

Bird Diapers 🦌 Bertha Dlugi of Milwaukee invented a nappy for pet
parrots, so that furniture and carpets would remain unblemished during exercise flights.

1960

An Octogenarian Stripper 🦌 (September) At the Haslemere Home
for the Elderly in Great Yarmouth, a male inmate suffered a fatal heart attack when fellow inmate, Gladys Elton (81), performed a striptease.

The Duck Liberation Front ☙ Foundation of the Basque separatist organization ETA (*Euskadi Ta Askatasuna*). In fact, it was originally called ATA (*Aberri Ta Askatasuna*), until activists realized that in some Basque dialects *ata* means 'duck'.

1961

Wanted: Motherly Soul to Deal with Trying Circumstances ☙ As the UK government made plans for the staffing requirements of a secret bunker for cabinet ministers in the even of nuclear holocaust, a civil servant outlined the need for a welfare officer, a 'kindly, fairly fat, motherly sort of soul, with a broad pair of shoulders on which people can weep. She need have no welfare experience ... but should be prepared to work hard in what would undoubtedly be trying circumstances.'

Only Obeying Orders ☙ (July) Stanley Milgram began a series of controversial psychological experiments at Yale University, in which subjects were instructed to give another subject (actually an actor) an electric shock if they failed to answer a question correctly. As the experiment continued, the strength of the electric shock apparently increased, and the recipient would mimic pain, screaming and begging for the experiment to stop. However, the person overseeing the experiment would instruct the subject to continue, and in many cases they did, even while expressing their unhappiness.

1962

Casus Belli ☙ (20 February) John Glenn made the first US manned orbital space flight. Just prior to this, the Joint Chiefs of Staff sent a memo to President Kennedy suggesting that if Glenn's rocket blew up on the launch pad, it could be blamed on Cuba and used as an excuse for invading the island.

Castro's Beard Targeted by Assassins

Castro's Beard Targeted by Assassins ❧ (16 March) The CIA briefed President John F. Kennedy on Operation Mongoose, a series of planned covert actions against Cuba. Among the ideas floated were projects to assassinate Fidel Castro using exploding cigars, a poisoned wetsuit and seashells planted with bombs, to be placed in areas where Castro was known to go diving. Another mooted plan was to use hair-removal powder to make Castro's beard fall out – as one CIA agent recalls, the idea was that 'the Cuban people would all fall over laughing at him and he would be ridiculed. This was a measure of our desperation.' As Castro himself once told a journalist, 'If surviving assassination were an Olympic event, I would win the gold medal.'

Trots in Space ❧ Formation of the Fourth International (Posadist), a breakaway Trotskyite group led by Juan Posada, an Argentinian who believed that UFOs come from a socialist future, or possibly another planet where socialism is already established. The Posadists – who largely disappeared following Posada's death in 1981 – also welcomed the prospect of global nuclear war, which they believed would clear the way for the establishment of socialism on Earth.

1963

Harold Wilson a KGB Agent, says CIA ❧ (9 April) Death of Hugh Gaitskell, leader of the Labour Party, at the early age of 56. The CIA believed he had been poisoned by the KGB, and that his successor, Harold Wilson, was a Soviet agent. This latter charge was repeated in 1967 by L. Ron Hubbard, founder of the Church of Scientology, after Wilson's government had banned foreign Scientologists from visiting Britain.

The Duchess and the Headless Man ❧ The Duke of Argyll sued his wife Margaret for divorce. Amongst the evidence he produced of her several adulteries were Polaroid photographs of Her Grace naked apart from three strings of pearls, in the act of fellating a man whose head could not be seen. For many years speculation was rife as to the identity of 'the Headless Man' – could it be Winston Churchill's son-in-law Duncan Sandys, or even the Duke of Edinburgh? But in 1999 it was revealed that the beneficiary of the Duchess's bounty was the American film star, Douglas Fairbanks Jnr.

His Tremendousness, Prince Georgio of Seborga ❧ The citizens of the small Ligurian village of Seborga, near the French border, elected the head of the local flower-growers' cooperative, Giorgio Carbone, as their head of state, with the title 'Giorgio I, Prince of Seborga'. Carbone had argued that Seborga had never been incorporated into Italy: it had originally been a small independent feudal state, and, although it was sold to the king of Savoy and Sardinia in 1729, the sale was never registered. Seborga was not mentioned at the Congress of Vienna in 1815, nor in the 1861 Act of Unification, nor in the constitutional instruments creating the Italian republic in 1946. However, relations between Seborga and Italy are peaceable and cooperative, the Seborghini for the most part obeying the laws of the republic, voting in Italian local and national elections, and welcoming the services provided by its larger neighbour. In 2006 Princess Yasmine von Hohenstaufen Anjou Plantagenet, who claims to be a descendant of the 13th-century Holy Roman Emperor Frederick II, and thus rightful ruler of Seborga, upset the villagers when she wrote to the Italian president offering to return the principality. 'The girl cannot give away something she does not own,' commented Prince Giorgio, who is addressed as 'Your Tremendousness' and has the virtually unanimous support of his fellow Seborghini.

1964

An Apology ❧ (17 October) As James Callaghan, the new chancellor of the exchequer, settled behind his desk at Number 11 Downing Street following Labour's election victory, his Conservative predecessor, Reginald Maudling, stuck his head round the door and said, 'Good luck, old cock. Sorry to leave it in such a mess.'

1965

The Spinning Bed &✦ Mr and Mrs Blonsky of the United States patented a spinning bed, designed to facilitate childbirth by the deployment of centrifugal force.

———

Second Thoughts &✦ In the document *Nostra Aetate*, the Vatican decided, after 2000 years, that it was time to stop blaming all Jews, past and present, for the death of Christ.

———

Dramatic Criticism &✦ (December) During a performance of *Mother Goose* in Southsea, the cast found themselves under fire from an air rifle.

1966

Erotica Calms Men Under Fire &✦ The classical scholar Sir Maurice Bowra published his memoirs, in which he recalled that while serving on the Western Front in the First World War his commanding office would calm his men during German bombardments by reading out passages from *The New Lady's Tickler: The Adventures of Lady Lovesport and Audacious Harry*, a classic of Victorian erotica by Captain Edward Sellon.

———

Mothman Sighted &✦ (12 November) In a cemetery in the Point Pleasant area of West Virginia, five men preparing a grave reported they had seen 'a brown human shape with wings' take off from nearby trees and fly over them. Several more sightings of what the press dubbed 'Mothman' occurred in the area through to the end of 1967; in some reports the creature had glowing eyes. Sceptics believe that the sightings were most likely of owls.

1967

The Zionists of Siam

The Zionists of Siam ❧ (June) Poland's communist government, determined to pin the blame for an outbreak of student unrest on the country's small surviving Jewish community, instructed workers' militias to demonstrate against the *syjoninci* (i.e. Zionists). Some pro-government workers duly carried placards bearing the legend '*Syjoninci do Syjamu*', which translates into English as 'Zionists back to Siam'.

Australian Premier Disappears

Australian Premier Disappears ❧ (17 December) The Australian prime minister, Harold Holt, disappeared. A keen snorkeller, he had been swimming off a beach near Melbourne, and had plunged into the surf and then had become hidden from view. A host of conspiracy theories immediately surfaced, among which the favourites were that he had been abducted by the Chinese aboard a submarine, or that the CIA had terminated him with extreme prejudice, believing he was about to withdraw Australian troops from Vietnam – although a year before Holt had won an election on the slogan 'All the Way with LBJ' – i.e. a policy of supporting US President Lyndon B. Johnson's strategy in Southeast Asia. There seems little doubt that he drowned when he was sucked down by a strong undertow. Somewhat ironically, he was commemorated by the Harold Holt Swimming Centre in the Melbourne suburb of Malvern.

Foundation of the Yippies

Foundation of the Yippies ❧ (31 December) A radical youth movement known as the 'Yippies' was founded at a marijuana-fuelled party in New York's Greenwich Village. Only later in the following year did the movement's founders, Abbie Hoffman and Jerry Rubin, decide that the name stood for the 'Youth International Party'. At the Democratic National

Pig for President: the Yippie leader Jerry Rubin
(second from the right) with Pigasus, his favoured
candidate for the presidency, Chicago, 1968. Shortly
afterwards, the little group were arrested.

Convention in August 1968, Rubin declared the candidacy of a pig for the US
presidency as part of the protests in Chicago against the Vietnam War. Both
Rubin and the pig were arrested. In 1970 Hoffman published *Steal This Book*,
a guide to alternative and subversive activity, which many bookshops refused
to stock, not least because of its title.

1968

The Dangers of Lust and Lentils

The Dangers of Lust and Lentils ❧ Stanley Green began his 25-year campaign in Oxford Street against the dangers of lust and lentils. His sandwich board (now in the possession of the Museum of London) proclaimed:

> LESS PASSION
> FROM LESS
> PROTEIN
> LESS FISH
> MEAT BIRD
> CHEESE
> EGG: PEAS
> BEANS, NUTS
> and SITTING

The Answer to Life, the Universe and Everything?

The Answer to Life, the Universe and Everything? ❧ (4 February) Neal Cassady, the inspiration for the character of Dean Moriarty in Jack Kerouac's Beat novel *On the Road*, died of exposure in Mexico after sleeping outdoors on a rainy night following a binge of alcohol and Seconal. His last words were, allegedly, 'Sixty-four thousand nine hundred and twenty-eight.'

Bobby Kennedy Gets His Hair Cut

Bobby Kennedy Gets His Hair Cut ❧ (March) As Senator Robert Kennedy pondered whether he should run for the Democratic presidential candidacy, he received a number of letters advising him to get his hair cut. 'No one wants a hippy for president,' one said. Kennedy did indeed have his hair cut after announcing his candidacy, but was assassinated on 4 June.

Italian Navy Blows Up Island Republic

Italian Navy Blows Up Island Republic ❧ (24 June) Establishment of the Republic of Rose Island on a platform measuring 400 square metres in the Adriatic Sea off Rimini. The artificial island included shops, a restaurant, bar, nightclub and post office (the republic had its own stamps). The official language was Esperanto. The Italian government interpreted the establishment of the republic as a dodge to avoid paying sales tax, and shortly after the declaration of independence the Italian navy blew up the place with dynamite.

Duelling Ronald Reagan with Marshmallows ❧ (October)
Speaking at a rally at Stanford University, Eldridge Cleaver, leader of the Peace and Freedom Party, challenged California governor Ronald Reagan to a duel to the death. 'Ronald Reagan is a punk, a sissy and a coward,' he said. 'I give him a choice of weapons – a gun, a knife, a baseball bat – or marshmallows.'

1969

Ireland Defeats West Indies at Cricket – Again ❧ (2 July)
Ireland's cricket side defeated the West Indies by nine wickets, having bowled them out for 25. The West Indies side included Clive Lloyd and Clyde Walcott. (*See also* 1928.)

The Football War ❧ (14 July) El Salvador launched an invasion of
neighbouring Honduras. Tensions between the two countries had been simmering for some time, the military governments of each country mounting xenophobic campaigns to distract their impoverished people from their economic problems. The crunch came with the North American qualifying round for the following year's World Cup finals. To the accompaniment of much violence and little sportsmanship, El Salvador lost away to Honduras on 6 June 1969, and a young Salvadoran woman who committed suicide at the outcome was given a state funeral. On the return leg, on 15 June, El Salvador won at home, Honduran morale having been dented when the

Salvadoran authorities raised an old rag instead of the Honduran flag. El Salvador also won the playoff match on 27 June, and the same day Honduras broke off diplomatic relations. On 14 July the Salvadoran air force bombed targets in Honduras, while the army crossed the border. The following day the Salvadorans captured the Honduran regional capital of Nueva Ocotepeque, but their advance came to a standstill as they ran out of fuel and ammunition. On 18 July the Organization of American States organized a ceasefire, and a peace treaty was eventually signed in 1980.

Rock and Roll Bakery 🐟 The cake on the cover of the Rolling Stones' album *Let It Bleed* was created by a then unknown Delia Smith.

Carnal Relations with the Deity 🐟 (5 December) Death of Princess Alice of Battenberg, mother of the Duke of Edinburgh. Enormously pious, but rarely in the best of mental health, she believed she was having carnal relations with Christ, and was only at the last minute dissuaded from turning up at the coronation of her daughter-in-law, Elizabeth II, in a nun's habit. One of her physicians, Dr Binswanger, diagnosed a 'neurotic pre-psychotic libidinous condition'. At the end of her life she asked to be buried in Jerusalem. Her son (with whom she had a difficult relationship) told her that this was a ridiculous notion, as he couldn't visit her grave there. 'Don't be silly,' she responded, 'there's a bus service.'

1970

Everything in the Garden is Lovely 🐟 A painter of biscuit tins at Huntley and Palmer got his own back for his imminent redundancy by adding some tiny details to his otherwise quaint picture of Victorian ladies taking tea in a cottage garden. His additions included a pot of jam with 'shit' on the label, and a pair of copulating dogs among the tulips. It was several years before the details were noticed and production of the tin halted.

Jesus said to be a Hallucinogenic Toadstool *❧* Publication of
The Sacred Mushroom and the Cross by John Allegro, lecturer in comparative
Semitic philology and Hebrew at the University of Manchester. Allegro
argued that Jesus was a hallucinogenic toadstool and Jehovah 'a mighty penis
in the heavens who in a thunderous climax of the storm ejaculated semen upon
the furrows of Mother Earth'.

Novelist Commits Ritual Suicide *❧* (25 November) The
Japanese novelist and nationalist, Yukio Mishima, committed seppuku (hara
kiri or suicide by ritual disembowelling) on a balcony in an army barracks,
having failed to persuade the soldiers to mount a right-wing coup to restore
the emperor to his former power. One of his companions was to complete
the ritual by cutting off Mishima's head (so bringing an otherwise slow and
agonizing death to a swift conclusion), but botched it, and another colleague
was obliged to finish the job.

1971

Lord of All the Beasts of the Earth *❧* (25 January) General Idi
Amin seized power in Uganda, and subsequently declared he was to be known
as 'His Excellency President for Life Field Marshal Al Hadji Dr Idi Amin,
VC, DSO, MC, Lord of All the Beasts of the Earth and the Fishes of the Sea
and Conqueror of the British Empire in Africa in General and Uganda in
Particular'.

Britain At Last Sees Reason *❧* (15 February) Britain eventually
adopted a decimal currency, 155 years after it was first proposed by the MP
John Croker.

———

A Ballet for Chamber Pots ❧ First performance of *Staatstheater*, a 'ballet for non-dancers' by the Argentine-born composer Mauricio Kagel. The piece is orchestrated for chamber pots and enema equipment.

1972

———

OED Includes F-Word ❧ For the first time, the *Oxford English Dictionary* included the word 'fuck'.

———

Artist Masturbates in Gallery ❧ (January) In *Seedbed*, the US artist Vito Acconci hid himself under a ramp in an art gallery. Here he masturbated while talking into a PA system about his fantasies involving the people walking above him.

———

A Way to Foil Hijackers ❧ Jack Jensen, of Fort Worth, Texas, patented a system for foiling aeroplane hijackers. Under each passenger seat would be positioned a hypodermic syringe, ready to inject any would-be hijacker with either a sedative or fatal dose, should the pilot deem it necessary. The airlines judged that passengers would not relax during their in-flight experience if they were aware that chemical death lurked only a centimetre beneath their bottoms.

———

Falling from Six Miles High ❧ (26 January) Vesna Vulović was a flight attendant aboard a Yugoslav DC-9 airliner when it was blown up by Croatian terrorists at a height of 10,000 m (33,000 ft). She fell to Earth still strapped to her seat, and amazingly survived as the speed of her fall was absorbed when she hit the snow-covered slopes of a mountain. She suffered extensive fractures – her skull, both legs, and several vertebrae – but made a full recovery.

A young woman about to sate the hunger of a giant rabbit; a still
from the 1972 film, *Night of the Lepus*.

Killer Rabbits 🙾 MGM released *Night of the Lepus*, a tale of giant killer
rabbits, based on Russell Braddon's novel *The Year of the Angry Rabbit*. One
critic deemed the film only suitable 'for insomniacs with lax standards'.

—

Wives Compared to Thoroughbred Mares ❧ (June) In a
Dublin court, in the course of an action for criminal conversation (by which a man could sue his wife's lover for damages), Mr Justice Butler declared, 'In this country a wife is regarded as a chattel, just as a thoroughbred mare or cow.'

—

An Experiment Worthy of Mengele ❧ It was revealed that the
Tuskegee Syphilis Study, which had begun in Alabama 40 years before, had deliberately withheld penicillin from its subjects – impoverished and often illiterate African Americans – so that the scientists conducting the study could examine how the disease spreads and what it does to the body in its final, fatal stages. Penicillin had been successfully used to cure syphilis since 1947.

1973

—

Lord Spliffy and the Call Girls ❧ Lord Lambton, a Conservative
government minister, resigned 'for personal and health reasons', after the *News of the World* carried photographs of him smoking cannabis while in bed with two prostitutes.

—

Peace and Order Ensured by Expelling Population ❧
The British government began expelling the native population of Diego Garcia, in the Indian Ocean archipelago of the Chagos Islands. They claimed to be furthering the 'peace, order and good government' of the UK overseas territory, but in fact cleared the 2000 indigenous Chagossians so that the USA could build a vast air base on the island. In 2006 two judges reviewing the case in the high court in London described the UK government's action as 'repugnant'.

British Rail Commissions Flying Saucer ❧ Plans for a vehicle designed for the British Railways Board were patented by its inventor Charles Osmond Frederick. The vehicle, which was broadly saucer-shaped, was intended to whiz passengers into space and around the Earth and was to be powered by a 'controlled thermonuclear fusion reaction'. As far as is known, British Rail did not get so far as building a prototype.

1974

Jazz Bagpipes ❧ Rufus Harley, of African American and Cherokee descent, made his London debut at Ronnie Scott's club, playing jazz bagpipes. He had traded his saxophone in for a set of bagpipes after hearing a pipe lament at President Kennedy's funeral in 1963.

Boom Boom ❧ During a performance by the Atlanta Symphony Orchestra of Tchaikovsky's *1812 Overture* – which calls for the repeated firing of a cannon at the climax – all 16 cannons went off at once by mistake. The audience was deafened, then blinded by clouds of smoke, and then sprayed with foam as the smoke detectors did their job.

The Last Warriors of World War II ❧ (March) Lieutenant Hiroo Onada of the Imperial Japanese Army emerged from the jungle of Lubang, in the Philippines, unaware that the Second World War had ended 29 years previously. He only agreed to surrender after talking to his former commanding officer. He was not the last to surrender, however. In April 1980 Captain Fumio Nakahira was found in the mountains of Mindoro in the Philippines.

Dodgy Minister Disappears ❧ (20 November) The British

Labour MP and former minister John Stonehouse faked his own death by leaving a pile of his clothes on a beach in Miami. He had in fact absconded to Australia with the intention of escaping official inquiries into his business affairs and setting up a new life with his mistress, Sheila Buckley. He was spotted in Melbourne by Australian police, who initially took him for Lord Lucan, and deported to the UK, where he was sentenced to seven years for fraud.

1975

Invention Provides 'Cheeky Derriere Relief' &. Julie Newmar, the actress known for her role as Catwoman on TV, was granted a patent for her 'Pantyhose with Shaping Band for Cheeky Derriere Relief'.

Dog Assassinated on Exmoor &. (24 October) Rinka, a Great Dane on loan to the male model Norman Scott, was shot on Exmoor by Andrew Newton, a former airline pilot, who then, according to Scott, pointed the gun at Scott himself. The following January Scott alleged in court that he had become the victim of a murder conspiracy following the end of a homosexual affair with Jeremy Thorpe, the leader of the Liberal Party. Thorpe resigned his post in May 1976, and three years later was acquitted of conspiracy to murder. At the 1979 election, the satirist Auberon Waugh stood for the Dog Lovers' Party against Thorpe in his own constituency. Although Waugh only polled 79 votes, Thorpe lost his seat. It has been suggested that the whole business was engineered by right-wing elements in the security services to discredit Thorpe.

The Slow Death of El Caudillo &. (20 November) Death of General Franco, the Spanish dictator. He had been kept just this side of death's door by his doctors for many weeks, allegedly so that his death could coincide with the date of the death 39 years earlier of the Falangist leader José

Antonio Primo de Rivera. In the USA newscasters had frequently noted that 'General Franco is still alive.' After Franco's death, on the Weekend Update segment of *Saturday Night Live*, Chevy Chase would announce, 'General Franco is still dead.' Franco was posthumously canonized by Pope Gregory XVII of the Palmarian Catholic Church, a right-wing Spanish sect.

1976

Literary Fisticuffs in Mexico

The Colombian novelist Gabriel García Márquez (later winner of the Nobel Prize) came to blows in a Mexican cinema with the Peruvian novelist Mario Vargas Llosa. The two had been close friends, and have never revealed the reasons for their falling out.

Defender Scores Four Goals

(20 March) Aston Villa's defender Chris Nicholl scored a remarkable four goals in a match against Leicester. Unfortunately two of them were against his own side.

Speaking Ill of the Dead

(12 August) Death of Tom Driberg, the Labour MP noted as a Soviet double-agent and friend of the gangsters Ron and Reggie Kray, and also as a flamboyant adherent of both homosexuality and the High Church tendency in the Church of England. In his will he required that at his memorial service, rather than the usual eulogy, he be upbraided for his many sins.

Emperor Bokassa, the Thirteenth Apostle

(4 December) Jean-Bédel Bokassa, dictator of the Central African Republic, renamed his country the Central African Empire. A year later Bokassa had himself crowned Emperor in a lavish ceremony modelled on the coronation of Napoleon I, and costing $20 million, one third of the country's annual budget. Bokassa was overthrown in 1979 and went into exile, but returned to face trial in 1986, charged with treason, murder, embezzlement and

The Napoleon of Africa: Jean-Bédel Bokassa assumes the
imperial mantle of the Central African Empire,
4 December 1976.

cannibalism. Only the last charge failed to stick, and he was imprisoned until
an amnesty in 1993. Before his death three years later, he let it be known that
he was the Thirteenth Apostle.

1977

A Girl's Guide to Whippings and Lashings &◆ Publication of
Whippings and Lashings by the Girl Guides Association. This useful little
volume contains the following advice: 'Do not fumble or use fancy methods.'

The Archipelago of San Seriffe ❦ (1 April) The *Guardian* published a supplement on the Sans Seriffe archipelago, whose two main islands are Upper Caisse and Lower Caisse and whose capital is Bodoni. The article also described how the country's dictator, a man called Pica, had come to power. The newspaper was subsequently the recipient of complaints from travel agents who were being badgered by people wishing to book holidays on the islands, and who had neither realized that all of the toponymy of Sans Seriffe was derived from typography, nor the date.

A Trap for Rogue Males ❦ (12 April) A design was lodged with the US patent office for a 'Penis locking and lacerating vaginal insert'. Its inventor, Alston L. Levesque, described the purpose of the insert thus:

> This device may find use for those women who have enormous fears of being raped. They may also be of value for those women who have extreme discomfort in the presence of a man even on such intimate terms as dating. With this device in her possession a woman may feel secure that if employed a male becoming intimate with her shall not receive pleasure from the experience. The penis may enter this device without great resistance and will activate the blade only upon the attempt of the man to withdraw the penis from the device.

The 'Bobby Charlton' Look Patented ❦ (10 May) The brothers Frank J. and Donald J. Smith patented 'a method of styling hair to cover partial baldness using only the hair on a person's head'. They went on to explain: 'The hair styling requires dividing a person's hair into three sections and carefully folding one section over another.' No one seems to have pointed out to the American inventors that Bobby Charlton had pioneered the 'comb-over' many years previously.

Adieu, Madame Guillotine ❦ (10 September) The last person to be guillotined in France, Hamida Djandoubi, went to his death.

1978

A Canine Comfort Station
The world's first public lavatory for dogs with flushing toilets opened in Paris.

Academics Discuss Nude Mice
Publication of *Proceedings of the Second International Conference on Nude Mice*, which won that year's award by the Diagram Group for Oddest Title of the Year.

US and Soviet Leaders One and the Same, Claims Lord Russell
John Conrad Russell, 4th Earl Russell, addressed the House of Lords for more than an hour on the desirability of abolishing law and order. He concluded by asserting that Leonid Brezhnev and Jimmy Carter were, in fact, the same person.

Resignation for Health Reasons
(28 April) President Mohammed Daoud Khan of Afghanistan was shot dead in a coup. The new government announced that he had 'resigned for health reasons'.

Death by Umbrella
1978 (7 September) On Waterloo Bridge, London, the Bulgarian dissident, Georgi Markov, was fatally stabbed in the leg with an umbrella tipped with ricin, a deadly poison. Soviet defectors later confirmed that it was the work of a Bulgarian assassin, supported by the KGB.

1979

Due Deference
(November) The Lord Chancellor, Lord Hailsham, spotted his friend Neil Marten MP in the Lobby of the House of Commons.

He waved his hand and called 'Neil!', upon which a group of tourists promptly dropped to their knees.

———

Bah, Humbug 🐚 (December) In Charlottesville, Virginia, an organization called SCROOGE was formed. The name is an acronym for 'Society to Curtail Ridiculous, Outrageous and Ostentatious Gift Exchanges'.

———

Parrot Slain in Vengeance Killing 🐚 Miss Ida Rubell, a theatrical landlady, was bound over to keep the peace after she had killed one of her lodger's performing parrots and served it up for dinner. Miss Rubell had objected to the parrot's constant complaints about the service in her establishment.

1980

An End to Joy 🐚 (3 January) Murder in Kenya of Joy Adamson, author of *Born Free*, the true story of Elsa the lioness. Adamson had a notably brisk way with servants, and the man convicted of her murder, Paul Wakwaro Ekai, claimed that he had killed her after she shot him in the leg. His error had been to complain that his wages were in arrears.

———

Director Accused of Pimping 🐚 Howard Brenton's play *The Romans in Britain* opened at the National Theatre. Outraged by the scene in which Roman soldiers rape a young druid, the censorship campaigner Mary Whitehouse, who brought a private prosecution against the play's director, Michael Bogdanov. Her lawyers claimed that under the Sexual Offences Act, Bogdanov had procured actors to perform an act of gross indecency on the stage. The case reached the Old Bailey, where it collapsed.

1981

Bed on Ben ❧ A group of medical students from Glasgow pushed a bed to the summit of Ben Nevis.

Sexual Deviation the Mainspring of Evolution ❧ Death of Dr Charlotte Bach, proponent of a new theory of evolution, the mainspring of which she held to be sexual deviation. It turned out that Dr Bach had in fact been a man called Karoly Hadju, the son of an impoverished Budapest tailor who had fled Hungary following the Soviet occupation. In England he went by the name Baron Carl Hadju, and in 1957 was exposed in the press as having defrauded donors to a fund ostensibly to aid Hungarian freedom fighters. He then adopted the name Michael B. Karoly, ScSc (Budapest), D Psy, CPE (Cantab), MBSH, and set himself up as a fashionable hypnotherapist in Mayfair and as the 'psychological expert' on *Today* magazine (penning such articles as 'Should Big Girls Be Spanked?'). Hadju/Karoly had for many years been a secretive cross-dresser, and later established him/herself as a dominatrix, before finally adopting, in 1968, the persona of Charlotte Bach PhD. Throughout the 1970s Dr Bach attracted a cult following, and some of her admirers – who included Colin Wilson, Desmond Morris and R.D. Laing – were quite taken aback when the post-mortem autopsy revealed she was anatomically male.

1982

Streaking for England ❧ Erica Roe performed her famous streak at Twickenham, prompting England scrum-half Steve Smith to remark to captain Bill Beaumont, 'Hey, Bill, there's a bird just run on the pitch with your bum on her chest.'

The Evil of Barcodes &. Mary Stewart Relfe published *The New Money System 666*, in which she asserted that barcodes secretly contain the Biblical number of the beast: 666. Her accusation was subsequently taken up by a host of other American fundamentalist Christian conspiracy theorists.

1983

'Studies on the Chemistry of Arsoles' &. Publication of 'Studies on the Chemistry of Arsoles', a paper by G. Markl and H. Hauptmann, in *J. Organomet. Chem.*, 248 (1983) 269. Arsole is the name of a ring-shaped molecule, the arsenic equivalent of pyrrole, and, contrary to expectations, is only moderately aromatic. Dr Paul May comments: 'The structure where arsole is fused to a benzene ring is called "benzarsole", and apparently when it's fused to six benzenes it would be called "sexibenzarsole" (although that molecule hasn't been synthesized yet).'

A Vignette of Minor Inconveniences &. The first winner of the Bulwer-Lytton Contest for the worst opening sentence of a novel was awarded to Gail Cain for the following:

> The camel died quite suddenly on the second day, and Selena fretted sulkily and, buffing her already impeccable nails – not for the first time since the journey began – pondered snidely if this would dissolve into a vignette of minor inconveniences like all the other holidays spent with Basil.

Wacko Shoes &. (26 October) A US patent was issued for the following invention:

> A system for allowing a shoe wearer to lean forwardly beyond his centre of gravity by virtue of wearing a specially designed pair of shoes which will engage with a hitch member movably projectable through a stage surface.

The device was commissioned for the singer Michael Jackson, who wished to repeat on stage the 45-degree-from-the-vertical walk he performed on his videos with the aid of wires and a harness.

My Enemy's Enemy ❧ (December) Donald Rumsfeld visited Baghdad as President Reagan's special envoy and shook hands with Saddam Hussein. During the 1980s the USA supported Iraq in its war with neighbouring Iran, which was then America's number-one bogeyman.

The First Battle of Little Sparta ❧ The Lanarkshire garden, known as Little Sparta, of the Scottish artist and concrete poet Ian Hamilton Finlay became the subject of a dispute with Strathclyde Region, who attempted to increase the rates, arguing that the garden was an art gallery. Finlay countered this by saying that the garden was a temple, and refused to pay. When the bailiffs arrived to seize artworks in lieu, Finlay and his supporters, in front of the television cameras, successfully resisted the incursion. Thus was fought the First Battle of Little Sparta.

1984

Bach Wanted by Tax Authorities ❧ The Hong Kong Philharmonic Society received an inquiry from the tax authorities inquiring why a certain J.S. Bach, who appeared to be associated with the orchestra, had not filed a tax return.

Doctor Diagnoses Demonic Possession ❧ The medical licence of Dr Ruth Bailey was withdrawn by the state of Indiana. The licensing authority found that she had 'knowingly and intentionally misdiagnosed her patients', attributing their ills to 'demons, devils and evil spirits'. Writing as Rebecca Brown, Bailey has subsequently written a number of books claiming a vast Satanic conspiracy involving the Roman Catholic Church, Free Masons and the practitioners of yoga.

1985

Smarty Pants ❧ A 13-year-old girl, Ruth Lawrence, was awarded a starred first-class mathematics degree at Oxford University, having completed the course in two years rather than the normal three.

Antipodean Tact ❧ At the World Cup qualifying match between Australia and Israel in Melbourne, the hosts caused a diplomatic rumpus when they played, in error, the German national anthem, 'Deutschland Über Alles'.

Undrinkable Plonk ❧ A bottle of 1787 Château Lafite went at auction for £105,000. Although quite undrinkable, the wine had come from the cellar of Thomas Jefferson, one of the founding fathers of the USA.

Meanwhile, Austria's wine industry was rocked by a scandal when it was revealed that some of the country's biggest producers had been adulterating their bottles with antifreeze.

1986

The Umbrella Hat ❧ (March) Jimmy Bates George Amor patented an umbrella hat, but people worried that they would look foolish wearing such a device, and it never caught on.

Monster Awarded Protected Status ❧ The local authorities in the Swedish county of Jämtland declared the Storsjöodjuret of Lake Storsjön an endangered species, and that anyone attempting to capture or kill it would be prosecuted. The Storsjöodjuret is a serpentine monster with a dog's head, sightings of which have been reported since the 17th century.

———

The Lake of Death 🪶 (26 August) In the northwest of Cameroon in West Africa, some 1700 people living in the valley below Lake Nyos mysteriously died. Lake Nyos lies in the crater of a dormant volcano, and on the evening in question a large amount of carbon dioxide had bubbled up out of the lake and asphyxiated nearly every living creature in the neighbourhood.

1987

Warhol the Church Goer 🪶 (22 February) Death of Andy Warhol from heart failure, having previously survived a shooting in 1968 by Valerie Solanas, founder and sole member of S.C.U.M. (The Society for Cutting Up Men). Intriguingly for the maker of such films as *Blow Job*, Warhol was a devout churchgoer, being a regular attender at St Vincent's, a Byzantine Rite Catholic church.

1988

At It Like Rabbits 🪶 Publication of *What Do Bunnies Do All Day?*, a children's book by Judy Mastrangelo.

———

'Antichrist' at the European Parliament 🪶 Dr Ian Paisley MEP was forcibly ousted from the European Parliament during an address by Pope John Paul II, whose speech he interrupted with shouts of 'Antichrist!'

———

Modern Crucifixions 🪶 In the town of San Pedro Cutud, north of Manila in the Philippines, Ruben Enaje, a carpenter, offered his thanks to God after he had survived a fall from a window by allowing himself to be crucified. He has subjected himself to this procedure – nails and all – every Passion Week since, and has been joined by various other men (including the British artist Sebastian Horsley).

Fly Like an Eagle, Drop Like a Stone Eddie 'the Eagle' Edwards, a British hopeful, came last by a considerable margin in the 70m ski jump at the Calgary Winter Olympics. The organizer of the competition at the games said, 'Edwards doesn't jump – he drops like a stone.' The Calgary Olympics also saw the début of the Jamaican bobsleigh team.

Humphrey, the Downing Street Cat Birth of Humphrey, the Downing Street cat. A year later he was found as a stray by a civil servant, homed at No 10 Downing Street as official mouser, and named after Sir Humphrey Appleby, the cunning permanent secretary in the TV comedy series *Yes, Minister*. The Cabinet Office paid £100 per year for Humphrey's maintenance, a snip compared to the previous pest-control contractor. Humphrey stayed in residence through the premierships of Margaret Thatcher and John Major, but with the arrival of the Blairs at No 10 in May 1997, there were rumours that Humphrey had been liquidated by the cat-hating Cherie. This slur was brushed aside when the press were summoned to an address in south London, which Humphrey had adopted as his retirement home. He passed away in March 2006.

1989

Prince of Wales Talks Dirty Prince Charles, in a telephone call to Camilla Parker Bowles, expressed his desire that he be reincarnated as her tampon.

Laws Governing Toilet Habits The Singapore government introduced a law making it an offence, punishable by a fine of $510, to leave a public lavatory unflushed. A team of inspectors roamed the city to enforce this law. The authorities in Singapore have also installed cameras and sensors in the lifts in apartment blocks to detect if anyone urinates in them. If an offender is detected, the lift doors stay locked until the police arrive.

Aurora or Flying Saucer?

Chris Gibson, who had served for 12 years with the Royal Observer Corps, sighted an unusual triangular-shaped aeroplane high above Galveston Key oilrig in the North Sea. It was being refuelled in midair, and was flanked by two USAF fighters. It is thought that this may have been the covert US spy plane known as 'Aurora', whose existence has been denied by the Americans. The following year there were various sightings in the north of Scotland of an object flying overhead at a tremendous speed. It is believed that Aurora (if it exists) can fly as high as 40 km (25 miles) and may be capable of speeds up to Mach 8 (8500 kph / 5300 mph), which would take it from London to New York in less than 40 minutes. An MoD report dating from 2000 investigating such sightings says that 'Certain viewing angles of these vehicles may be described as saucer-like.'

Alone in a Cave for 130 Days

As an experiment, an Italian interior designer, Stefania Follini, spent 130 days alone in a cave with no access to daylight or any other means of timekeeping. For the most part she would remain awake for 20 to 25 hours, then sleep for 10. Her menstrual cycle stopped. In 1992–3 another Italian volunteer, sociologist Maurizio Montalbani, spent 366 days underground, although he himself reckoned only 219 days had passed.

1990

Rock Music as a Tactical Weapon

(3 January) General Noriega, military ruler of Panama, surrendered to US forces who had invaded the country. Noriega had taken refuge in the Vatican embassy, and US

troops tried to dislodge him by playing loud rock music outside the building, until the Vatican complained to President George Bush. Noriega was taken to Florida to face charges relating to drug trafficking and other misdemeanours.

Lies, Damned Lies and Public Relations • (October) 'Nurse Nariyah' testified before the US Congress that she had worked in a maternity hospital in Kuwait at the time of the Iraqi invasion, and that she had witnessed Iraqi troops pulling infants out of incubators and dumping them on 'the cold floor to die', prior to walking off with the machines. It later turned out that 'Nurse Nariyah' was the daughter of the Kuwaiti ambassador to the USA and had never worked in a Kuwaiti maternity hospital. She had been coached to give her fabricated testimony by the PR company Hill & Knowlton, which had been hired by the US government and Citizens for a Free Kuwait to promote the Gulf War.

1991

The Physics of Fast Food • Publication of *The Thermodynamics of Pizza* by Harold J. Morowitz.

A Good Night Out • After he had been shot by a rival gangster outside a disco in south London, 'Mad' Frankie Fraser commented, 'It was good fun, good action, it made for a good night out.'

The Number of the Beast • The Driver and Vehicle Licensing Authority in Swansea cease to issue car number plates that include 666, 'the number of the Beast' in Revelation.

Boy Raised by Monkeys • A six-year-old boy called John Ssebunya was found living wild in the jungles of Uganda, where he had been raised by a group of African grey monkeys for several years.

———

Reptiles Rule the World 🐾 The former footballer and sports commentator, David Icke, was dropped as a spokesman for the Green Party following his claim to be the son of God, and his assertion that the world is ruled by the Babylonian Brotherhood, a group of extraterrestrial lizards, including George W. Bush, Bill Clinton, the Queen Mother and Kris Kristofferson.

1992

Chewing Gum Banned 🐾 Singapore banned the importation, sale or possession of chewing gum.

———

Fergie the Foot Fetishist 🐾 (August) Photographs of a topless Duchess of York having her toes sucked by her financial adviser appeared in the English tabloid press.

———

Farewell to Limbo 🐾 Pope John Paul II dropped the concept of Limbo from the catechism. The idea of Limbo had been concocted in the 13th century to provide a place where unbaptized babies and virtuous people born before Christ could go after death, given that they were not allowed into Heaven.

———

Tory Toff Sleeps with Judge's Wife and Daughters 🐾 The former Conservative minister, Alan Clark, was cited in a divorce case in South Africa, in which it emerged that he had had flings not only with the wife of a judge, but also with her two daughters. His own wife commented. 'Well, what do you expect when you sleep with below-stairs types?'

Christ visits Limbo, as depicted by Albrecht Dürer. In 1992 the Vatican decided
that the place did not, after all, exist.

1993

Thirty Years of Bananas 🍌 Oxford University Press (Nairobi) published *Thirty Years of Bananas* by Alex Makula.

Hotel Falls into Sea 🍌 (June) The Holbeck Hall Hotel, Scarborough, fell into the sea, when the cliff on which it was built collapsed.

'Ello, 'Ello, 'Ello 🍌 Mrs Julie Amiri (35) was arrested for shoplifting in Oxford Street, London. In her defence she said that she was compelled to perform acts likely to lead to arrest, as only in such circumstances could she achieve orgasm. Doctors supported her contention, and she was acquitted.

A Schoolboy Impersonator 🍌 Having been ousted from Glasgow Medical School after repeatedly failing his exams, 30-year-old Brian Mackinnon, still determined to become a doctor, decided to re-start his academic career by changing his appearance and adopting the persona of a 16-year-old Canadian orphan. Under this guise he enrolled at Bearsden Academy, near Glasgow, where he had been at school many years before, and successfully retook his Higher exams without any of the teachers (many of whom had taught him previously) noticing anything untoward. He was accepted as a student by Dundee Medical School, but his imposture was discovered in 1995 and Dundee withdrew its offer. He was subsequently reduced to sleeping rough in his car.

1994

Boston Tea Party Loses Election 🍌 The journalist and real-ale campaigner Richard Boston stood in the European elections for the Boston

Tea Party, with the slogan 'It's a big trough, and I want to get my nose in it.' He won 1018 votes.

The City of Bielefeld Does Not Exist ❦ (16 May) A German computer science student, Achim Held, posted a piece on an internet newsgroup asserting that the somewhat anonymous city of Bielefeld, in North Rhine-Westphalia, does not actually exist, but is a creation of a sinister body called SIE (German for 'they'). Held's satirical conspiracy theory has had an enduring life on the internet ever since.

Boris the Bibulous ❦ (30 September) Boris Yeltsin, the Russian president, failed to emerge from his aircraft at Shannon Airport for a scheduled reception with the Irish taoiseach Albert Reynolds. Russian officials at first said the president was asleep, and then that he was ill. In fact he was just dead drunk. Reynolds denied that it was a snub. 'I completely understand,' said the taoiseach. 'Mr Yeltsin was acting on the orders of doctors who said it would be better for him not to get off the plane.' The president himself later explained, 'The security services did not let in the people who were due to wake me – of course I will sort things out and punish them.'

You Cannot Be Sirius ❦ In 1994–5 dozens of members of the New Age cult, the Order of the Solar Temple, were found dead in various locations in France, Canada and Switzerland, having committed ritual suicide. Some were poisoned, others shot, and many had plastic bags tied over their heads. In some cases, such as the mass suicide that took place in the clearing in the French Alps known as the Well of Hell, the 16 bodies were laid out in a star shape, feet to the middle, and heads pointing outwards. The Order, which alludes to various myths associated with the medieval Knights Templar, was founded in the 1980s by Joseph di Mambro, who persuaded a number of wealthy neophytes to hand over large amounts of

money in the expectation that after death they would be reborn on a star called Sirius.

1995

Freak Waves {❦ (1 January) The first 'freak' or 'monster' wave – long suspected to be responsible for the disappearance of large ocean-going ships – to be positively confirmed was recorded on the Draupner oil platform in the North Sea off Norway. The wave had a peak elevation above sea level of 18.5 m (61 ft) – and measured 26 m (85 ft) from trough to crest. This height was exceeded by a wave scientifically measured in February 2000 by a British oceanographic vessel near Rockall to the west of Scotland: this wave measured 29.1 m (95.5 ft) from trough to crest – the height of a ten-storey building.

Regarding the Perambulation of Pet Pigs ❦ Britain introduced a law requiring those who wish to walk their pet pigs to possess a licence.

Clairvoyance Explored by Intelligence Services ❦ The US government withdrew funding from a secret intelligence project – Project Stargate – initiated in the 1970s to research the uses of clairvoyance, or 'remote viewing' as its adherents preferred to call it. Apparently things had gone downhill since 1989, when new personnel had attempted to involve witches, tarot cards and channelling. A key supporter of the research had been Major General Albert Stubblebine, head of US Army intelligence in the early 1980s, whose own experiments had included attempts to walk through walls.

The Last Slave State ❦ The state of Mississippi ratified the 13th Amendment to the US Constitution, first introduced in 1865. The 13th Amendment abolished slavery throughout the United States, and Mississippi was the last of the 36 states in existence in 1865 to ratify it. It took them 130 years.

1996

Prayer No Good for Health, Study Finds

Prayer No Good for Health, Study Finds 🏵 A large scientific survey was embarked upon in America, to determine if praying for those who are ill improves their chances of recovery. A decade later the study concluded that it does not.

Ars Longa, Vita Brevis 🏵 Publication of *Hepatopancreatoduodenectomy*, a surgical textbook edited by F. Hanyu providing all the information you need to cut out the liver, pancreas and duodenum.

1997

Mandela Awed by Spice Girls 🏵 The Spice Girls met Nelson Mandela, who, apparently without irony, declared, 'This is one of the greatest moments of my life.'

Cult Followers Believe *Star Trek* to be the Literal Truth 🏵 (26 March) The bodies of 39 followers of the Heaven's Gate cult – all dressed in identical black clothes with white trainers – were found in a mansion in San Diego. They had taken barbiturates washed down with vodka, and had secured plastic bags over their heads, just to make sure. Their intention was to catch a ride in the spaceship that they believed was waiting for them in the tail of the Comet Hale-Bopp, then shining brightly in the sky. The members of the cult apparently believed that *Star Trek* was non-fiction, and many of the men had earlier submitted willingly to castration.

Getting Up the Arse of the White House 🏵 (November) Jonathan Powell, chief of staff to prime minister Tony Blair, briefed the new ambassador to Washington, Christopher Meyer, with the following curt injunction: 'We want you to get up the arse of the White House, and stay there.'

Boxer Bites Opponent's Ears ❧ (28 June) Boxer Mike Tyson bit a chunk out of the ear of his opponent Evander Holyfield. He received a two-point deduction from the referee, but, undeterred, went on to bite Holyfield's other ear. He was then disqualified.

1998

Puffing Through Purgatory ❧ Pope John Paul II announced that anyone giving up smoking or drinking would be entitled to a reduction of their time in Purgatory.

Painting with Elephant Dung ❧ Chris Ofili won the Turner Prize for *The Adoration of Captain Shit and the Legend of the Black Star Part Two*, a painting that incorporated elephant dung.

1999

Brothers Pull a Fast One ❧ Similar-looking brothers Fika and Sergio Motsoeneng swapped places with each other during a 90-km (56-mile) running race in South Africa, enabling Sergio (who hitched a lift in a car for part of the distance) to finish ninth. Their cheat was revealed when video film shows that they wore their watches on different wrists.

Shakespeare Banned ❧ Shakespeare's *Twelfth Night* was briefly banned in schools in Merrimack, New Hampshire, as it was believed to contravene an act prohibiting 'alternative lifestyle instruction'. The school board was troubled by the cross-dressing aspects of the play, in which Viola, a young woman originally played by a boy, disguises herself as a young man, Cesario, with whom Olivia (also originally played by a boy) falls in love.

———

Mallory Found on Everest 🐦 (1 May) The frozen body of George

Mallory was found on the north face of Mount Everest, at a height of 8155 m (26,755 ft). He had last been seen heading for the summit along the north-east ridge 75 years previously, on 8 June 1924. From the twisted position of his leg and other evidence, it was clear that Mallory had fallen down the north face from the ridge high above. No trace of his companion on that day, Andrew Irvine, has yet been found, although in 1975 a Chinese climber reported finding an 'old English dead' near the summit. Mountaineers are divided as to whether they might have reached the top, although on balance it is thought unlikely.

———

President Abducted by Aliens 🐦 Kirsan Ilyumzhinov, president

since 1993 of the impoverished Russian republic of Kalmykia, on the Caspian Sea, claimed he was abducted by aliens. 'They took me from my apartment and we went aboard their ship,' he recalls. 'We flew to some kind of star. They put a spacesuit on me, told me many things and showed me around. They wanted to demonstrate that UFOs do exist.' Ilyumzhinov, who owns a fleet of Rolls Royces, once campaigned under the slogan 'A wealthy president is a safeguard against corruption,' and promised a mobile phone for every shepherd. Ilyumzhinov is also head of Fide, the World Chess Federation, and has made chess a compulsory subject in Kalmykian schools.

2000

———

Holocaust Denier Addresses Judge as *Mein Führer* 🐦

(15 March) During the course of his unsuccessful libel action against Penguin Books and Deborah Lipstadt, publisher and author of *Denying the Holocaust*, David Irving, the right-wing historian and biographer of Hitler,

addressed the judge as '*Mein Führer*'. On 20 February 2006 an Austrian court sentenced Irving to three years' imprisonment for denying the Holocaust.

Bulbs Spell 'Bollocks' 🦋 (April) Along one of the main roads in Rotherham, the daffodils coming into bloom spelt out the words 'Shag' and 'Bollocks'. The bulbs had been planted the previous autumn by a gang of thieves doing community service.

Salford Bullfighter Practises on Shopping Trolley 🦋 (July)

The British bullfighter Frank Evans – known to his fans as El Ingles – was tossed in a ring near Malaga. With a show of stiff upper lip, Evans told the press as he was taken to hospital that he had been hit harder by his wife. Evans learnt his craft back home in Salford using a supermarket trolley (albeit one with horns) to stand in for the bull. He killed his first bull in 1966, and retired in 2005, at the age of 63, following a knee injury.

The Real X Files? 🦋 DI55, a cell within Defence Intelligence in the Ministry of Defence, completed a report called *Unidentified Aerial Phenomena (UAPs) in the UK Air Defence Region*. Having examined some 10,000 eyewitness reports, the report concluded that it is 'indisputable' that UAPs exist, and that they 'clearly can exhibit aerodynamic characteristics well beyond those of any known aircraft or missile – either manned or unmanned'. It blamed some of the most mysterious sightings on airborne plasmas, formed during complex atmospheric and meteorological conditions, or during meteor showers. The report, which came to the same broad conclusions as that produced by the government's Flying Saucer Working Party in 1952, was only released in May 2006, after a request under the Freedom of Information Act.

2001

Foundation of the World Toilet Organization

The World Toilet Organization was established, and a World Toilet Summit was held in Singapore. This has become an annual event, and 19 November is now World Toilet Day. The WTO is a serious organization, dedicated to improving standards of public facilities around the world.

The Rotenburg Cannibal

(March) Having advertised on the internet, the German cannibal Armin Meiwes was delighted to welcome into his home Bernd Jürgen Armando Brandes, a manager at Siemens AG, who had responded to Meiwes's appeal for a willing victim. Brandes initially asked Meiwes to bite off his penis so that they could eat it together, but this proved impractical, so Meiwes used a knife. Brandes found that his penis was too chewy to eat raw, so Meiwes sautéed it with garlic and seasoning. He then dosed his victim with quantities of alcohol and pain killers before dispatching and butchering him, storing the parts in his freezer for later consumption. Meiwes videotaped the whole procedure. At his first trial Meiwes was found guilty of manslaughter given that his victim had voluntarily gone to his death, and Meiwes was sentenced to only eight and a half years, but at a retrial in 2006 he was found guilty of murder and sent to prison for life.

Rejection of a Dead Man's Hand

Surgeons were obliged to amputate the world's first transplanted hand, because the recipient, a 50-year-old New Zealand man, found it 'hideous and withered', and could not face a dead man's hand on the end of his arm. Similarly, in 2006, a Chinese man asked surgeons to remove a penis transplant that had been grafted on to the 1 cm stump he had been left with after an accident. Although the transplant was a success, with blood vessels and nerves being linked up and no sign of rejection, neither the man nor his wife found they could live with another's man's penis.

2002

Lioness Adopts Young Antelopes 🐾 A lioness dubbed
Kamuniak ('blessed one') in the Samburu National Park in northern Kenya adopted a succession of baby oryxes, attempting to protect them from other predators, and allowing their own mothers to feed them.

Tome Raider 🐾 William Jacques, a graduate of Cambridge University,
was jailed for four years for stealing hundreds of rare books from the British Museum Reading Room and the university library at Cambridge. The press dubbed him 'Tome Raider'.

Career Development for Sex Workers 🐾 The Brazilian ministry
of employment published an online manual for sex workers, offering tips on how to please clients ('use loving nicknames', 'wash their clothes', 'offer them specialities') and detailing suitable courses (safe sex, beauty, personal finance).

The World's Most Expensive Whisky 🐾 (4 December) A bot-
tle of 62-year-old Dalmore whisky was sold for £25,877.50. In 2006 the marmalade makers Duerrs celebrated their 125th anniversary by creating a 1 kg jar including edible gold leaf, vintage champagne, and £3450 worth of Dalmore 62.

2003

Santa Moves to Greenland 🐾 The 40th Father Christmas World
Congress declared that Santa's home was in fact in Greenland. No delegate from Lapland was present.

Blunkett Condemns Bellicosity *❧* (15 February) Following the million-strong antiwar march in London, David Blunkett– apparently without irony – noted in his diary, 'I think Tony has stood up very well to the enormous turnout – frighteningly intimidatory, and people so bellicose.'

Music as Torture *❧* US military interrogators 'softened up' Iraqi captives by repeatedly playing the song 'I Love You' by Barney the Purple Dinosaur.

Protest at 'Fart Tax' *❧* Farmers in New Zealand blocked the streets of Wellington to protest against the government's 'fart tax' – a per capita tax on sheep and cattle imposed because of the amount of methane they pump into the atmosphere, thus contributing to global warming.

The Full English *❧* The artist Mark McGowan spent 12 days immersed in a bath of baked beans with a string of sausages wrapped round his head and a chip up each nostril, as a *homage* to the full English breakfast.

The Lowest Note in the Universe *❧* (September) Astronomers detected the lowest note in the Universe yet 'heard'. Ripples emanating from the black hole at the centre of the Perseus cluster of galaxies (some 250 million light years distant from Earth) have a wavelength of 35,000 light years, and a frequency of 10 million years. The note is quite some way deeper than any that can be detected by human ears, but it is a B flat, pitched 57 octaves below middle C.

2004

Help! A couple in Stanley, County Durham, were surprised when police burst into their home. They had inadvertently dialled 999 while rolling over the phone in the throes of passion.

The Mongolian Cow Sour Yogurt Super Girl Contest Chinese TV launched its version of *Pop Idol / American Idol*, sponsored by a dairy company. The programme had the catchy title *The Mongolian Cow Sour Yogurt Super Girl Contest*.

Moonie Saves Souls of Hitler and Stalin The Revd Sun Myung Moon informed the world that he had saved the souls of Adolf Hitler and Joseph Stalin, and that they had confirmed that the Revd Moon was 'none other than humanity's Saviour, Messiah, Returning Lord and True Parent'.

Beyond the Catacombs (September) Police in Paris found a vast underground chamber beneath the fashionable 16th arrondissement. The cavern had seating carved out of the rock, a fully working cinema, a large collection of films and a well-stocked bar.

There are some 270 km (170 miles) of rock-hewn tunnels and connected chambers under the French capital. They were largely dug out at the time of the Romans, as a source of stone for the buildings of the city. Tourists may visit Les Catacombes, a small area of tunnels where the bones of some 6 million people were transferred in the 18th century from the city's overcrowded cemeteries. The rest of the complex has been forbidden to the public for security reasons since 1955. However, various secret societies of so-called *cataphiles* have explored the underground system.

Following the discovery of the secret cinema in 2004, the police returned three days later with technicians from the French electricity board, intent on finding where the power supply was coming from. They found the cables had been cut, and a note that said: 'Do not try to find us.'

Ovine Opera Lovers ☙ (December) A bale of top-quality Australian wool sold for over £90,000. The farmer who produced the wool attributed its fine quality to his habit of playing Italian opera to his sheep.

2005

Welshman Castrates Himself After Team's Victory ☙

A Welshman swore while he was watching an England–Wales rugby match that 'If Wales wins, I'll cut my balls off.' They did, and so did he. He was a winner of that year's Darwin Awards, which 'salute the improvement of the human genome by honouring those who accidentally kill themselves in really stupid ways'.

The Costs of Mrs Blair's Hair ☙ (April–May) The Labour Party

spent £7700 on Cherie Blair's hair during the general election campaign.

Drunken Elks and Other Animal Tales ☙ Police in Sweden had

to disperse a herd of drunken elks surrounding an old people's home. The giant deer had become inebriated through eating fermented apples. The same year an outbreak of exploding toads occurred in Hamburg, while in Croatia a new reality TV show set sheep against sheep. The winner became the subject of poems, while the losers were barbequed. In Burma, meanwhile, a 40-year-old woman gave suck to two orphaned tiger cubs from Yangon Zoological Gardens. Finally, three houses in Newcastle, Australia, were attacked by frozen chickens. Police believe the chickens may have been fired from a 'very big catapult'.

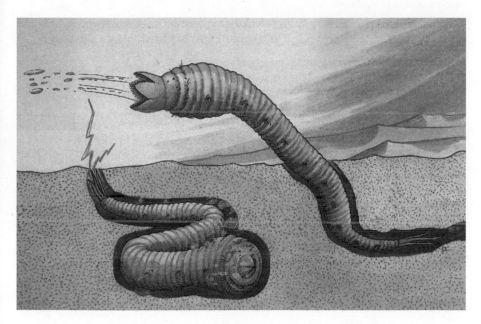

An artist's impression of the Mongolian death worm, sought by an expedition to the Gobi Desert in 2005.

———

Virtual Rage Leads to Murder 🐛 Qui Chengwei, an aficianado of online fantasy gaming, was angered when Zhu Caoyan allegedly stole his virtual sword and sold it to another player. So incensed was Mr Qui – especially when the police refused to take any action over the 'theft' – that he paid Mr Zhu a visit and stabbed him to death. He was given a suspended death sentence.

———

In Search of the Mongolian Death Worm 🐛 A cryptozoological expedition was mounted to the Gobi Desert to find the *allghoi khorkoi* ('blood-filled intestine worm'), known as the Mongolian death worm. This fabulous creature is said to resemble a cow's gut and be capable of killing its victims by squirting a yellow acid at them. It is also reported that it can generate electric shocks capable of felling a camel. The expedition found no sign of the fabled worm, but some believe it could exist in the closed region along the Chinese–Mongolian border. It is possible that it was the Mongolian death worm that inspired the giant man-eating centipedes of Tibet, encountered in *Biggles Hits the Trail* (1935).

2006

The Coming of the Cyborgs ❧ (8 March) DARPA, the US Department of Defense's Defense Advanced Research Projects Agency, put out the following advertisement: 'DARPA seeks innovative proposals to develop technology to create insect-cyborgs, possibly enabled by intimately integrating microsystems within insects during their early stages of metamorphoses.' Such part-natural, part-robotic devices might be used to detect explosives, or to 'bug' conversations.

The Birth of Chav Lit ❧ (10 March) It was reported that the 20-year-old footballer Wayne Rooney had signed a £5 million deal with the publishers HarperCollins for a five-volume autobiography. Quite where he will find the half million or so words required to fill all these pages is difficult to tell, given the brevity of his life and the fact that his vocabulary on the field is largely restricted to the F-word, as in this remark to a referee: 'You f***ing t***, you're a f***ing disgrace.' Sir Winston Churchill's memoirs of the Second World War ran to a more expansive six volumes, so Rooney's ambitions are relatively modest. 'Hopefully,' he was quoted as saying, 'there will be a lot of things to read about.' Two months later another publishing giant, Random House, signed up Chantelle, the 'fake celebrity' who won the 2006 *Celebrity Big Brother* competition, for a more modest £300,000 – but then she was only expected to produce a single volume of autobiography. Comments on Chantelle's website included the following: 'I fink she shud def rite an ortobiografy but i don't fink i wud reed it cuz i aint red a buk in me lyf!' Another fan opined that 'reedin iz 4 geekz n sad ppl'. The news of

Chantelle's literary ambitions broke in the same week that HarperCollins published the memoirs of Jade Goody, another star in the *Big Brother* firmament. Not to be outdone, by the end of May Wayne Rooney's girlfriend Coleen McLoughlin had signed up with HarperCollins. She said that her book, *Welcome to My World*, would contain fashion tips and would be a light read, 'not just words, words, words'.

Nude Cyclists a Danger to Themselves ❧ (March) The mayor of Tasman district in New Zealand's South Island banned the annual nude cycle ride on the grounds that participants would not be wearing helmets.

Storing One's Parents in the Deep-Freeze ❧ (March) Rémy Martinot's long battle with the French courts over his dead parents came to an end. According to French law, corpses must be buried, cremated or donated to science, whereas M. Martinot, adhering to his parents' wishes, had kept them in a deep-freeze in his chateau in the Loire. His mother had died 22 years before, and his father, a doctor and a believer in cryogenics, had installed her in the freezer, helping to pay for the large electricity bills by charging guests to visit the cellar where she lay. Dr Martinot died in 2002, and was stored alongside his wife. Sadly, a freezer malfunction in 2006 obliged Rémy Martinot to unpack the bodies and have them cremated.

Judge Consults Imaginary Dwarves ❧ (April) Judge Florentino Floro of the Philippines was sacked by the Supreme Court after he confessed to consulting three imaginary mystic dwarves called Armand, Luis and Angel prior to arriving at his judgements. 'They should not have dismissed me for what I believed,' said Floro. The Supreme Court said it was not within its expertise to say whether Floro was insane; the judge was instead sacked for incompetence, bias and contempt for court procedure.

Mysterious Organ Up the Ben ❧ (May) Volunteers clearing litter from the summit plateau of Ben Nevis found, buried beneath large rocks, what they thought was a grand piano, complete apart from the keyboard. No one knew how or when it got there, but inside it was found a biscuit wrapper with a best-before date of 1986. Subsequently a Mr Kenneth Campbell of Bonar Bridge let it be known that it was possibly the organ he had spent three days carrying to the summit in 1971, in aid of a cancer charity. When he got to the summit he played 'Scotland the Brave', but was unable to carry the instrument back down to the valley.

Serbian Navy Landlocked ❧ (May) Montenegro voted to secede from Serbia. This left the Serbian navy – comprising 2900 sailors, eight submarines and three frigates – without access to the sea.

Japan's Low Birth Rate Explained ❧ (June) A survey by the Japanese Family Planning Association found that 44 per cent of those questioned felt a relationship with someone of the opposite sex was either 'tiresome' or 'very tiresome'.

'A.N. Wilson is a Shit' ❧ (August) It was revealed that the waspish writer and former 'Young Fogey' A.N. Wilson had been the victim of a hoax in his recently published biography of John Betjeman. The hoax took the form of a supposed love letter from the poet to Honor de Tracy, indicating that Betjeman had had a hitherto unknown affair with her. The letter had been forwarded to Wilson by a certain 'Eve de Harben'. It turned out that Eve de Harben is an anagram of 'ever been had', while the letter itself contained an acrostic, in which the first letter of each sentence read 'A.N. Wilson is a shit.' Wilson's rival biographer, Bevis Hillier, although initially denying any involvement, eventually admitted his responsibility for the hoax. He had

been galled by Wilson's 2002 review of the second volume of his Betjeman biography, which Wilson had dismissed as 'a hopeless mishmash of a book'. Wilson further derided Hillier in 2004 for 'dripping resentment like the dottle from a smelly churchwarden's pipe, and with so little in his life that he has to worry his sad old head about a book review'. For his part, Hillier told the *Sunday Times*, when news of the hoax broke, that he found Wilson 'despicable'.

———

More Sex Demanded for Dutch Farm Animals ❧ (August)

A Dutch pressure group called Sex voor Dieren launched a petition to get a hitherto overlooked aspect of animal welfare discussed in Parliament. The *Brabants Dagbad* newspaper quoted a spokesperson for the group: 'There are 1.3 million cattle, 10 million pigs and who knows how many chickens in the Netherlands, and all will die virgins.' And the barrier to true love? The almost universal use of artificial insemination.

———

Sleeping at Work Improves Performance ❧ (October)

Scientists at Massey University, New Zealand, concluded that 'sleeping at work can improve performance'.

———

Eunuchs Extract Unpaid Taxes ❧ (18 October) It was reported

that the authorities in Aurangabad, in Bihar state, India, had decided to paint the town pink in an effort to reduce the crime rate. Meanwhile, in November came the news that the authorities in Patna had devised a new method of collecting unpaid taxes: they sent eunuchs with drums and loud music to the doors of defaulters, who only too willingly paid up to end the embarrassment.

———

Pelican Devours Pigeon ❧ (24 October) In St James's Park, London,

after a 20-minute struggle, a pelican swallowed a pigeon.

2007

—

'Shit' Permitted in Parliament ❧ (9 January) Sir Michael Lord, the Deputy Speaker of the House of Commons, ruled that the word 'shit' was not necessarily 'unparliamentary language'. It had been uttered by Fiona Mactaggart, Labour MP for Slough, in the context of a discussion about sewerage, and Sir Michael stated that it was perfectly appropriate 'to use the word in the way that the Hon. Lady used it'. The phrase 'Pecksniffian cant' continues to be forbidden to members, however.

—

Picture Acknowledgements

Mary Evans Picture Library Page 8, 10, 53, 58, 72, 102, 120, 135, 189, 241, 246, 270. Topfoto / Alinari Page 18.

Topfoto / Fortean Page 82, 344, 357. Topfoto / Charles Walker Page 98. Topfoto Page 289. Corbis Page 22, 233.

Corbis / Leonard de Selva Page 80. Corbis / Bettmann Page 116, 208, 277, 303. Corbis / Hulton-Deutsch Collection

Page 148, 299. Bridgeman Art Library / Private Collection / Ken Welsh Page 25. Bridgeman Art Library /

Bibliothèque des Arts Decoratifs, Paris Page 40. Bridgeman Art Library / Private Collection/ Archives Charmet

Page 63. Getty Images / Rischgitz Page 90, 200. Getty Images / Hulton Archive Page 157, 184, 219. Getty Images /

Pierre Jahan / Roger Viollet Page 255. Getty Images / Julian Wasser / Time Life Pictures Page 320. Getty Images /

Keystone Page 331. Kobal Collection / UFA Page 262. Kobal Collection / MGM Page 326.

Jacket: Bridgeman Art Library, Corbis, Getty Images.

Picture Research: Elaine Willis.